ANTHROPOLOGY AND ETHNOGRAPHY
ARE NOT EQUIVALENT

Methodology and History in Anthropology

Series Editors:
David Parkin, Fellow of All Souls College, University of Oxford
David Gellner, Fellow of All Souls College, University of Oxford
Nayanika Mathur, Fellow of Wolfson College, University of Oxford

Recent volumes:

Volume 41
*Anthropology and Ethnography Are Not Equivalent:
Reorienting Anthropology for the Future*
Edited by Irfan Ahmad

Volume 40
*Search after Method: Sensing, Moving, and Imagining in
Anthropological Fieldwork*
Edited by Julie Laplante, Ari Gandsman, and Willow Scobie

Volume 39
After Society: Anthropological Trajectories out of Oxford
Edited by João Pina-Cabral and Glenn Bowman

Volume 38
Total Atheism: Secular Activism and Politics of Difference in South India
Stefan Binder

Volume 37
*Crossing Histories and Ethnographies: Following Colonial Historicities in
Timor-Leste*
Edited by Ricardo Roque and Elizabeth G. Traube

Volume 36
Engaging Evil: A Moral Anthropology
Edited by William C. Olsen and Thomas J. Csordas

Volume 35
Medicinal Rule: A Historical Anthropology of Kingship in East and Central Africa
Koen Stroeken

Volume 34
Who Are "We"? Reimagining Alterity and Affinity in Anthropology
Edited by Liana Chua and Nayanika Mathur

Volume 33
Expeditionary Anthropology: Teamwork, Travel and the "Science of Man"
Edited by Martin Thomas and Amanda Harris

Volume 32
Returning Life: Language, Life Force and History in Kilimanjaro
Knut Christian Myhre

For a full volume listing, please see the series page on our website:
http://berghahnbooks.com/series/methodology-and-history-in-anthropology

ANTHROPOLOGY AND ETHNOGRAPHY ARE NOT EQUIVALENT

Reorienting Anthropology for the Future

Edited by
Irfan Ahmad

berghahn
NEW YORK • OXFORD
www.berghahnbooks.com

First published in 2021 by

Berghahn Books

www.berghahnbooks.com

© 2021, 2024 Irfan Ahmad
First paperback edition published in 2024

All rights reserved. Except for the quotation of short passages for the purpose of criticism and review, no part of this book may be reproduced in any form or by any means, electronic or mechanical, including photocopying, recording, or any information storage and retrieval system now known or to be invented, without written permission of the publisher.

Library of Congress Cataloging-in-Publication Data

Names: Ahmad, Irfan, 1974– editor.
Title: Anthropology and Ethnography Are Not Equivalent:
  Reorienting Anthropology for the Future / Edited by Irfan Ahmad.
Description: New York: Berghahn, 2021. | Includes bibliographical
  references and index.
Identifiers: LCCN 2020048762 (print) | LCCN 2020048763 (ebook) |
  ISBN 9781789209884 (hardback) | ISBN 9781789209891 (ebook)
Subjects: LCSH: Anthropology—Cross-cultural studies. | Ethnology—
  Cross-cultural studies.
Classification: LCC GN25 .A576 2021 (print) | LCC GN25 (ebook) |
  DDC 301—dc23
LC record available at https://lccn.loc.gov/2020048762
LC ebook record available at https://lccn.loc.gov/2020048763

British Library Cataloguing in Publication Data

A catalogue record for this book is available from the British Library

ISBN 978-1-78920-988-4 hardback
ISBN 978-1-80539-343-6 paperback
ISBN 978-1-78920-989-1 web pdf
ISBN 978-1-80539-450-1 epub

https://doi.org/10.3167/9781789209884

To My Teachers Who Are No More

Mahmood Alam
[Madrasa Islamia 'Arabia, Dumri, Sheohar, Bihar, India]

Gerd Baumann (1953–2014)
[University of Amsterdam, The Netherlands]

Joginder Singh Gandhi
[Jawaharlal Nehru University, New Delhi]

Johan Goudsblom (1932–2020)
[University of Amsterdam, The Netherlands]

Mustafa Master
[Madrasa Islamia 'Arabia, Dumri, Sheohar, Bihar, India]

Abdul Moghni
[B. N. College Patna, Patna University, Bihar]

Bikram Narayan Nanda
[Jamia Millia Islamia, New Delhi]

SM Akram Rizvi
[Jamia Millia Islamia, New Delhi]

Yogendra Singh (1932–2020)
[Jawaharlal Nehru University, New Delhi]

CONTENTS

List of Figures	viii
Acknowledgments	ix
Introduction. On the Equivalence between Anthropology and Ethnography *Irfan Ahmad*	1
Chapter 1. Beyond Correspondence: Doing Anthropology of Islam in the Field and Classroom *Hatsuki Aishima*	20
Chapter 2. Anthropology as an Experimental Mode of Inquiry *Arpita Roy*	36
Chapter 3. Graphic Designs: On Constellational Writing, or a Benjaminian Response to Ingold's Critique of Ethnography *Jeremy F. Walton*	53
Chapter 4. Non-correspondence in Fieldwork: Death, Dark Ethnography, and the Need for Temporal Alienation *Patrice Ladwig*	71
Chapter 5. Commitment, Correspondence, and Fieldwork as Nonvolitional Dwelling: A Weberian Critique *Patrick Eisenlohr*	93
Chapter 6. A New Holistic Anthropology with Politics In *Irfan Ahmad*	112
Afterword *Tim Ingold*	141
Index	153

FIGURES

0.1. Cat at Irfan Ahmad's souterrain apartment during the
Coronavirus quarantine   x

3.1. The new mosque in Thessaloniki, Greece   61

4.1. Worker of a local crematorium, presenting offerings to
spirits, Thailand   78

4.2. Mortician (*sappaloe*) in front of an open coffin, Thailand   79

6.1. Absent political anthropology in four-field
anthropology   116

6.2. Heterogeneous singularity about equation between
Islam and terrorism   123

ACKNOWLEDGMENTS

The idea of this volume organically emerged from a discussion that took place in September 2017 at the Max Planck Institute for the Study of Religious and Ethnic Diversity in Göttingen, Germany. The aim of the discussion was to reflect on Tim Ingold's influential recent interventions concerning the relationships between anthropology and ethnography. One of the questions the discussion addressed was: "Is 'that's enough about ethnography' enough?"

I thank Nate Roberts who enthusiastically supported the idea of the discussion as well as lent help in its organization. As the Director of the Max Planck Institute, Peter van der Veer graciously facilitated the discussion as well as took part in it. I am thankful to him. Several months after this event, I contacted Tim Ingold, inviting him to respond to the writings brought together in this volume, which critically engage with his exposition. I thank him for accepting my invitation and offering multiple rich suggestions in the subsequent stages of this project. Of course, I am thankful to the contributors for writing their chapters and attending to my comments, suggestions, and queries.

I am greatly thankful to the two anonymous reviewers who offered constructive criticisms and helpful suggestions about the volume as well as specific chapters. Their incorporation has hopefully made the volume richer and more refined. Their comments have enabled me to sharpen some points in the Introduction as well as organize the volume. My thanks also go to the editors of the Methodology & History in Anthropology series, of which, I am pleased, this book eventually became part, and whose editors also made instructive comments. Tom Bonnington, Assistant Editor at Berghahn, efficiently supervised the peer review process, offered useful advice along the way, and, yes, sent me uplifting timely reminders. Early on, Marion Berghahn, Director of Berghahn Books, enthusiastically took interest in the book proposal. I am extremely grateful to her. In its penultimate stage, my partner, Sana Ghazi (herself an anthropologist), has contributed to this book in many ways. I wonder if "thank you" to her is a suitable phrase to say.

Figure 0.1. Cat at Irfan Ahmad's souterrain apartment during the Coronavirus quarantine, Göttingen, Germany. © Irfan Ahmad.

Much of the revision, including the editorial, of this volume was done during "social distancing" in order to fight (escape?) the coronavirus. The friend with whom I interacted most during this strange period was the black-and-white cat in my neighbourhood who visited me regularly. Our friendship is over one year long. Initially, I offered her milk, which she had no interest in. Unlike cats in India, cats in Germany eat meat dishes. So, based on my new knowledge, I began to buy special cat food from the supermarket. As I used to get Alnatura organic corn flakes for myself, I began to buy organic food for her too, which the cat liked more than the nonorganic type. "Desire for others," so goes a *hadīth*, "what you love for yourself."

Engrossed in revision one day, I did not immediately notice her quiet arrival at the window—her special door—asking to come into my apartment. Was I unconsciously protecting myself from the virus? She sat facing the window glass and me for half an hour. Later, when I opened the window to let her in, she jumped in to lovingly circle around my legs. She did not at first eat the organic food I offered. She waited until I had caressed her. We were then faced with the humanity of animals and the animality of humans.

In Bollywood films, heroes often curse and threaten the villains saying, "You will die a dog's death." Do dogs curse one another saying, "You will die a human's death"? What would the cat have said to her fellows and herself about me not opening the window for half an hour?

As I see it, questions such as these are integral to the ideas of correspondence, attentionality, resonance, and anthropology *a la* Tim Ingold, as well as to the reorienting of the discipline for the future and public imagination writ large. Turn the page, dear readers, or scroll down.

Irfan Ahmad
Göttingen, 31 March 2020

INTRODUCTION

ON THE EQUIVALENCE BETWEEN ANTHROPOLOGY AND ETHNOGRAPHY

Irfan Ahmad

It is somewhat a common practice for towering anthropologists close to or after their retirements—for instance, Edmund Leach (Kuper 1986), Lévi-Strauss (Massenzio 2001), and Clifford Geertz (Panourgiá 2002)—to be interviewed for their life-long contributions to the discipline. It is rare, however, to be interviewed for writing a single article. In *Cultural Anthropology*, Susan MacDougall (2016) interviewed Tim Ingold to know about the reactions generated by his 2014 article "That's Enough about Ethnography." Ingold's article "sparked a conversation" beyond the pages of *Cultural Anthropology*, both on Twitter and in open anthropology cooperative. An animated debate ensued in *HAU: Journal of Ethnographic Theory*, where his views first appeared. More accurately, Ingold had enunciated his thesis originally in 2007 at the A. R. Radcliffe-Brown lecture, which was published a year later in *Proceedings of the British Academy*. The combined citations of its many versions, according to the Google Scholar in August 2020, are over one thousand. As a "no-holds-barred critique of its [anthropology's] own raison d'être" (da Col 2017: 2) and approximating a manifesto, in some ways Ingold's article rocked the field. It received, in the main, two caricaturist responses. While some held that Ingold was dead opposed to ethnography, others maintained that he was "right in challenging the [notion that] anthropology should be a mirror image of ethnography" (da Col 2017: 2). It is true that Ingold challenged the mainstream view that anthropology and ethnography are more or less substitutes. However, it would be simplistic to reduce the depth and range of his contribution to the twin formulaic reactions.

Rationale for the Volume

This volume—*Anthropology and Ethnography Are Not Equivalent*—moves beyond a polarising and caricatured reception of Ingold's intervention as laudatory or antiethnography and instead recognises its fundamental contribution in its generative capability. It takes his multilayered thesis as important in opening up an analytically productive space to fruitfully revisit many of the common notions about and practices in ethnography as well as those in anthropology. At stake here, then, is not whether or not one agrees with Ingold but how an engagement with his writings enables us to examine some of the most entrenched assumptions anthropologists hold, as do practitioners of other disciplines, about their discipline and ethnography. To this end and in consonance with Ingold's overall objectives, the volume sheds fresh light on the diverse ways in which to renew anthropology's potential for the future, especially when the discipline is faced with precariousness and challenges in the contemporary neoliberal times, including its decreasing voice and relevance in the public arenas.

The six contributors in this volume respond to Ingold in various ways. Whereas some defend the very notion of ethnography, which Ingold subjects to a thorough criticism, by invoking Weber on a specific topic (but without relating it to his overall thoughts such as the idea of "value-free" science and its putative objectivity based inter alia on the surgical separation between fact and value; see Allen 2004: 4; Pollock 1993: 85, 119n11; Weber 1946), and the notion of the disciplinary calling, others, enthralled by the poetic appeal of Ingold's writing, find it less than relevant in conducting research on, for example, themes relating to "dark anthropology." Yet others enthusiastically welcome Ingold's intervention but find his intervention wanting in many respects and less than radical in others. Thus, the contributors aim to further push the frontier of the discourse in directions unthought or underthought in Ingold's original contribution. The sites of engagement are richly diverse ranging as they do from anthropology of science to anthropology of religion, anthropology of terrorism to anthropology of ethnicity and language, and from locations as diverse as Egypt, Greece, India, Laos, Mauritius, Thailand, and Switzerland. The range of engagements—thematic and geographical—goes to demonstrate the salience of Ingold's far-reaching interventions, which the volume in your hands or on your screens further broadens.

This volume engages with Ingold to addresses two set of questions: (1) those about the relationships between ethnography[1] and anthropology that are explicitly at the core of his writings, and (2) additional and implied questions, which his writings enable but do not elaborate or enunciate. Patrick Eisenlohr and Patrice Ladwig take up the first set of questions. Unlike Ingold, both seem to be mostly committed to the "traditional" ideas about ethnography and find the concept of "correspondence" between participant observers and people they work with less than helpful. Based on their respective fieldworks in Mauritius, Laos, and Thailand, they demonstrate their unease with Ingold's idea of correspondence. For Eisenlohr, this takes the form of radical incongruence between his commitment to anthropology (also to his own ideology) and those of his interlocutors who were wedded to the ethnic and religious ideology of Hindu nationalism. In his study of the Buddhist death rituals and while working in crematoria in Laos and Thailand, Ladwig, contra Ingold, felt the need for noncorrespondence as well as a temporal objectification.

As concerns the second set of questions, other contributions take the debate in unexpected (but connected) directions. For instance, if ethnography is so problematic, as Ingold has it, then is there an alternative to it? If not ethnography, what sort of -graphy should we practice? Drawing on Walter Benjamin and his own recent works on historical–cultural memory in Europe and the place of architecture therein, Jeremy Walton proposes an alternative graphic form, "constellational writing," in conjunction with what he arrestingly calls "textured historicity." Irfan Ahmad takes on elision of the political (Ahmad 2018) and international relations (IR) in Ingold to foreground a reformulated notion of holism by scaling it up to a horizon anthropologists have hitherto been reluctant to approach—holism on an awkward global scale with politics, IR, and other fields as its lynchpins. He also examines the category of "the people," which is at the heart of Ingold's definition of both anthropology and ethnography. Tracing the changing trajectory of the subject matter of anthropology from "other culture," "race," "the native," "the primitive," and "simple society" to "the people," Ahmad asks if the replacement of earlier terms with "people" solves the problem or instead raises more questions, especially from the perspective of political theory and IR. Based on her research in Egypt among intellectuals and concerning the role of media, Hatsuki Aishima asks if and to what extent Ingold's exposition on relationships between and conceptualizations of ethnography and anthropology work in anthropological studies of Islam in the Middle East. She also relates these questions to her role as a lecturer teaching courses on Islam at the University of Manchester—a subject unmentioned by Ingold. Based on her fieldwork with particle physicists at CERN (Conseil Européen pour la Recherche

Nucléaire—the European Organization for Nuclear Research, Switzerland), Arpita Roy aims to shift the focus from Ingold's emphasis on the ontological to the impersonal and the logical to note the limits of ethnography. Viewing anthropological research as a form of experimental mode of inquiry, she observes that the logical relations—contradictions, dualisms, separations, oppositions, and the like—are no less human. Taking the Socratic approach to inquiry, she asks if and how ethnography can, viewed mainly as an ontological encounter, account for the logical.

Questions such as these relate as much to the past of anthropology as to its present and future. And since the future of anthropology is predicated on the future of other disciplines—indeed the future of the world at large, including the transformation in/of academy—these contributions likewise touch on these multiple futures. In the context of this volume, these questions are clearly linked to the relationships between ethnography and anthropology, as understood conventionally by anthropologists as much as by nonanthropologists (see below).

Thanks to the prevailing consensus that practicing anthropology amounts to practicing ethnography (Clifford Geertz being its one prominent example—see Aishima, this volume) and the increasing embrace of "ethnographic methods" by nonanthropologists, there is a superabundance of publications on ethnography. For example, practitioners of political science such as Schatz (2009), Wedeen (2010), and Priyam (2016) have made a strong case for political scientists to adopt what they see as anthropology's "ethnographic method." While for Wedeen it is ethnographic method in plural, for Priyam it is in singular. In contradistinction to rational choice and game theories preponderant in political science, especially in its dominant behaviorist model, Wedeen (2010: 257) defines ethnography as "immersion in the place and lives of people under study." However, as Ingold rightly notes in his response to his interlocutors in this volume, contra Wedeen, immersion is far from an innocent idea. Along lines similar to Wedeen, for Priyam (2016: 119), "ethnographic method" is characterized by "small n" and it distinguishes itself from the quantitative method marked by "Large N." Concerned as she is primarily with election studies, for Priyam, anything that is based on conversation with voters and is not derived from surveys or opinion polls conducted by psephologists or media houses briskly passes as "ethnographic."

Even without giving examples of how social scientists other than political scientists think of anthropology and ethnography (for an account by a sociologist, see O'Reilly 2012), needless to say, anthropologists themselves have published too many books on the topic to list here. However, most such books—both by anthropologists and nonanthropologists—often adopt the taken-for-granted view of ethnography as a method, tool, technique, procedure, and so on (e.g., see Eriksen 2001, Gingrich 2012, Kottak 2008, Kuper 1983, Robben and Sluka 2007; these examples are obviously representative, not exhaustive). In contrast, this volume approaches the subject quite differently. It is distinctive in three respects.

First, at the center of this volume are the diverse, engaged, and critical responses to Tim Ingold's recent interventions (Ingold 2008a, 2008b, 2014, 2017), which are probably among the very few to comprehensively and systematically interrogate the received wisdom on the equivalence between ethnography and anthropology. To the best of my knowledge, I cannot think of another volume that discusses this subject so substantively and pointedly.

Second, contrary to the consensual view of ethnography as a method or tool, the volume follows Ingold in going past the construal of ethnography as a method to relate it to the very constitution, aims, and objectives of anthropology as a discipline, which in turn brings into question the very idea of method and ethnography. Put differently, it is this dialectical take on ethnography and anthropology, whereby both become simultaneously the subjects of critical examination and renewal or reorientation, that makes this volume distinct.

Third, although the single-authored books by McLean (2017) and Rees (2018) address, albeit quite differently, some of the questions Ingold raises, this volume is distinct because unlike these two books, which solely propound the views of their respective authors, this volume foregrounds a multiplicity of standpoints. This multiplicity is also distinguished by its thematic and spatial diversity. Rather than being preoccupied with specific concepts (of aesthetic theory, in the case of McLean), this volume approaches the issues from a fairly broad, more diverse set of theoretical frameworks, not to speak of the variety of cultural settings ranging from Europe and the Middle East to the Indian subcontinent and Southeast Asia. The respective subfields from which contributors to this volume engage with and expand Ingold's propositions are likewise diverse: anthropology of science, anthropology of religion, anthropology of terrorism, and anthropology of ethnicity and language. The diversity of viewpoints and cultural settings this volume presents further opens up the field for future dialogues with a range of scholars and interlocutors working in varied cultural sites and political milieus.

Anthropology, Ethnography, and the Future

In my reading, Ingold's multiple intervention consists of two connected propositions. First, his exposition on the idea that anthropology equals ethnography is crucially tied to the larger goal of securing "the kind of impact in the world" anthropology "deserves" and that "the world so desperately needs" (2014: 383, 384). This goal will remain unfulfilled, he observes, as long as there remains a conflation between ethnography/fieldwork and participant observation (PO). This precisely is his second point. Ingold's article is a diagnosis of this double conflation to rescue anthropology "under threats"—a concern earlier expressed by fellow anthropologists such as Bruce Kapferer (2007) and Marshall Sahlins (1999).

In Ingold's view, the conflation between anthropology and ethnography did not operate in the past, at least in British anthropology, which he heavily draws on to foreground his contention. They became "virtually equivalent," he observes, "over the last quarter of a century" (2008b: 69). There is something odd about Ingold's assertion here. Broadly the same period during which he thinks the conflation between the two took place, however, also saw many anthropological works that were seldom ethnographic, as conventionally construed. These works also became popular, even canonical in some ways. Some examples are as follows: Appadurai's (1996) *Modernity at Large*; Asad's (1993, 2003) *Genealogies of Religion* and *Formations of the Secular*; Mamdani's (2005) *Good Muslim, Bad Muslim*; Trouillot's (1995) *Silencing the Past*; van der Veer's (1994, 2001) *Religious Nationalism* and *Imperial Encounters*; and Eric Wolf's (1982) *Europe and People Without History*. Obviously, examples cited here are by no means exhaustive, and they bear the mark of the editor's interest (perforce his limitations too). My point is that the subfields of historical anthropology (as distinct from anthropology of history—on which, see Palmié and Stewart 2016) and comparative anthropology (see below)—historical and comparative are not mutually exclusive—flourished independently of ethnography. Needless to point out, ethnography was not even possible in the kind of work and questions that Sidney Mintz's (1985) *Sweetness and Power: The Place of Sugar in Modern History* undertook. In the book's Acknowledgments, Mintz expresses gratitude not to "informants" but instead to librarians of various libraries across the Atlantic. Concerned with the production of sugar in the Caribbean and its consumption in Europe and North America, Mintz aimed to chart out the entangled but asymmetrical historical relations, in place since 1492, between the colonies and the metropolis. To this end, he mapped out the history of sugar consumption in Great Britain from 1650 until 1900, when it had become an everyday item in most households. Remarkably, as an anthropologist—and unlike Robben (2010: vi) in a different context—Mintz rightly felt no need to offer an apologia that his inquiry was not ethnographic and lacked long-term fieldwork. For him, a historical inquiry was well within the precinct of anthropology, an undertaking that was neither conterminous with nor reducible to ethnography.[2]

As for the second conflation, between ethnography/fieldwork and PO, Ingold advises dropping the former. He takes ethnography as "*writing about the people*" (2014: 385—italics in original). A monograph that records "the life and times of a people may justifiably be called ethnographic." However, according to Ingold, it is misleading to call "our encounters with people, to the fieldwork in which these encounters take place, to the methods by which we prosecute it, or to the knowledge that grows therefrom" ethnographic. For Ingold, to choose PO rather than ethnographic fieldwork is to underline the "ontological commitment" to the people with whom anthropologists work. The pivot of this ontological commitment is educational in that anthropology itself becomes "a practice of education" (Ingold 2014: 388).[3] Against ethnography that sees encounters with people in terms of reportage or description of that which is already past, Ingold conceives PO as a correspondence between the anthropologist and people, the goal of which is the coimagining of possible futures rather than ethnographizing the past. As an intersubjective enterprise, PO "couples the forward movement of one's own perception and action with the movements of others, much as melodic lines are coupled in musical counterpoint." Ingold names this coupling of movements as *correspondence*. Thus conceived, the difference between PO and ethnographic fieldwork, and correspondence and description respectively, comes to its full glare. The "appeal to ethnography holds anthropology hostage to the popular stereotype of the ethnographer" as chronicler of particularism thereby preventing it from "having the wider, transformative effect" (2014: 392–93). In contrast, PO as a correspondence and educational-learning practice attends to the potential and to the "co-imagining of possible futures" (2014: 389–91). It is the PO, not ethnography, that will restore anthropology to its due place, concludes Ingold.

What is anthropology, however? Ingold discusses it in much detail in his Radcliffe-Brown lecture. Ethnography is concerned with the particular, whereas anthropology deals with generalizations. Here, Radcliffe-Brown, who conceptualized anthropology as a nomothetic and theoretical as opposed to an ideographic (e.g., history) discipline (also see Goldthorpe 2000), seems to be Ingold's source of inspiration (2008b: 70–79, 90). Ingold appears to suggest that it is by (re)turning to Radcliffe-Brown's conception of anthropology as a nomothetic discipline that anthropology can regain its voice. However, the precise contours of this proposition, if such is his proposition in the first place, are far from clear and not adequately laid out. That is, how can one arrive at generalizations in a world marked by sheer diversity? What is the arche in the Leibnizian mould (Dillon 1996: 12–13) from which generalizations and philosophizing would be undertaken? In fact, Ingold concludes by asking: "With its dreams of generalizations shattered, where should anthropology go?" Instead of answering the question pointedly, he suggests a move toward philosophy—a philosophy different from that of philosophers, however. Ingold's philosophy is "not in the arm chair but in the world." He offers the definition of anthropology as "philosophy with the people in" (2014: 393). It is indeed a terse definition, which Ahmad's chapter ahead subjects to a detailed critique.

Ingold's decoupling of the second conflation is markedly relevant. Part of this decoupling, including the conflation between anthropology and ethnography, may seem somewhat more stylistic than substantive, however. Many anthropologists practiced it without expressing it precisely in the same terms Ingold uses. For instance, Asad wrote:

> Most anthropologists are taught that their discipline is essentially defined by a research technique (participant observation) carried out in a circumscribed field and that as such it deals with particularity—with what Clifford Geertz, following the philosopher Gilbert Ryle, called "thick description." . . .
>
> In my view, anthropology is more than a method, and it should not be equated—as it has popularly become—with the direction given to inquiry by the pseudoscientific notion of "fieldwork." . . . What is distinctive about modern anthropology is the comparison of embedded concepts (representations) between societies differently located in time or space. (2003: 16–17)

As the quote above demonstrates, Talal Asad (re)asserts the comparative and theoretical objectives of anthropology. Importantly, such a comparative anthropological pursuit is not premised on equivalence between anthropology and fieldwork or participant observation. This is not the proper place to go into an in-depth treatment of comparison in anthropology, including the reassessment of its epistemological and methodological assumptions in the history of the discipline over *longue durée* and its return in the contemporary moment (on which, see Candea 2019; Gingrich 2012; Gingrich and Fox 2002; Holy 1987; cf. Boas 1896). For the purpose of the present discussion, I want to briefly discuss van der Veer's (2016) book on comparison in anthropology. In the vein of Mintz, in *The Value of Comparison*, van der Veer pursues as well as outlines the task of anthropological comparison without necessarily tying it to the indispensability of ethnography. This is not to say that the book does not use ethnographic materials, those of others as well as his own. It most certainly does. But it equally deploys works by historians, sociologists, scholars of religion, political theorists, novelists, and others. What is clear is that van der Veer rejects the types of anthropological comparison that he terms "the macro sociological form of ethnic profiling," and which, in his view, characterized holism-inspired works such as *Patterns of Cultures* by Ruth Benedict, *The Cultural Background of Personality* by Ralph Linton, as well as works by Abraham Kardiner and Francis Hsu (in Ahmad 2020: 16–17). Fox and Gingrich (2002: 3) make a similar contention as they too abandon what they call "holocultural comparison."[4]

Clearly, the aim of the above discussion about ethnography and its place vis-à-vis historical and comparative anthropology is not to undervalue Ingold's intervention but instead to situate his argument and concerns in relation to earlier and other writings on anthropology in general and ethnography in particular (Mauss 2007; Parkin and Ulijaszek 2007; Reed-Danahay 2017; Robben and Sluka 2007; Wolf 2001). More importantly, the generative qualities of his writings allow us to ask questions that connect with and at times also exceed Ingold's interventions, which, as noted earlier, have generated an important debate, animating anthropologists worldwide.

Outline of Contributions

Before closing this Introduction with an outline of chapters to follow, two disclaimers are in order. First, this volume deals with a fragment of Ingold's otherwise multifarious and prolific list of publications, which span nearly half a century. By its very nature, this volume is problem-oriented rather than corpus-specific. Readers who maintain that a scholar's contribution to a specific subject can properly be appreciated only in relation to her entire corpus can undertake such an exercise on their own. Second, to see various contributions to this volume in dualistic terms of detractors or admirers of Ingold would be close to defeating its very purpose (with the possible exception of

Eisenlohr's essay in the former category). All contributors regard Ingold's interventions as salient enough to engage with, though their modes of engagement and the manner in which they (dis)agree with them are evidently diverse. Overall, their critique is immanent, not transcendental (Ahmad 2017). Risking the charge of reductionism, including slinking away from their multilayered density and diverse points of entry, the arrangement of chapters proceed from application or operationalization of Ingold's reflections and near agreement with them to intense disagreement, questioning and expanding themes and points implied, silent or unsaid therein. It follows that readers can modify the existing organization of chapters to suit their intellectual tastes and priorities.

By discussing two types of select writings in her contribution—those on anthropology of Islam in general and on anthropology of Islam in Egypt in particular—Aishima critically assesses if and how Ingold's observation sheds light on those specific writings and the implication arising therefrom for an anthropology of Islam. Put differently, she works to determine if and how the practices of correspondence operate in the anthropology of Islam. Here, she discusses the changing nature of works on Islam in the Middle East after Edward Said and Talal Asad's interventions and relates these changes to Ingold's (re)formulation of anthropology. Along the way, she also dwells on the postmodern debates on crisis of representation in anthropology. More importantly, she observes incongruence between her role as an ethnographer, which, in Ingold's terms, is oriented toward learning from people with whom one works, and her role as a teacher when she taught courses on Islam. Aishima finds Ingold's thesis about anthropological research as study *with* rather than *of* Egyptians/Muslims as fruitful (and echoing Asad's formulation of Islam as a discursive tradition), while wondering if the same holds true for classrooms where her many Muslim students sharply object, for instance, to her views about sectarian differences within Islam. She adds further richness to her analysis by reflecting on her own subject position.

Against the possible (mis)reading of Ingold as seeking to renounce ethnography, Roy thoughtfully reads him as arguing for correspondence and attending to others. Beyond the ontological imperatives, Roy, however, pleads for a Socratic dialogue whereby fieldwork becomes more than an intersubjective correspondence to pursue the larger dialectic of anthropological craftsmanship. To foreground her contention, Roy draws on her extensive fieldwork with practitioners of "hard science" at CERN, Switzerland. Central to her contention is the primacy of the logical and impersonal relations vis-à-vis the ontological, which she analyses with unusual brevity and in a flowing prose. In the tradition of anthropological thinking such as Uberoi's (2002), she asks: To what extent and how can logical relationships in the forms of contradictions, dualisms, separations, and oppositions be accounted for through ethnography, putatively conceived as an intersubjective enterprise alone?

In his contribution, Walton interrogates the strict distinction between anthropology and ethnography that Ingold proposes. Noting that Ingold rightly identifies serious problems in the ideas and practices of ethnography, he finds Ingold grappling with a "graphic" dilemma that his argument logically entails: If not ethnography, what sort of -graphy should anthropologists, then, practice? Based on this reading—Ingold finds it a misreading bordering on "accusation"—Walton takes on the challenging task of proposing an alternative, which he calls "constellational writing." Drawing on Walter Benjamin, especially his publications on the practices of writing, and relating them ethnographically to a mosque in Thessaloniki, Greece, he shows what an alternative to ethnography might look like. At the center of his alternative proposal lies the notion of time. Unlike anthropologists–ethnographers who write about people with whom they work in the past tense, in Walton's reading, Benjamin dialectically viewed the present as a "past future."

Taking the subject of "correspondence" head on, in his contribution, Ladwig provocatively argues—along the "counterpoint" method of thinking associated with Dutch anthropologist–sociologist W. F. Wertheim (1974)—for a "noncorrespondence." While recognizing its relevance elsewhere, he argues that practicing "correspondence" in what Sherry Ortner calls "dark anthropology" is less than easy, to some extent even undesirable and impossible. Discussing the dynamics of Buddhist death rituals in Laos and Thailand, Ladwig instead argues in favor of establishing distance and noncorrespondence with his informants as a more reasonable practice. Largely sympathetic to Ingold's "idealist" vision imbued as he finds it with a theological baggage, in practice, Ladwig finds it unworkable because fieldwork is equally marked by circumstances with cracks and fault lines. In contrast to Ingold's rejection of objectification, he instead offers qualified justifications for it, noting how temporal alienation may well be a useful strategy to deal with such tough situations as during his own fieldwork.

Along partly similar but markedly different lines, Eisenlohr defends the conventional and what some might take as an "old-fashioned" idea and practice of ethnography. To this end, Eisenlohr dwells, inter alia, on the significant difference between knowledge interests and institutional and professional commitments of anthropologists on the one hand, and those of their informants or interlocutors on the other. Due mainly to this difference, what Ingold calls "correspondence" and "ontological commitment" as hallmarks of participant observation, Eisenlohr maintains, do not fully work. If they do, they do only precariously, even indefensibly. Eisenlohr's analysis is based on his long-term, extensive fieldwork in Mauritius where he finds a radical incongruence between his own goals and those of the activists–interlocutors committed to an explicitly ethnic, anti-Muslim Hindu nationalist cause. In disagreement with Ingold and invoking Max Weber, he notes that anthropological fieldwork is more like a Weberian calling rather than a process of becoming or coimagining of futures in Ingoldian registers.

While in agreement with Ingold's questioning of the substitution between ethnography and anthropology, Ahmad critiques Ingold for his failure to fully account for politics and international relations (IR) in any enterprise to reimagine anthropology. To this end, Ahmad focuses on "the people"—a term at the center of Ingold's definitions of both anthropology and ethnography. Ahmad asks how the replacement of earlier terms—such as other culture, the primitive, race, tribe, simple society, and so on—with "the people" serves the purpose of renewing anthropology. Drawing on his fieldwork with journalists and media's reporting on terrorism in India, Ahmad calls for a reformulated notion of holism with political theory and IR as its lynchpins. He also argues that beyond the cliché of anthropology as studying "others," anthropology should also study "us," asking how people become "other" or "us." For anthropology to be a voice beyond the university silo, so goes his contention, it should concern itself more with the true than with what is merely real. After an extensive critical engagement with Ingold, Ahmad offers his own definition of anthropology as "political philosophy with 'people' in."

Addressing the key issues that various contributions have raised, the volume concludes with a detailed and an animated response from Ingold. His response lucidly clarifies many issues and answers several questions raised here. Ingold deftly spells out the distinctions—once more—between ethnography and anthropology; he also dwells on the pitfalls emanating from their hurriedly assumed union. Reflecting on objections to the term "correspondence" by some interlocutors, he relationally and vividly elaborates on the associated concepts of "harmony" and "resonance" to clarify and assert the significance of "correspondence" as a term. Particularly illuminating is his exposition, albeit too brief—in response to Eisenlohr with whom no other contributor seems to share the ground—on the disciplinary boundaries and the continuing image or claim of academia as an institution of autonomous knowledge. It is also the case, however, that Ingold does not address every issue or argument that contributors make, at least not comprehensively enough. To take one among many examples, Ingold's response to the questions of truth and the true that Ahmad and Roy broach are certainly instructive. However, it does not offer an elaborate treatment of their various components and the interrelationships among them; much less resolve these thorny questions. No response, including the texts, from which the response emanates and is directed at (here Ahmad and Roy), can truly answer these questions. That would indeed tantamount to closure of conversations, or what Ingold in his response tellingly calls a "final resolution." In that very spirit to continue rather than resolve the conversations, Ingold's response demonstrates the generosity and openness characteristic of a true scholar. This is manifest, for instance, in Ingold's willingness, in light of Ahmad's interdisciplinary critique (at the intersections of political theory, international relations, and the related fields), to revise his earlier definition of anthropology—anthropology is "philosophy with the people in"—as follows: "I was naïve not to anticipate the way in which the idea of 'the people' would be mobilized in the rhetoric of contemporary populism, as the signs were already there. In retrospect, it would have been better to leave out the offending article, rendering anthropology thus as 'philosophy with people in.'"

However, on occasions, I tend to think that I have been misunderstood, as does Ingold vis-à-vis the critiques of him by the contributors to this volume. For instance, the spirit of my critique pertained not to "the people" only but equally to people without the definite article "the" and which Ingold offers as an alternative to earlier terms anthropology used to describe their subject matter: "tribe," "the primitive," "simple society," "the non-West," "other cultures," and so on. Likewise, my critique of anthropology's holism as delinked from politics and IR relates to dominant practice of holism undertaken in the discipline more widely and not to its sectional or private understandings by some (Wittgenstein 1953). It is puzzling to read that Ingold finds that my reformulated notion of holism involves "totalization," a word that I never use nor do I convey its sense through other words. Like him, I too am no fan of totalization. Even more astonishing is Ingold's inference that my critique of him about his idea of people torn apart, inter alia, from the fields of politics and IR amounts to rejection of his definition of anthropology, "people" being one of the keywords. Put simply, my submission is that "people" with or without "the" is not an innocent word or term; instead, it is deeply connected to and predicated on politics, from which Ingold's exposition maintains quite a distance. Other contributors may have impressions of similar misreading of their own expositions. As is often the case, misunderstanding is not foreign to discussions, especially of the sort this volume broaches in greater depth. During the years ahead, contributors to this volume, Ingold, as well as readers and future interlocutors will likely have the opportunity to clarify and articulate their standpoints more thoroughly and pointedly. Knowledge, or more appropriately wisdom (*ḥikma/ḥikmat* in Islamic and Islamicate traditions), is a process in collective thinking—impermanence and openness being its marked features.

Given the regnant substitutive identification between anthropology and ethnography and Ingold's sustained examination of it, which this volume critically expands, enhances, and enriches, anthropologists as well as the wider community of social scientists who are receptive to ethnographic and anthropological insights will hopefully find this volume of great interest, engaging with its (de)merits.

Irfan Ahmad (PhD in anthropology, University of Amsterdam) is Senior Research Fellow, Max Planck Institute for the Study of Religious & Ethnic Diversity, Göttingen, Germany. Previously, he acted as an associate professor of political anthropology at Australian Catholic University and senior lecturer at Monash University. He is author of *Islamism and Democracy in India* (Princeton University Press, 2009) and *Religion as Critique: Islamic Critical Thinking from Mecca to the Marketplace* (University of North Carolina Press, 2017). Recently, he coedited *The Algebra of Warfare-Welfare* (Oxford University Press, 2019). He has taught at Australian and Dutch universities. Founding coeditor of *Journal of Religious & Political Practice*, he is on editorial boards, inter alia, of *Public Anthropologist* and *South Asia*. In 2018, he wrote the "Renewing Political Anthropology" column for *Anthropology News*. He also contributes to debates in global media.

Notes

1. Since many contributors to this volume are professionally affiliated with institutions in Göttingen, it is additionally important to note that the word "ethnography" originated in the university town of Göttingen. Historian of anthropology Han F. Vermeulen (1995: 39–40, 43, 50, 53) records that linguist–historian August Ludwig Schlözer of Göttingen first used *Ethnographie* in German in 1771. Vermeulen thus contests the

demotic belief that this word was first used in Britain in the 1830s. In France, the word *Ethnographie* appeared in the 1820s. Used as an equivalent of *Völkerkunde* and in relation to *Volkskunde*, *Ethnographie* meant historical and descriptive study of peoples or nations, "the history of nations or Völkergeschichte" (also see Vermeulen 2006). See also note 4 below.
2. Elsewhere, Mintz (Undated) observed that without his earlier "on-the-ground-fieldwork," he could not have written the kind of historical anthropology he did. He considered it important to clarify that he was trained in anthropology, not in history. See Walton, this volume, on the purity of disciplines and methods. For a more recent engagement of history, historicity, and memory in relation to anthropology, see Walton (2019).
3. Talal Asad's (2020) following remark is worth quoting: "participant-observation is not merely the distinctive method of a particular academic discipline but the essence of all learning."
4. Meanings of the word *comparison* vary within as well as outside a discipline. Though many take comparison as integral to anthropology, others do not. In one reading, based on participant observation, ethnography focuses on a single culture from an emic frame pertaining to the local-particular. In contrast, ethnology studies cultures; it is comparative, broad, and theory-driven. Further, as ethnologists analyze finished ethnographies rather than conducting their own, their standpoint is etic (Flemming 2011). In another account, while ethnography addresses "what," "when," and "where," ethnology answers the questions of "why" and " how" to transcend "simple description" and arrive at "analysis and comparison" (Eisenberg 1971: 298). The interpretative turn and Geertz's advocacy of thick description, writes Welz, proposed "not to generalize across cases but to generalize within them" (in Welz 2001: 4,864). Absent from Welz's discussion is Geertz's *Islam Observed*, which went beyond generalizing within. Elsewhere I have argued (Ahmad 2018) how *Islam Observed* belonged to the genre of Cold War anthropological works (see Chapter 6) engaged in producing "national personality" and "national identity" (Fabian 1983). Dotted with orientalism, Geertz's work exemplified "holocultural comparison" between Indonesia and Morocco. Notably, definitions in general, including those of a discipline, are an exercise in the drawing of boundaries. Not set in stone, definitions shape and are shaped by power matrix: academic, political–economic, and the like.

References

Ahmad, Irfan. 2017. *Religion as Critique: Islamic Critical Thinking from Mecca to the Marketplace*. Chapel Hill: University of North Carolina Press.
———. 2018. "On the Absence of Political in Four-Field Anthropology." *Anthropology News*. Online. 22 March. https://anthrosource.onlinelibrary.wiley.com/doi/10.1111/AN.804.

———. 2020. "The Oeuvre of Peter van der Veer." MMG Working Paper 20-01, ISSN 2192-2357. Max Planck Institute for the Study of Religious and Ethnic Diversity, Göttingen. https://www.mmg.mpg.de/540549/WP_20-01_Ahmad-The-Oeuvre-of-Peter-van-der-Veer.pdf.

Allen, Kieran. 2004. *Max Weber: A Critical Introduction*. London: Pluto.

Appadurai, Arjun. 1996. *Modernity At Large: Cultural Dimensions of Globalization*. Minneapolis: University of Minnesota Press.

Asad, Talal. 1993. *Genealogies of Religion: Discipline and Reasons of Power in Christianity and Islam*. Baltimore: Johns Hopkins University Press.

———. 2003. *Formations of the Secular: Christianity, Islam, Modernity*. Stanford: Stanford University Press.

———. 2020. "Thinking about Religion through Wittgenstein." *Critical Times*.

Boas, Franz. 1896. "The Limitations of the Comparative Method of Anthropology." *Science* (NS) IV, no. 103: 901–8.

Candea, Matei. 2019. "Comparison, Re-Placed." In *Going to Pentecost: An Experimental Approach to Studies in Pentecostalism*, edited by A. Eriksen, R. L. Blanes, and M. MacCarthy, 179–86. New York: Berghahn Books.

Comaroff, Jean, and John Comaroff, 2003. "Ethnography on an Awkward Scale: Postcolonial Anthropology and the Violence of Abstraction." *Ethnography* 4, no. 2: 147–79.

da Col, Giovanni. 2017. "Two or Three Things I Know about Ethnographic Theory." *HAU: Journal of Ethnographic Theory* 7, no. 1: 1–8.

Dillon, Michael. 1996. *Politics of Security: Towards a Political Philosophy of Continental Thought*. London: Routledge.

Eisenberg, Lonard. 1971. "Anthropological Archaeology: Ethnography or Ethnology?" *Plains Anthropologist* 16, no. 54: 298–301.

Eriksen, Thomas. 2001. *Small Places, Large Issues: An Introduction to Social and Cultural Anthropology*. 2nd ed. London: Pluto.

Fabian, Johannes. 1983. *Time and the Other: How Anthropology Makes Its Object*. New York: Columbia University Press

Flemming, Isabelle. 2011. "Ethnography and Ethnology." In *21st Century Anthropology: A Reference Handbook*, edited by H. J. Birx, 153–61. London: Sage.

Fox, Richard, and Andre Gingrich 2002. " Introduction." In *Anthropology, by Comparison*, edited by A. Gingrich and R. Fox, 1–24. London: Routledge.

Gingrich, Andre. 2012. "Comparative Methods in Socio-Cultural Anthropology Today." In *The SAGE Handbook of Social Anthropology*. Vol. II, edited by R. Fardon et al., 201–14. London: Sage.

Gingrich, Andre, and Richard Fox, eds. 2002. *Anthropology, by Comparison*. London: Routledge.

Goldthorpe, John. 2000. *On Sociology: Numbers, Narratives, and the Integration of Research and Theory*. Oxford: Oxford University Press.

Holy, Ladislav, ed. 1987. *Comparative Anthropology*. Oxford: Blackwell.

Ingold, Tim. 2008a. "Anthropology Is *Not* Ethnography." *British Academy Review* 11: 21–23.

———. 2008b. "Anthropology Is *Not* Ethnography." *Proceedings of the British Academy* 154: 69–92.
———. 2014. "That Is Enough About Ethnography." *HAU: Journal of Ethnographic Theory* 4, no. 1: 383–95.
———. 2017. "Anthropology Contra Ethnography." *HAU: Journal of Ethnographic Theory* 7, no. 1: 21–26.
Kapferer, Bruce. 2007. "Anthropology and the Dialectic of Enlightenment: A Discourse on the Definition and Ideals of a Threatened Discipline." *The Australian Journal of Anthropology* 18, no. 1: 72–94.
Kottak, Conrad. 2008. *Anthropology: The Exploration of Human Diversity*. 12th ed. Boston: McGraw-Hill.
Kuper, Adam. 1983 [1973]. *Anthropology and Anthropologist: The Modern British School*. London: Routledge.
———. 1986. "An Interview with Edmund Leach." *Current Anthropology* 27, no. 4: 375–382.
MacDougall, Susan. 2016. "Enough about Ethnography: An Interview with Tim Ingold." Society for Cultural Anthropology. 5 April. https://culanth.org/fieldsights/enough-about-ethnography-an-interview-with-tim-ingold.
Mamdani, Mahmood. 2005. *Good Muslim, Bad Muslim: America, the Cold War, and the Roots of Terror*. New York: Three Leaves Press, Doubleday.
Massenzio, Marcello. 2001. "An Interview with Claude Lévi-Strauss." *Current Anthropology* 42, no. 3: 419–425.
Mauss, Marcel. 2007. *Manual of Ethnography* (edited with an introduction by N J. Allen). New York: Berghahn Books and Durkheim Press.
McLean, Stuart. 2017. *Fictionalizing Anthropology: Encounters and Fabulations at the Edges of the Human*. Minneapolis: University of Minnesota Press.
Mintz, Sidney. 1985. *Sweetness and Power: The Place of Sugar in Modern History*. New York: Penguin.
———. Undated. "Anthropology and History." Accessed 18 March 2020. https://sidneymintz.net/history.php.
O'Reilly, Karen. 2012. *Ethnographic Methods*. 2nd edition. London: Routledge.
Palmié, Stephan, and Charles Stewart. 2016. "Introduction: For an Anthropology of History." *HAU: Journal of Ethnographic Theory* 6, no. 1: 207–36.
Panourgiá, Neni. 2002. "Interview with Clifford Geertz." *Anthropological Theory* 2, no. 4: 421–431.
Parkin, David, and Stanley Ulijaszek, eds. 2007. *Holistic Anthropology: Emergence and Convergence*. New York: Berghahn Books.
Pollock, Sheldon. 1993. "Deep Orientalism: Notes on Sanskrit and Power beyond the Raj." In *Orientalism and the Post-colonial Predicament: Perspectives on South Asia*, edited by Carole Breckenridge and Peter van der Veer, 76–133. Philadelphia: University of Pennsylvania Press.
Priyam, Manisha. 2016. "Notes on Method: Political Ethnography as a Method for Understanding Urban Politics and Elections in India." *Studies in Indian Politics* 4, no. 1: 119–27.

Reed-Danahay, Deobrah. 2017. "Participating, Observing, Witnessing." In *The Routledge Companion to Contemporary Anthropology*, edited by S. Coleman, S. B. Hyatt, and A. Kingsolver, 119–27. Abingdon: Routledge.

Rees, Tobias. 2018. *After Ethnos*. Durham: Duke University Press.

Robben, Antonius. 2010. "Preface." In *Iraq at a Distance: What Anthropologists Can Teach Us about War*, edited by A. Robben, vii–ix. Philadelphia: University of Pennsylvania Press.

Robben, Antonius, and Jeffrey Sluka, eds. 2007. *Ethnographic Fieldwork: An Anthropological Reader*. Malden, MA: Blackwell.

Sahlins, Marshall. 1999. "What Is Anthropological Enlightenment? Some Lessons of the Twentieth Century." *Annual Review of Anthropology* 28: i–xxiii.

Schatz, Edward, ed. 2009. *Political Ethnography: What Immersion Contributes to the Study of Power*. Chicago: University of Chicago Press.

Trouillot, Michel-Rolph. 1995. *Silencing the Past: Power and the Production of History*. Boston: Beacon Press.

Uberoi, J. P. S. 2002. *European Modernity: Science, Truth, Method*. New Delhi: Oxford University Press.

van der Veer, Peter. 1994. *Religious Nationalism: Hindus and Muslims in India*. Berkeley: University of California Press.

———. 2001. *Imperial Encounters: Religion and Modernity in India and Britain*. Princeton: Princeton University Press.

———. 2016. *The Value of Comparison* (The Lewis Henry Morgan Lectures). Durham: Duke University Press.

Vermeulen, Han F. 1995. "Origins and Institutionalization of Ethnography and Ethnology in Europe and the USA, 1771–1845." In *Fieldwork and Footnotes: Studies in the History of European Anthropology*, edited by H. B. Vermeulen and Arturo Alvarez Roldán, 39–59. London: Routledge.

———. 2006. "The German Invention of Völkerkunde." In *The German Invention of Race*, edited by S. Eigen and M. Larrimore, 123–45. Albany: State University of New York Press.

Walton, Jeremy F., ed. 2019. "Ambivalent Legacies: Political Cultures of Memory and Amnesia in Former Habsburg and Ottoman Lands." Special issue, *History and Anthropology* 30, no 4.

Weber, Max. 1946. "Science as a Vocation." In *From Max Weber: Essays in Sociology*, translated by by H. H. Gerth and C. Wright Mills. New York: Oxford University Press.

Wedeen, Lisa. 2010. "Reflections on Ethnographic Work in Political Science." *Annual Review of Political Science* 13: 225–72.

Welz, G. 2001. "Ethnology." In *International Encyclopedia of the Social & Behavioral Science*. Amsterdam: Elsevier.

Wertheim, W. F. 1974. *Evolution and Revolution: The Rising Waves of Emancipation*. Harmondsworth: Penguin Books.

Wittgenstein, Ludwig. 1953. *Philosophical Investigations*. Oxford: Basil Blackwell.

Wolf, Eric. 2001. *Pathways of Power: Building an Anthropology of the Modern World*. Berkeley: University of California Press.
———. 2010 [1982]. *Europe and People Without History*. Berkeley: University of California Press.

Chapter 1

BEYOND CORRESPONDENCE

DOING ANTHROPOLOGY OF ISLAM IN THE FIELD AND CLASSROOM

Hatsuki Aishima

In this chapter, I critically engage with Tim Ingold's repeated calls to establish a clear boundary between anthropology and ethnography. Ingold's goal, it seems, is to redefine how anthropologists relate to people they meet during their fieldwork as well as back home. He aspires to liberate anthropology from its long-lasting dilemma of representation by assigning its task of description and objectification to ethnography. In this way, he hopes to repatriate anthropologists' authority to write about a "society," "culture," and more recently about "self" or "ethics." Ingold's proposals allow me to revisit and compare my own experiences of engaging with Muslims in Cairo and Manchester. Whereas the Prophet Muhammad advised his followers in the seventh century Arabian Peninsula to "seek knowledge even unto China," Ingold alerts us that in the increasingly globalizing world, not only the everyday life in the distant fieldwork sites but also life at home are the significant spaces for epistemological inquiry.

Ingold's call to distinguish anthropology from ethnography is important because for a long time, ethnography had indeed become anthropologists' trademark. The ethnographic approach has certainly become fashionable in both the social sciences and humanities. When I reflect upon meeting colleagues and those working on Egypt—whether historians, political scientists, or a developmental project manager—they come to Cairo to carry out fieldwork, and many of them claim to employ ethnographic methods. This was indeed the main concern of the workshop "Ethnographies of Islam" that was held in London in 2009 (see Dupret, Pierret, Pinto, and Spellman-Poots 2012). Many participants in that workshop felt the urge to discuss how the ethnographic approach we employ in anthropological studies of Islam differed from that of other disciplines. We concluded that the difference was in a distinctive type of personal relations we form with our interlocutors. Researchers of other disciplines tend to "fly in" to conduct interviews and "fly out" within a week. Their ethnographies are based on a series of one-off interviews. They don't see the necessity for getting to know the personal backgrounds of their interviewees. In contrast, anthropologists have conversations with people they meet during the fieldwork. They must form personal relationships with their interlocutors by each learning about the other. Our understanding of anthropological ethnography was quite similar to Ingold's notion of "anthropology as correspondence." However, it never occurred to me that anthropology could be divorced from ethnography. While I agree with Ingold's assertion that the purpose of anthropology is "to join people in their speculation about what life *might* be or *could* be like," it makes me wonder what an anthropological work would look like after removing ethnographic details from its writing (Ingold 2013: 4—emphasis in original). Unlike many other anthropologists who tear the work of fellow anthropologists apart, Ingold does not give much clue to what exactly he sees as good and bad practices in current anthropology. As a result, we are only left to speculate.

After situating Ingold's project on separating anthropology from ethnography in the debates over anthropological writing, this chapter mainly discusses works on the anthropology of Islam in Egypt to demonstrate the ways in which his observations have a bearing on such works. Then I revisit my own work on the Egyptian middle classes as well as my experience teaching anthropological scholarship on Islam at the University of Manchester to compare and contrast the types of relationships I formed with my interlocutors and students. I conclude with observations about Ingold's warning against the conflation between anthropology and ethnography and the extent to which it is applicable when teaching Islam at a university setting. My contribution will demonstrate that by redefining the purpose of social anthropology as educational, Ingold provides an invaluable clue to overcome the crisis of representation. However, a problem arises when applying Ingold's insight about ideas and practices of doing research in the context of teaching anthropology in classrooms. I truly admire the ways in which Ingold practices anthropology in his lectures and in the field, yet I struggle to find ways to replicate his model when teaching Islam in university classrooms (see also Eisenlohr, this volume).

From Description to Correspondence

What distinguishes social anthropology from other disciplines is a combination of participant observation and field notes. Writing field notes allows anthropologists to reflect upon conversations with interlocutors as well as contextualize the incidents they experienced during participant observations. As James Clifford (1990: 67—emphasis in original) has aptly characterized, "the construction of 'thick' cultural descriptions involves a *turning away* from inscription and transcription to a different form of writing." Although there is a temptation to document the entire event in a holistic manner, field notes are more like snapshots. We strategize and select scenes from our experience before writing them down, with the hope of eventually using this piece of writing as "an ethnographic example."

While there is no denying that writing field notes is at the core of the anthropological discipline, the definition of ethnography has been widely debated. For Clifford Geertz, ethnography and anthropology were almost synonymous when he characterized a good anthropological writing as "thick description." "In anthropology, or anyway social anthropology, what the practitioners do is ethnography. And it is in understanding what ethnography is, or more exactly *what doing ethnography is*, that a start can be made towards grasping what anthropological analysis amounts to as a form of knowledge" (Geertz 1973: 5–6—emphasis in original). Acknowledging the centrality of ethnography in social anthropology, edited volumes such as *Writing Culture: The Poetics and Politics of Ethnography* (Clifford and Marcus 1986) and *Fieldnotes: The Making of Anthropology* (Sanjek 1990) have problematized the nature of ethnographic and field note writing in terms of anthropologists' authority to represent and objectify their research subjects. The atmosphere of postcolonial discomfort of the 1970s brought into question the unequal power relations Western anthropologists continue to exert vis-à-vis their interlocutors during their fieldwork.

However, Ingold's project of defining ethnography and anthropology as two different types of intellectual inquiries brought this debate to another level. In his formulation, whereas ethnography aims to describe in detail and with accuracy a sociocultural phenomenon, anthropology "seek[s] a generous, comparative but nevertheless critical understanding of human being and knowing in the one world we all inhabit" (Ingold 2008a: 69). Since his 2007 Radcliffe Brown Lecture, Ingold has continued to assert that anthropology was stuck in a cul-de-sac of the crisis of representation because many scholars confuse "observation" with "objectification" (see Ingold 2008b, 2013, 2014, 2017). Anthropology is "a practice of observation grounded in participatory dialogue" (Ingold 2008a: 87), which requires one to acquire an art to observe and converse attentively. Anthropological writing is derived from such "correspondence" with our interlocutors (Ingold 2008a: 87)

Anthropologists who depersonalize their encounters in the fields by characterizing them as mere "case studies" perplex Ingold. For him, anthropological engagements are essentially educational and transformative. We are learning from one another. "The distinction between the kinds of work done with the little words *of* and *with* is all-important here. It is the *of* that converts observation into objectification" (Ingold 2017: 23—emphasis in original). By redefining the subfields of anthropology as an enterprise *with* rather than *of*, he assigns a new task to anthropology that is an epistemological inquiry into everyday life both in the field and at home. For him, anthropology is essentially a mutual learning process, not mere ethnographic data gathering and writing about them.

Arjun Appadurai (1996) and others have criticized anthropological techniques of circumventing a "local culture" and producing a "fieldwork site" as an isolated space, although large portions of ethnography would be written at "home," long after leaving the field. Ingold takes this issue a step further. The work in the field, for Ingold, extends well beyond the distant, exotic places we visit to conduct research. Anthropology ought to be an everyday practice. We should regard university offices and lecture halls as the sites of anthropological engagement as much as, for instance, Cairo or Calcutta, the cities we write about. He alerts us about the fictional boundary we construct between "ethnographic data" we gather in the field and "knowledge" we impart in lecture halls. Ethnographic reality is disconnected from that of academia (Ingold 2014: 391–92). He is deeply concerned that in order for anthropology to remain relevant in the neoliberal age, the goal of anthropological writing should shift from a mere description *of* to correspondence *with* people, both inside and outside the ivory tower.

Toward an Anthropology of Islam with Muslims

It seems to me that Ingold is showing us the way out from the long, dark tunnel from which both cultural and social anthropologists have been striving to find an exit, namely the crisis of representation. Not unlike other fields of social anthropology, those of us working on Islam in the Middle East have grappled with the ways to demarcate and conceptualize the subject of our study. Edward Said's (1978) *Orientalism* revealed the process in which "the exotic Other" that was produced through Orientalist artwork, literature, and scholarship justified the European colonial presence in the Middle East. Research in the wake of Said has demonstrated how the asymmetrical power relations between the West and the Middle East made European scholarship on Islam and the Middle East appear credible and authentic, and helped to shape Middle Easterners' imagination of their religion, culture, and history. Timothy Mitchell's (1988) *Colonizing Egypt* furthered Said's project by demonstrating how overarching the colonial power of representing "the truth" was, starting from the Paris Expo of 1889 to the introduction of the mobile printing press in Egypt. He illustrated how the sense of order validated by colonial power in the late nineteenth-century Egypt was crucial in distinguishing what constituted valid knowledge and what did not. If we were to follow faithfully postcolonial theory, however, there seems to be no way out of knowledge-power syndrome. Imbalance of power between the studying subject and the studied object preconditions the knowledge we gain from studies. Our aspiration to know, no matter how innocent it seems, cannot escape the web of colonial power dynamics.

Talal Asad's (1986) *The Idea of an Anthropology of Islam* was a direct response to the issue of Orientalism in anthropological studies of Islam and Muslim societies. Asad reminds us of the significance of observing attentively the socioeconomic conditions and power dynamics, which define traditions and the issues of what is authentic and inauthentic. He criticized Ernest Gellner and Geertz for simply observing and describing what Muslims *do* without remotely showing any interests in what they had to say about their own beliefs and practices. Through his subsequent study of Christianity, Asad (1993) demonstrated the degree to which anthropological studies of Islam were uncritically dependent on Western understandings of "religion." He suggested an approach that would conceptually liberate anthropological studies of Islam and Muslim societies from the tradition of western religious studies: "If one wants to write an anthropology of Islam one should begin, as Muslims do, from the concept of a discursive tradition that includes and relates itself to the founding texts of the Qur'an and the Hadīth. Islam is neither a distinctive social structure nor a heterogeneous collection of beliefs, artifacts, customs, and morals. It is a tradition" (Asad 1986: 14). If we were to employ Ingold's expressions, Asad was proposing to anthropologists to study Islam *with* Muslims, rather than following the path paved by Orientalists. In Asad's definition, "tradition" is not set in stone; instead it is a highly contextual and nuanced set of ideas and practices. Qur'an and hadīth (authoritative accounts of the Prophet Muhammad) provide vocabularies and values that Muslims can tap into when in need of justifying their beliefs and practices. Asad employs the metaphor of "tradition" because by invoking Prophet Muhammad's authority, Muslims strive to show their connection to the past and divinely inspired history. It would be useful to some extent for non-Muslim researchers to gain a first-hand experience of how Muslims perform daily ritual prayers or how Sufis chant *dhikr* during *hadra* gatherings. However, gathering empirical data regarding Islamic beliefs and practices in everyday life of Muslims does not qualify as an anthropological study of Islam. We must trace the genealogy of their ideas and situate them in the web of knowledge-power dynamics.

Asad's approach to Islam as a discursive tradition and his thesis had lasting impact on anthropological studies of Islam. For instance, John R. Bowen's (1993) *Muslims through Discourse* is a comparative study of Muslims located in various parts of Indonesia. He analyzed the diverse ways in which individuals defined the meanings of rituals by evoking a variety of authoritative traditions, and then situated their discussions in the geopolitical and sociohistorical contexts of Indonesia. However, compared to more recent anthropological studies of Islam, there is a divorce between anthropological theory and ethnographic description in Bowen's (1989) writing because he reduced daily ritual prayers as a "case study" vis-à-vis the larger anthropological study of rituals (cf. Ahmad 2017). Although he listens to what Indonesian Muslims have to say about their religious rituals, rather than simply describing them as Geertz did, he is keen on labeling and classifying groups of people. The authority to interpret a discourse resides with Bowen, not Indonesian Muslims he met in the field.

Drawing on Asad, Gregory Starrett (1998) stated that Muslims who received modern school education are more in need of "tradition" than their parents' generation. He illustrated the historical process in which Egyptian Muslims started to objectify their religious heritage and discuss Islamic teaching in terms of socioeconomic functions after the government's introduction of Islam as a state school curricular subject. Charles Hirschkind further developed Asad's thesis in his anthropological study of Islam by focusing on "ethics of listening" shared among working-class men in Cairo. In *The Ethical Soundscape*, Hirschkind (2006) discussed how young men listening to cassette recordings of mosque sermons were not passive agents; rather, they employed those sermons as a means to transform their moral dispositions. The penultimate section of the book recounts Hirschkind attending the funeral of a preacher that his friends adored and then going home together to listen to his sermon. Regardless of the extent to which he appreciated this preacher's sermon, I could gather from this passage that he was putting into practice the ethics of listening in anthropological terms. His writing shows what Ingold (2008a: 87) calls "a practice of observation grounded in participatory dialogue." Hirschkind engaged in "verbal correspondence" (Ingold 2008a: 88) with professional preachers, specialists of Islamic law, as well as ordinary Muslims of Egypt who strive for a better life in this world and hereafter.

Ingold's statement that in anthropology, "there can be no distinction between the theory of a discipline and a method—that both were indissoluble aspects of the practice of a craft" (2014: 390) reminded me of Amira Mittermaier's (2011) *Dreams that Matter*. In it, she illustrated the highly complex genealogy of Islamic dream interpretation in contemporary Egypt by mapping out how Muslims employed vocabularies of Sunni legal theory, Sufism, Islamic modernism as well as Social Darwinism and Freudian psychoanalysis interchangeably. In her work, theories and experiences of dream interpretations that Egyptian Muslims shared with Mittermaier and the relevant studies in social anthropology and related fields are seamlessly woven together. There is no divide between ethnographic description and anthropological theory. Dream interpretation might appear as a typical research interest of Orientalists that further exotifies the Muslim other, yet Mittermaier's treatment of the subject situates the fear and aspirations of Egyptians in what Ingold (2008a: 69) called "in the one world we all inhabit."

After the publication of *Orientalism*, it had become almost unethical to ignore the global political economy of knowledge production when studying Islam; yet anthropological studies since Asad illustrate the creative ways in which Muslims make their way around the postcolonial conditions they experience in everyday life without being completely captured by the web of knowledge-power dynamics.

So far, I have critically discussed Ingold's exposition about separating anthropology from ethnography and the issue of representation in anthropological writing. To demonstrate the ways in which his observations have a bearing on works on the anthropology of Islam in Egypt, I have looked for examples of what Ingold might deem good anthropological practices in my own research field. In the section that follows, my contribution will critically engage with the challenges in employing Ingold's differentiation between anthropology and ethnography in a pedagogical practice in a university classroom.

Practicing Anthropology in the Classroom

As I stated earlier, Ingold situates participant observation at the heart of anthropological quest for knowledge. By acquiring the lens through which we observe social phenomena attentively, we learn to engage with other members of the society. Anthropology, as Ingold views it, is synonymous with education (Ingold 2018). The place we carry out the fieldwork is our schools (Ingold 2018: 63–65). I wholeheartedly support Ingold's project of separating anthropology from ethnography in this regard; yet it remains unclear to me how to teach students "the art of inquiry" without discussing ethnographic details. I shall further interrogate Ingold's notion of "correspondence" when practicing anthropology in the context of higher education.

As a model for integrating an anthropological way of knowing into university education, Ingold gives highly insightful examples of his collaborating with those who work on art, architecture, and archaeology at Manchester and Aberdeen (Ingold 2013: 8–11). He states, "The aims of the course [on the 4 As (i.e., Anthropology, Art, Architecture, and Archaeology)] were to train students in the art of inquiry, to sharpen their powers of observation, and to encourage them to think *through* observation rather than *after* it" (Ingold 2013: 11). Although I am extremely envious of such an intellectually rewarding exchange, I wonder in what precise ways and to what extent this approach could be applicable to my professional experience of teaching modern Islam at the University of Manchester's Middle Eastern Studies program. When appointed in the early 2010s, my job title was Lecturer in "Modern Islam" with an expectation that I would teach not only Islam in historical contexts but also the lives of modern-day Muslims through sociological and anthropological approaches. During my tenure at Manchester, I was the course unit coordinator of three undergraduate-level courses related to Islamic studies as well as a contributor to team-taught courses as the expert of modern Islam. Each course unit consisted of a three-hour lecture per week and ran over twelve weeks.

Class sizes were small for the University of Manchester. The largest class I taught had forty-five students.

Whereas my role in the field was that of a learner of Islam, in university settings, I was responsible for teaching students how to study Islam as an academic subject. There seems to have been a crucial incongruence between these two roles—as a learner in the field (in Cairo) and as a teacher in the classrooms (in Manchester). This is the context in which I see the challenge of practicing "the anthropology of Islam with Muslims" approach. It is not my intention in the slightest to assert that Islam is essentially different from other subfields within social anthropology or arts and humanities subjects at large. Rather, I attempt to highlight that Islamic learning that takes place in educational environments in which secular modern has become the norm stands divorced from "everyday Islam" that anthropologists study.

Manchester is home to diverse Muslim communities with multiple ethnic backgrounds and intellectual currents (see Webner 2002; Spellman-Poots 2012). In fact, it is those Muslims who formed a large population in the Islamic studies courses at the University of Manchester. When I accepted my appointment as a lecturer in 2012, I was unaware of the diverse socioeconomic backgrounds of my students. I was least aware about the young British Muslims who saw my lectures as the vital occasion to display their eagerly cultivated pious selves. In my very first lecture, I said, "You will not become a better Muslim by taking this course." Yet many of them returned in the following weeks. I designed my courses to teach students how to study Islam as an academic subject, a pursuit different from acquiring correct knowledge of Islam *to live* as a better Muslim. Similar to Ingold, my goal was to teach my students the art of inquiry. By objectifying one's essentialist views about Islam, I aspired to help students gain awareness that there were diverse approaches to the divine in Islam. Learning to study about Islam and its history allows both Muslim and non-Muslim students to situate their version of Islam in a variety of intellectual currents. Exploring the ways of knowing rather than simply accumulating correct knowledge of Islam could be a steep learning curve for Muslim students because most of them were exposed to only one version of Islam at home or in their own communities.

Learning about the diversity within Islamic tradition is not exclusive to secular intellectual exercise. Al-Azhar Mosque in Cairo is famed for its double-headed minaret, which is the gesture of acknowledging the verdicts from all the four Sunni Orthodox Schools of Law. Students at the Faculty of Islamic Missionary of al-Azhar University, for instance, learn about other religions as well as the diverse approaches to the divine within Islam to facilitate their engagements in polemical debates. Their knowledge of religion should serve as a skill when engaging in missionary activities with Muslims and non-Muslims. In contrast, studying Islam for intellectual pleasure or cultural enrichment, divorced from institutionalized religious practices, is essentially a highly secularized approach to religion (van der Veer 2009). In this sense, approaching Islam merely as an academic subject requires disciplining one's secular subjectivity.

"Mapping out Islam" according to academic terms such as Sunni and Shi'a, literalist and rationalist, as well as Sufism and Salafism (Islamic reformism) is an artificial exercise derived from a fictionally objective version of Islam that ordinary Muslims are not exposed to on a daily basis. Although many students learned to appreciate the highly insightful contradictions within the discursive traditions of Islam (Ahmed 2015), there was more than one occasion when Salafis fought with Sufis, Sunnis denied Shi'a interpretation of Islam, and British-born students talked about "their village" in India, Pakistan, or Indonesia as the backward version of Islam. On such occasions, my lectures were turned into a microcosm of "the Muslim World" (Aydin 2017), and I would have loved to take a distance from the unfolding saga and write the interactions up as an ethnography.

Nadia Fadil and Mayanthi Fernando (2015) criticized Samuli Schielke's (2009) approach, which focused on the dilemmas and contradictions of Muslim subjectivity as "everyday Islam" produces a fictional view that those who follow piety movements or Salafism are an exception. Fadil and Fernando do not acknowledge that the path to Ultimate Truth is never straightforward. As Schielke asserts, aspirations and failure to lead a pious lifestyle are part and parcel of everyday Islam in Egypt and a mundane life of being a Muslim around the globe, including those who subscribe to Salafism. My point is that although there is an expectation that courses on "Modern Islam" are supposed to teach "everyday Islam," "everyday Islam" that is dealt with in anthropological literature would be quite different from classroom Islam. The demand for impartial and objective representation of Islam in the secular university setting produces a version that is catered for classrooms. Put differently, lectures on modern Islam are far from teaching students the everyday lives of modern day Muslims. The following is an example from my classroom.

Once, during a seminar discussion about Ashura rituals commemorating Imam Husayn's death, a veiled female student who subscribed to a Salafi-leaning movement was eager to correct my erroneous views on Sunni–Shi'a divide in Islam. This seminar took place after a two-hour lecture on the historical contexts in which the divide between Sunni and Shi'a evolved after the martyrdom of Husayn at the Battle of Karbala in 680 CE. Yet this student insisted, "There is only one Islam, no Sunni nor Shi'a." Some Sunni Muslim students supported her claim, yet others looked perplexed and speechless. "Sectarian divide" in Islam, as we see on news programs, was visible in the class too. When she continued, saying, "Those who claim to be Shi'a have been given wrong information about Islamic history from their parents," I felt obliged to intervene. However, by defending Shi'a as a well-established school of thought within Islam, I had inadvertently evoked my scholarly authority and presented my version of Islam as "true" and "authentic." In this seminar, I intended to discuss the ways in which we could study a ritual. To this end, I selected an anthropological study of Ashura rituals in the UK as the seminar reading. Before reaching the discussion on theoretical or methodological questions in analyzing an Islamic ritual practice, we had to go through a Shi'a "fact-check." For instance, the followers of 'Ali believe that Muhammad appointed 'Ali to be his successor before his passing, but Sunni do not acknowledge the authenticity of this hadīth. Likewise we discussed what happened in Karbala and the differences between Imamate and Caliphate. In the enlightened liberal imagination, the quest for knowledge might appear like an innate human desire. Yet, asking conceptual questions or having interests in such a subject requires intensive honing of anthropological sensibility through an accumulation of ethnographic details. Because of the sharp divide between the anthropological category of everyday Islam and what might be called lecture hall Islam, I struggled to find a way to apply an "Anthropology of Islam with Muslims" approach in educational settings.

Seeking Knowledge of Islam

For my doctoral thesis project, I studied the life and thought of 'Abd al-Halim Mahmud (1910–78), a French-trained Egyptian scholar of Sufism, and explored how his audience in contemporary Egypt employ his work when performing their middle-class ideals. My participant observation in Cairo consisted of debating with my interlocutors the strengths and weaknesses of 'Abd al-Halim Mahmud's works. I participated in weekly Sufi *hadra* gatherings, learned some verses of the Qur'an, and went on pilgrimages to Sufi mausoleums (*ziyara*) with Sufi friends. However, such experience did not improve my overall understanding of Sufism. In contrast, when reading 'Abd al-Halim Mahmud's publications and listening to radio recordings of his lectures with my interlocutors, I began to understand how educated Egyptians appreciated his formulation of Sufism. Such conversations made me aware of the significant place "culture talk" occupied in Egyptian social class formations (Aishima 2016). It was indeed the experience of being "led *out* into the world" (Ingold 2014: 388—emphasis in original). Furthermore, I hope these were somewhat equally enriching experiences for my interlocutors who went through the texts of 'Abd al-Halim Mahmud and shared with me their views on his works.

However, after reading Ingold's formulation of the differences between anthropology and ethnography, I am concerned with the extent to which my work would qualify as anthropology. Ingold (2013: 3) gives examples of the difference between learning to play the cello and studying a famous cellist when illustrating the difference between anthropology and ethnography. According to Ingold, anthropology is an art of learning to correspond with people from other societies and observe their social phenomenon. Participant observation should be equivalent to learning to herd sheep or weave a carpet, rather than simply observing and depicting how others work. In this regard, I am kept in suspense. I wonder how I could apply Ingold's assertion when studying about Islam in Egypt. There would be a stark contrast in the nature of knowledge accumulated by an Indonesian student at Azhar University and me in Cairo because the respective purposes of our learning would be different. Both of us could aspire to immerse ourselves in studying the discursive traditions of Islam. As a Muslim, the Indonesian student could also put into practice the knowledge of Islamic legal theory and worship he acquired to lead the everyday life of a good Muslim. In contrast, my knowledge and understanding of Islam would remain merely abstract and academic, unrelated to my personal life as a Buddhist. Whereas the Indonesian student would be expected to accumulate enough knowledge to give a legal verdict on Islamic faith, it would never be my professional duty to deliver judgments about *halal* and *haram* (legally impermissible) in Islam. My knowledge would remain theoretical, never employed as a practical skill. I am curious to know if my understanding of Islam would qualify as anthropological in Ingold's formulation.

Conclusion

In this chapter, I engaged with Tim Ingold's proposal to clearly demarcate the role of anthropology and ethnography and divide the two as different fields of academic inquiries. First, I situated Ingold's thesis in the dilemma of representation that anthropologists have been tackling since Clifford's and Marcus's *Writing Culture*. By redefining the purpose of anthropology as educational and the art of inquiry, Ingold is showing us the way to overcome the crisis of representation that anthropologists have debated for so long. We need to find a way to speak for ourselves without relying on our authority as an ethnographer who "witnessed" exotic cultural practices. Second, because it was unclear from Ingold's work which study would qualify as a good practice, I looked at anthropological research on Islam, especially those on Egypt, in light of his assertions. Talal Asad's thesis that Islam is indeed a discursive tradition was an anthropologist's response to Edward Said's *Orientalism* in which he exposed the problems in the ways that non-Muslim scholars of Europe represented Islam. If we were to employ Ingold's expressions, Asad urged anthropologists to study Islam *with* Muslims, rather than employing the theoretical frameworks established by Orientalists.

However, I was faced with a dilemma when I reflected on my fieldwork in Egypt and teaching experiences in the UK to examine how Ingold's proposal would be applicable to my own work. I struggled to find a way to teach the anthropological art of inquiry and observation without dwelling on ethnographic details. Higher educational institutions in a secular setting assume that while the Islamic knowledge Muslims possess is biased or merely subjective, academic approaches to Islam are "impartial" and "objective." In other words, there is a sharp divide between the anthropological category of everyday Islam as a subject of research and Islam as taught, for instance, by a Buddhist lecturer–anthropologist to a largely Muslim class in a university setting such as the British one. If we were to correspond with students by practicing an anthropology of Islam *with* Muslims in classrooms, there is an inherent risk of a lecture turning into a mere exchange of detailed personal knowledge of Islamic beliefs and practices because individual views on Islam would be quite diverse. It is not my intention to assert that my knowledge of Islam is superior to that of practicing Muslims. My point instead is that the Islamic knowledge gained through study in the field versus teaching at universities is, though related, quite different.

The core of Islamic faith is supported by a number of philosophical principles, which are applicable to both Muslims and non-Muslims. To that extent, studying Islam certainly enriched my life. However, because I have no necessity to employ my knowledge of Islam in the way Muslims do, my research, following Ingold's formulation, is more in the realm of ethnography rather than anthropology. To use Ingold's metaphor, it is equivalent to studying a famous cellist rather than learning how to play the instrument. Corresponding with the others, whether people we encounter at home or away from home, is never an easy task. Ingold's is a highly stimulating proposal; to critically grasp its full significance we must carry on the debate.

Acknowledgments

I am grateful to Irfan Ahmad, Fukachi Furukawa, Christian Goeschel, and two anonymous reviewers for reading and commenting on the earlier versions of my chapter.

Hatsuki Aishima is Associate Professor at the National Museum of Ethnology in Japan. She has also held appointments at the University of Manchester in UK and Freie Universität Berlin in Germany. She is an anthropologist working on public culture in the contemporary Middle East. Her monograph, *Public Culture and Islam in Modern Egypt: Media, Intellectuals and Society* (IB Tauris, 2016) explored the roles of mass media and modern education in shaping the public knowledge, scholarly culture, and literary traditions of Islam. Her publications have appeared in *Culture and Religion*, *Die Welt des Islams*, and *Journal of the Royal Anthropological Institute*.

References

Ahmad, Irfan. 2017. *Religion as a Critique: Islamic Critical Thinking from Mecca to Marketplace*. Chapel Hill: The University of North Carolina Press.
Ahmed, Shahab. 2015. *What Is Islam? The Importance of Being Islamic*. Princeton: Princeton University Press.
Aishima, Hatsuki. 2016. *Public Culture and Islam in Modern Egypt: Media, Intellectuals and Society*. London: IB Tauris.
Appadurai, Arjun. 1996. *Modernity at Large: Cultural Dimensions of Globalization*. Minneapolis: University of Minnesota Press.
Asad, Talal. 1986. *The Idea of an Anthropology of Islam*. Occasional Paper Series. Washington, DC: Georgetown University, Center for Contemporary Arab Studies.
———. 1993. *Genealogies of Religion: Discipline and Reasons of Power in Christianity and Islam*. Baltimore: Johns Hopkins University Press.
Aydin, Cemil. 2017. *The Idea of the Muslim World: A Global Intellectual History*. Cambridge, MA: Harvard University Press.

Bowen, John R. 1989. "Salat in Indonesia: The Social Meanings of an Islamic Ritual." *Man*, New Series 24, no. 4: 600–619.

———. 1993. *Muslims through Discourse: Religion and Ritual in Gayo Society*. Princeton: Princeton University Press.

Clifford, James. 1990. "Notes on (Field)notes." In *Fieldnotes: The Makings of Anthropology*, edited by Roger Sanjek, 47–70. Ithaca: Cornell University Press.

Clifford, James, and George Marcus, eds. 1986. *Writing Culture: The Poetics and Politics of Ethnography*. Berkeley: University of California Press.

Dupret, Baudouin, Thomas Pierret, Paulo G. Pinto, and Kathryn Spellman-Poots, eds. 2012. *Ethnographies of Islam: Ritual Performances and Everyday Practices*. Edinburgh: Edinburgh University Press.

Fadil, Nadia, and Mayanthi Fernando. 2015. "Rediscovering the 'everyday' Muslim: Notes on an Anthropological Divide." *HAU: Journal of Ethnographic Theory* 5, no. 2: 59–88.

Geertz, Clifford. 1973. "Thick Description: Toward an Interpretive Theory of Culture." In *The Interpretation of Cultures: Selected Essays*, 3–30. New York: Basic Books.

Hirschkind, Charles. 2006. *The Ethnical Soundscape: Cassette Sermons and Islamic Counterpublics*. New York: Columbia University Press.

Ingold, Tim. 2008a. "Anthropology Is *Not* Ethnography." *Proceedings of the British Academy* 154: 69–92.

———. 2008b. "Anthropology Is *Not* Ethnography." *British Academy Review* 11: 21–23.

———. 2013. "Knowing from the Inside." In *Making: Anthropology, Archaeology, Art and Architecture*, 1–16. London: Routledge.

———. 2014. "That's Enough about Ethnography!" *HAU: Journal of Ethnographic Theory* 4, no. 1: 383–95.

———. 2017. "Anthropology contra Ethnography." *HAU: Journal of Ethnographic Theory* 7, no. 1: 21–26.

———. 2018. *Anthropology and/as Education*. Abington: Routledge.

Mitchell, Timothy. 1988. *Colonising Egypt*. Berkeley: University of California Press.

Mittermaier, Amira. 2011. *Dreams that Matter: Egyptian Landscapes of the Imagination*. Berkeley: California University Press.

Said, Edward W. 1978. *Orientalism: Western Conceptions of the Orient*. London: Penguin Books.

Sanjek, Roger, ed. 1990. *Fieldnotes: The Makings of Anthropology*. Ithaca: Cornell University Press.

Schielke, Samuli. 2009. "Being Good in Ramadan: Ambivalence, Fragmentation, and the Moral Self in the Lives of Young Egyptians." *Journal of the Royal Anthropological Institute* Special Issue: S24–S40.

Spellman-Poots, Kathryn. 2012. "Manifestations of Ashura among Young British Shi'is." In *Ethnographies of Islam: Ritual Performances and Everyday Practices*, edited by Baudouin Dupret, Thomas Pierret, Paulo G Pinto,

and Kathryn Spellman-Poots, 40–49. Edinburgh: Edinburgh University Press.
Starrett, Gregory. 1998. *Putting Islam to Work: Education, Politics, and Religious Transformation in Egypt*. Berkeley: California University Press.
van der Veer, Peter. 2009. "Spirituality in Modern Society." *Social Research* 76, no. 4: 1097–120.
Webner, Pnina. 2002. *Imagined Diasporas Among Manchester Muslims: The Public Performance of Pakistani Transnational Identity Politics*. Oxford: James Currey.

Chapter 2

ANTHROPOLOGY AS AN EXPERIMENTAL MODE OF INQUIRY

Arpita Roy

In *Meno*, one of Plato's most influential dialogues, Socrates tenaciously questions a slave boy who has not received a formal education; and after several wrong attempts by the boy, Socrates obtains from him the answer to a complex geometrical proof. By systematically interrogating him, Plato demonstrates how Socrates had through a series of questions "stirred up in him" and recovered the knowledge that the boy did not know he possessed. This process of inquiry, with Socrates as the gadfly questioner eliciting responses through sustained interlocution, is an attempt by Plato to establish that knowledge is the transformation of latent beliefs contained in embryonic form via the provocation and mediation of a fitting catalyst. As an adventure whose aim and activity is the consciousness of birthing a new knowledge, anthropological fieldwork shares an inimitable affinity with the Socratic dialogue. Several aspects of Plato's systematization of the dialogue form—such as, how thinking is conducted in conversation, knowledge may unfold in street corners or cafés, beliefs are judged on the altar of truth, higher truths are not taught but awakened in the questioning mind—are relevant here. But one overarching frame, which enables the diverse epistemological trajectories, is the Socratic demand for self-reflection (i.e., the examination of our subterranean beliefs and values) to arrive at the power and limits of thinking itself. However, that is a question that seldom makes it to the forecourt of anthropology meaningfully.

The oversight is surprising given that as a professional field of inquiry, anthropological fieldwork has continued to repose on the "I was there" mode of testimony since the blazing manifesto of Malinowski (1922), who established the principal contours of participant observation, a versatile method of inquiry by which a researcher gains an intimate familiarity with diverse aspects of social life. More recent debates, which acknowledge the improvisatory stance of anthropology, are also tethered to physical, and almost soulless, dynamics of alignment and assemblage, locked in the self-sufficiency of immediate sense experience (Miller 2013; Rabinow 1996). Even postmodernism, which speaks on the hazards of arriving at conclusive interpretations owing to a veritable "crisis of representation" that captured attention a few decades ago, stages the claims of anthropological knowing in the actual, empirical complexity of the world that is made significantly worse by fragmentation, colonialism, relativism, and so on (Clifford and Marcus 1986). In other words, anthropological categories and methods of knowledge production have consistently been grounded in the idiom of sense data and experience. Yet anthropological fieldwork is not simply the unfolding of empirical experience. It is the staging of an experiment, as Marcus (2013) rightly reminds us, a way of confronting the known and the unknown, the real and the possible. What, we are led to ask, is the movement by which a fleeting impression is arrested and turned into a reflection? How is a sense of acquaintance with lived reality transformed into definite consciousness? Where are we to locate the source or stimulation awakening our interest in alien modes of being?

Tim Ingold has recently addressed some of these questions. He is forthright in recognizing that what lies at the heart of the anthropological dilemma is the relation between knowledge and care. For him, the reflexivity of anthropology can justly be cultivated in the milieu of relations encompassing the knower and the known. To this end, however, he thinks we may have gotten the wrong end of the stick when substituting the diversity of representations with the closed syntax of descriptions. Accordingly, the burden of his criticism centers on ethnography and its ideal of descriptive fidelity. As far as I know, the incisive scrutiny of why description should matter to the anthropological craft has never before been drawn so adroitly. Ingold (2018) assiduously desires to raise anthropology to greater sensitivity about itself, while at the same time admonishing us to decouple it from any simplistic "transmission of information." I wholeheartedly agree with Ingold that anthropological fieldwork remains mute unless we locate in ourselves the means of making it speak. It is not arbitrary, and constitutes our very métier.

Where I part company with Ingold, however, is on his emphasis of ontological oneness to convey the singularity of anthropology, and the consequent neglect of impersonal, logical relations of contrast, difference, inversion, separation, or contradiction. Ingold's writings on attentional living, mutual flourishing, and intersubjective unfolding serve, in my opinion, limited explanatory purpose in analyzing innovations that break free from context, and one is "left with an uncomfortable suspicion that it is impossible to inspect anything for the first time" (i.e., in cases where one has to), a criticism that Santayana directs at Dewey's similar emphasis on oneness or holism (1925: 678). We need only to reflect on the endeavors of language, labor, or science to realize that breaks in the sedulous chain of reasoning, turning points in the use of tools, or the arbitrariness of initial conditions in cosmology are deserving candidates in need of anthropological explanation. Ingold's critique means little to the analysis of sudden transitions or radical separations, and it is in the fulfillment of this task that the method of Socratic inquiry holds promise and to whose precise development this chapter is devoted.

Against Ingold's understanding of participant observation as an ontological commitment that serves to "attend to persons and things" (2018: 61), which has a decidedly moralistic ring to it, I wish to emphasize participant observation as the drama of ideas and argument, one that is rooted in language, thought, and truth. What is important about anthropological fieldwork is what enables it to function, not the various ontologies or theories which it suggests. The activity of fieldwork is linked to a bewildering variety of relations of reflection, opposition, contrast, inversion, and even separation—and that question belongs to logic, not to metaphysics. Of course, nobody has in mind here the study of logical relations as an exact calculus. The point rather is that a thesis on the ontological commitments of anthropology has no bearing on the modes of reasoning and codes of conduct employed within research. Ingold, in attending to the complexity between care and learning, and then shifting the weight back to care, abandons the intellectual order of concepts, principles, and relations, and actually settles for a sophisticated empiricism—one that is sensitive to the ethical dimensions of education, much like Dewey's. By contrast, I am anxious to insist that anthropological fieldwork is indefinitely open-ended and evolving because "we look not to things, not to the world, but instead to the validity of what we know about things or the world" (Gellner 1974: 28), and the basis for that lies not in some ontology but in the crisscrossing of logical relations—that is, to read logical relations as preconditions that help us judge reality and not as facts or abstractions derived from reality. The Socratic dialogue is an excellent illustration of talking about possibilities of thought through which we can go beyond the critical limits of observation, experience, and even existence itself in pursuit of truth.

Elaborating on the basis of my own specialty, anthropology of science, with fieldwork conducted at the particle accelerator complex, CERN, near Geneva in Switzerland, I shall argue for the substrate of logical relations like binary oppositions and separations, which account for epistemic mediation as well as autonomy, and can encompass extremely heterogeneous orientations of the kind that Ingold favors. More generally, it helps if we conceptualize these relations as impersonal, though not divested or separated from the social and material context of experience. It might seem odd that in a chapter reflecting on Ingold's emphasis on attentionality, correspondence, and mutual flourishing, I should fling the word "impersonal" in the readers' direction, but in what mode could the observation and depiction related to cases of novelty be better recognized? In the first few critical months of fieldwork I spent among particle physicists, I was struck by how often physicists made assertions about discoveries of new particles that required breaks in the threads that bind them to existing contexts. Indeed, cases of discoveries implicitly throw up the whole tangled question of the relationship between the possible and the real. This conjunction provides the following rejoinder to Ingold: ontology by itself is unable to set limits on the possible. At issue here is the concept of limits concerning knowledge, and to open a space for forms of knowing without predetermined ontology. Such a move allows us to link novelties in science to novelties in anthropological fieldwork. In short, the problem is to grasp how thinking can be both bound and free (from context). Drawing on my understanding of contemporary particle physics, this chapter pleads for the retrieval of logical and impersonal relations in the impulse of anthropological knowing, which reinforces the limitations of ethnography that Ingold has meaningfully outlined.

Beyond Ontology

I shall commence the discussion on the disciplinary aims of anthropology with Ingold's critique of ethnography. The gist of his contention relates to the question whether the objectives of ethnography completely exhaust or coincide with anthropology. Students of anthropology ought to be beholden to Ingold for reflecting so decisively on a problem normally glossed over. Every question we ask, whether in fieldwork or in writing, touches on the craft of knowledge production. It is in this direction that Ingold finds ethnography to be both inadequate and perverse. Inadequate because ethnography aims at description—to describe reality with great fidelity—whereas anthropology "is an inquiry into the conditions and possibilities" of social life (Ingold 2008: 79). With this succinct formulation, Ingold illustrates at once that gaining an insight into a community's way of life is not simply a receptive process, but a transformative one, where grasping the inner abundance of interlocution and exchange means that knowledge, in so far as it exists, comes into being; it passes from potentiality to actuality. In this respect, descriptive fidelity certainly appears inadequate. Since it must adhere to what is a state of affairs, description cannot address how a state of affairs comes to be.

It also happens that the adumbration of ethnography is perverse. We have often been taught that ethnography is *the* method, which realizes the ends of anthropological inquiry. But in this ethnography lays claims to a false monumentality. It was never meant to be the "formal procedural means designed to satisfy the ends of anthropological inquiry" (Ingold 2008: 88). Here, Ingold brings some ancient wisdom to the table, like the views of A. R. Radcliffe-Brown, Alfred Kroeber, and C. Wright Mills, to show how the substitution of ethnography for anthropology has moved through the years. The debate on idiographic versus nomothetic, in particular, is an interesting portrait of an intellectual mood. However, Ingold's evaluation does not demonstrate at what point in the history of our discipline the boast of ethnography becomes exhaustive. He mentions the baleful influence of the "crisis of representation" debate, but it is more in the form of a throwaway suggestion. Be that as it may, Ingold's apprehensions with how ethnography becomes a major force leading anthropology to become hostage to observation and description is strikingly set forth.

Abstract methodology is perhaps the dreariest of areas in anthropology. Therefore, it is heartwarming to find that Ingold does not flinch from scrutinizing and rejecting the notions that anthropology is nothing but empirical documentation, that encounters with people are "data" that one writes about, or that a lifetime of studying with people ceases with the trumpeting of "case studies." Yet all such concerns would remain mere truisms unless they were illuminated in the spirit of anthropological craft. For what is crucial to the search and renewal of anthropological knowledge is that while it may lie in the everyday cognition of social life, it has to be raised to a form of conversation, wrought to life by the catalytic figure of the researcher, as I said earlier. Ingold is right to remind us that anthropology can transcend its scholasticism because it triumphs in the practice of life. The poignancy of knowledge entwined with human interests is what he terms "ontological commitment," which he also identifies as the "educational" aim of anthropological research (2014). This is supported by his further claim that anthropological standpoints are yielded in the movement of intersubjectivity, in the correspondence of articulations, in the ecology of "living attentionally" (Ingold 2014: 389).

"Correspondence" is a key term for Ingold to designate the intellectual collaboration that takes place between knower and known. However, he is careful to explain that correspondence does not imply disregarding disagreements or conflicts:

> Indeed, I might profoundly disagree with them. Participant observation can be uncomfortable, and we certainly don't have to go into it thinking that everything the people tell us is true or wonderful. They may do or say things that we find awful or abhorrent. Our task, then, is not to mask this abhorrence with a veil of sympathy, or present an artificially sanitized account of their words and deeds, but directly to take issue with them. (2017: 24)

Ingold's recommendation is not that anthropologists should conclude their research with a vision of harmony, which is often erroneously attributed to him, but instead that they must underline the importance of development and growth as knowledge accrues. Ingold is even mindful that to talk of fusion suggests prior breakage and separation. What may truly be exclaimed in praise of Ingold's anthropology is that it is critical "because we cannot be content with things as they are" (2017: 22).

Yet oddly enough, Ingold's analysis at this point becomes bland and prescriptive. He writes that anthropology is an exercise in "what we owe to the world for our development and formation" (2014: 388). If one were to adopt such a sweeping recognition, then even a dream would qualify as knowledge, which clearly it is not. In the craft of anthropological knowing, it is a formidable challenge to distinguish between misleading statements and true observations, both of which we owe to the world in every research. The real point at issue is that an ontological commitment is simply a functional point of departure—X cannot exist without Y—that does not reflect on the motor and movement of anthropological knowledge production in its specificity. For the sake of logical reasoning, surely, it must be admitted that anthropology is concerned with possibilities that lie beyond the range of what is experienced in fieldwork encounters. A generic subordination of knowing to being is in danger of overlooking the real extent to which epistemic inferences have grounds other than perceptual attunements or lived experience. Let me clarify, I am not denying what

Ingold has said; instead, I am stressing something that is left unsaid, and which is just as significant for our research.

That something is the domain of logical relations, which may be abstruse, but no less human on that account. The issue is so important that it is perhaps worthwhile to state it bluntly: relations can never be cobbled out of experience. They are orthogonal to experience. In *Phaedo*, for instance, Plato compellingly argues that the notion of equality is not extracted from the perception of equal things; the sight of equal things is an occasion to recall or reflect on the general notion of equality (Plato 1977). Marx similarly reflects on modes of production, both as circuits of capital and as social reproduction of labor, in the form of relations that facilitate and explain the comparison of many actual types (1964). Durkheim puts the matter lucidly when he writes, ". . . how it comes that we can see certain relations in things which the examination of these things cannot reveal to us" (1965: 27). There is nothing mystical in this. Relations of identity, difference, opposition, or contradiction are an indispensable middle term between thoughts and things (Russell 1958). If I understand Ingold's view—that anthropology is an inquiry into "the conditions and possibilities" of human life—then a position against simple description should have more to say on the matter of how impersonal relations are the medium through which anthropological knowledge is fomented and communicated. Let me present an illustration from my research to underscore how impersonal, logical relations turn on the dialectic of the mind and the world, and furnish the means of understanding an anthropological encounter even when they are not proffered in the immediacy of lived experience.

Intellectual Midwifery

I carried out anthropological fieldwork for two and a half continuous years at CERN (Conseil Européen pour la Recherche Nucléaire), the world's leading laboratory for particle physics, near Geneva in Switzerland. Dwelling among the particle physics community at CERN, I observed that conceptions of matter and energy were derived from submerged assumptions about how the universe works. These assumptions took the form of proscriptions and dualisms: values do not affect physical reality, the mind does not participate in the universe, human conventions have little bearing on laws of physics, and so on. However, the intellectual core of these assumptions does not become apparent unless one retreats from external forms of observation to pause over the matrix of relations guiding modern science, in particular the stark oppositions of subject and object, fact and value, or theory and practice. These dualisms are all the more strongly indicated when we recall the amplified emphasis on the logic of scientific novelties, and the vehement discord with the social sciences. Volumes have been penned to describe the logic of discoveries in the sciences and their tension-laden interface with the social sciences (Biagioli 1999; Latour 2004; Snow 1964). A humanistic protest against these oppositions also runs through Ingold's writings, but the question is of form, not content, I submit. This is especially true of the ways in which discoveries are recognized that demand judgment, and hence the use of conceptual relations. The case of discovery of new particles is particularly interesting and perplexing: how to recognize what is not known. The question makes sense within an overarching system of beliefs, provided that the system can set what matters. What I want to highlight next is how that determination is set using conceptual relations like binary oppositions.

Now, binary classifications are a common feature of many cultures (Needham 1973; Sahlins 1976). In some instances, they pertain to specific structural spheres, such as the opposition of state and church. In others, they are coterminous with a social group, for example, the division of a tribe into moieties or clans. However, a few resilient forms of binary classification exhibit an absolute character, cutting across communities and subsuming every aspect of social life, such as the division of sacred and profane that Durkheim (1965) propounds. In this category of binary relations, I place the oppositions of fact and value, subject and object, and theory and practice, which constitute the point of departure of all creative activity in modern science. I will produce a snippet from a conversation I had with a theoretical physicist in the summer of 2009, which is exemplary because it is so typical and routine, to argue that intersubjectivity is a necessary but not a sufficient condition in drawing out conceptual assumptions sustaining nature and society. The conversation was set in motion by the physicist expressing his bafflement with how supersymmetry, a theory that relates two classes of subatomic particles called mesons and baryons, has managed to keep a hold on particle physics "without any basis in nature."

Physicist: Supersymmetry is not real physics. It is an aesthetic choice.

Anthropologist: What is real physics?

Physicist: Physics works on evidence. The Standard Model was accepted after evidence was found for it. We have no evidence for supersymmetry.

Anthropologist: String theory is not physics then since it has no evidence; but nobody says Edward Witten, a Fields medalist, is a terrible physicist.

Physicist: You see, evidence is separate from people. Witten is a genius. But it is up to nature to prove Witten right or not.

Anthropologist: Then what is it that you [theorists] do?

Physicist: We make predictions. We use models and theories to understand nature. Experimentalists do the calculations and test the theories and tell us if our predictions are right.

Anthropologist: But experimentalists often present results with 3-sigma evidence. In those cases, who decides if it is real physics or a detector effect—nature or people?

Physicist: Look, whatever they may say, they know deep down that it is not evidence. The previous collider found some evidence of the Higgs boson. They didn't have good statistics, but the data did show some signs of the Higgs particle. But for supersymmetry, nothing so far. In those days, we could go to the experimentalists and get the numbers and include them in our theories. Now, it is too much bureaucracy. Hundreds of groups analyzing every result, different results have to be integrated. They guard it like some state secret. They don't tell anyone the numbers. You should study that. That is sociology.

Anthropologist: You don't think this is sociology, that nature behaves one way and humans another?

Physicist: Come on, that is how the world is. What is there to study?

Here in this exchange, we have the strange feeling of a set of beliefs about which at first no ready notion can be formed. And yet the feeling of reality attaches so strongly that one's perspectives and actions may be affected through and through by the content of the belief; and yet that belief itself, for purpose of a definite description, can hardly be said to be there. Ostensibly, the discussion is about the merits of a new theory in physics, supersymmetry, and the biases of some of the scientists in favor of this theory. Yet the means of establishing these biases follow from a steady belief in the opposition of objective evidence and subjective inclinations. Time and again, I observed that models may be debated, biases dispelled, or evidence recounted, but the separation of human existence from physical nature is presupposed with an unfailing inertia; it is followed without being justified—or to use the hackneyed analogy, it is like people being unconscious of the grammar of their language but feeling obliged to follow it for any communicative act. Informants dismiss with irritation any question of why it must be believed that nature acts independently of human beings. The universe *is* like that. Yet from a comparative anthropological perspective, one could easily argue the Achuar of Amazonia (Descola 2013) or the Kabyle of Algeria (Bourdieu 1977) are not perplexed at the intimacies of the human and the natural world.

During the two and a half years I spent at CERN, I was struck by the particle physics community's assumption of every kind of separation, be it of theory and application, means and ends, subject and object. These dualisms were rarely given overt, articulate expression. Moreover, it fell to my analytical faculties to successfully elicit these submerged assumptions as well as determining their soundness, which led me to reflect on how well the Socratic dialogue commends itself to anthropological fieldwork. The position I have adopted is that anthropological fieldwork involves the spectacular element of what Plato called "intellectual midwifery," or causing a turn-about, a transformation, in the passage of latent beliefs into knowledge by a curious inquirer. "My art of midwifery is in general like theirs. . . . And the highest point of my art is the ability to prove by every test whether the offspring of a young man's thought is a false phantom or instinct with life and truth. I am so far like the midwife . . . and the common reproach is true, that, though I question others . . . I myself have no sort of wisdom" (Plato 1957: 26). Plato's insistence that the inquirer does not introduce any new knowledge to the participants, but through a systematic prompt of questions enables them to arrive at the knowledge themselves, is well known. What merits attention is that intellectual questioning cannot be completely subsumed under an empirical inventory any more than the subject of truth (addressed later in the following section). However, it would be a mistake to conclude that midwifery brings forth something once and for all. That would be contrary to Plato's way of thinking. In fact, Socratic midwifery is a passage never concluded; it makes progress by dialectical turns and twists, which include drama, doubt, hesitation, error, and *aporia*. That is to say we should not consider knowledge so much as an inevitable given, but rather we should look into the steps that lead up to it.

Contemporary scholarship has so often and so forcefully elucidated the "dialogic" dimension of fieldwork (Clifford and Marcus 1986) that one is at a loss as to why the Socratic dialogue has never been alluded to (e.g., *Writing Culture* does not invoke Plato once). Could it be that an ingrained antipathy toward rationalism precludes this? However this matter may stand philosophically, it is clear that if the turf of conceptual relations can precipitate distinct forms of knowledge, it is because they are impersonal. They have an enduring character since they form part of a community's habits and habitus. Otherwise skeptical of every statement that presents itself as self-evident, the physicists I spoke to rarely wondered if the absolute bifurcation of theory and practice or fact and value could be eliminated or displaced. It is the most vital and most arbitrary part of their belief system; but for that very reason, it is the most zealously guarded. To probe these presuppositions of physics is to inquire into the conditions of its possibility.

The consideration of logical relations also proves fruitful in disclosing the universe of conflicting moral precepts and prohibitions, while shutting out none of the difficulties and obstacles of anthropological knowing (Douglas 1986; Uberoi 2019). The ethics of anthropological consciousness are not always moral. Faustian bargains are struck in the apprehension of higher learning. It is erroneous to maintain that anthropological education is feasible only when there is care or commitment to others. Sometimes, from the depths of human weakness and moral confusion knowledge arises. Therefore, we should not be so sensitive to departures in moral commitments to our field site or to our interlocutors. And yet there are standards and limits to which we are answerable. Ingold's writing on this aspect is somewhat veiled but more suggestive and shows meanings more profound than those currently available. Reckoning the intellectual depths of participant observation, he reaches the question of what it is that has receded from the vision of anthropology. And that is the distinction between reality and truth.

Truth versus Reality

Ingold is on the mark to insist that we cannot just write anything as anthropologists. "In what I write I can at least argue for what I consider it be true, or as close to truth as I can attain, in the light of my reading, the conversations I have had, and my own critical reflection." (Ingold 2017: 23). These lines engage the nub of the problem and, what is more to our purpose, hold the clue to the secret of intellectual life. Now, what is truth per se is hard to define, but this fact should not terrorize us. In a sense, things that are out there in reality are said to be true. But sustained reflection shatters any such simplistic notion of truth as a synonym of reality. The manner in which we carry out our appraisals makes it plain that while as anthropologists we are obviously concerned with reality, what we implicitly enact is the notion of truth as a measure of reality (Roy 2017). For in reality, there is nothing of which the contrary may not be maintained, and we may never reach any understanding. And this is the gist of what Ingold is arguing: only when any event or custom is represented against the criterion of truth can we take cognizance of it.

In recent years, postmodernism has led us to believe that questions of truth appear in the guise of power and in the ideological expression of that power in terms of who can represent the "other" (Foucault 1980). It is meant to give us a warning that absolutely no area of human social existence is free from the exercise of power (Goody 1995). Bourdieu talks of the heroic self-deception necessary to the continuation of social life, where social actors can pursue meaningful action only by living in *illusio* to "schemes of thought and perception [that] can produce the objectivity that they do produce only by producing misrecognition of the limits of the cognition that they make possible" (1977: 164). Rabinow argues that owing to this necessary misrecognition, an unsavory power dimension is introduced to the relationship of researcher and interlocutor in that "only the sociologist is capable of understanding what is really and truly going on" (1996: 9). That is why, according to Rabinow, running through Bourdieu's argument is a dangerous assumption that the anthropologist parasitically produces knowledge by occupying "a position of exteriority to the social field" (1996: 9). This is indeed questionable. That the mutuality and conflict of concerns place definite restrictions on the kinds of exchange engendered by fieldwork, that varieties of observations are translatable only because they are relative, and that the truth of generalizations is far removed from the concreteness of lived life are valid forebodings emanating from the postmodern turn. But I am vexed at the reasoning that the great distance between knower and known should be bridged by resorting to an insipid idealism and a fanatical realism. In monograph after monograph, we are exhorted, on the one hand, to write in the fragile subjectivity of the first person, and on the other, to thicken our descriptions with all-too-real effects of statecraft, colonialism, or history. Gellner has commented with penetrative insight on the facile vacillation sweeping through our discipline "between political liberation and cognitive subjectivity" (1992: 27).

Ingold is fully aware of how fraught and dangerous idealistic aspirations are: "With its dreams of generalization shattered, where should anthropology go?" (2008: 90). But this is not a cry of despair. Nor is it a call to radicalism. On the contrary, he tells us, without sentimentality, that the shaping impulses of anthropology are embedded in the nooks and recesses of life itself, just like embarking on a walk or attending a university (Ingold 2018: 23–32). A model of epistemology on Cartesian-Kantian lines, which overlooks the possibility of living "attentionally," cannot transcribe the miscellaneous demands flowing out of life. From this recognition, Ingold arrives at the key concordance of abstract and physical that makes participant observation the defining pivot of anthropology. Stemming from an anthropologist who is steeped in the morphological tradition of Johann Wolfgang von Goethe and D'Arcy Wentworth Thompson (Ingold 2016), Ingold's unlocking of the earthy stance of participant observation is of immense interest. D'Arcy Thompson's (1961) kaleidoscopic insight that morphology cross-weaves motion and matter, such as hexagonal forms developing spontaneously when heat is applied to limewater, speaks of a rebellious gaiety unknown to the great sum of modern science. Topology is likewise a welcome exception, and in its fluid grammar, the rich afterglow of Ingold's contention that anthropology is "a generous, open-ended, comparative, and yet critical inquiry" (2018: 58) comes alive.

Perhaps we may profitably remind ourselves at this juncture that the finesse of participant observation entails the tuning fork of truth. The worthiness of truth deserves attention because, in a paradoxical sense, it stands higher than any experience and, at the same time, informs every experience. That truth is not a thing located in reality, but rather a relation, a judgment on reality, needs to be untiringly urged (Russell 1958). One can speak of "the exemplary pursuit of truth" (Ingold 2018: ix) to the extent that one recognizes that truth is an awakening, a going forward, which comes to us not extraneously, but in the ambit of self-discovery. That is why Goethe could express in monumental form: If I know my relation to myself and to the outer world, I call it truth. And thus everyone can have his own truth, and yet it is always one and the same. Ingold deserves credit for the breathtaking boldness with which a rational and speculative element like truth has been made an ingredient in the renewal of the anthropology he has in mind. In this respect, I believe, Ingold's critique is vastly more decisive than Dewey's, who substituted, and in consequence diluted, "inquiry" for "truth" as the fundamental concept of logic and epistemology. Ingold discloses that the pulse of transformation brought about by anthropological awareness is not the labored abstraction to any fixed commitment, but is instead the path of its own uneven movement in truth.

Ingold's writing is as far from the specious punditry that turns anthropology into paroxysms of "reaction of the anthropologist to his own reactions to his observations of the society" (Gellner 1992: 23) as he is from the mood of despondency, which denies the generation of "original insights" or at best seeks to objectify them in dogmatic descriptions (Ingold 2014: 392). The very liveliness of his questioning gives to Ingold's endeavor its widest scope as an interpretive method of inquiry. Although he is personally apologetic about using the term "method," which for him carries the whiff of positivism, I am thrilled with his methodological appeal to renounce descriptive finesse in favor of the persuasive powers of imagination and truth. Rituals, myths, tools, or languages that we study index the extraordinary leaps of human thought without in any way obliterating the dangers and risks associated with them. Their pursuit constitutes the distinguished catalog of anthropology. However, as argued earlier, Ingold's emphasis on ontological oneness is too slender a basis for analyzing breaks or leaps, which are qualitative and structural and may involve protracted processes but do not signify genetic linkages or continuity of any normal development. The power of innovations to rupture and remake contexts is a truth that finds an enduring home in the field of science. I should add that just as majestically, the strain of Socratic questioning—which confounds equivalences, upends reciprocity, and wreaks havoc with context—reflects the profound open-endedness of anthropological endeavors.

Conclusion

In the winter of 1917, Max Weber gave a lecture at Munich deploring the bureaucratic professionalization of higher learning, which had ravaged the integrity of "calling" intrinsic to science and scholarship. He also did not shy away from asserting that most of the dangers, in particular to the joys of learning, emanated from *wissenschaft* itself. In the 105 years since Weber's eloquent warning, the challenges to academic writing and reflection have multiplied and vitiated the air to such an extent that anthropology, which appears to be a delightful venture, has been filled with burdensome circumlocutions. In addition to troubling presuppositions of power and hegemony permeating every fieldwork encounter, we are further plagued by postmodern angst of what we can know, how we portray others, or if there are even definite "others." In this regard, it is a relief to find that Ingold understands that the passionate avowal of ethnography is a symptom of an abdication in the communication of higher truths. Of course, what higher truths are suffers from a vagueness, which is undeniable and hard to eradicate. But the unease is not dissimilar to Platonic wisdom, where concepts and methods seem diffuse and playful to begin with, but become useful and abundant in their suggestions.

I have emphasized the case of impersonal, logical relations of separations, bifurcations, or ruptures for the manner in which these facilitate the comprehension of different life worlds. These relations go beyond the simplicity of ontological commitments binding a subject and an object of inquiry, and can even establish the determination of their mutual movement. Ingold's writings mark an acknowledgment of ontology and correspondence that is positive but also in need of further critical elaboration. To disregard logical relations of rupture, opposition, separation, or contradiction is to condemn anthropological fieldwork to tame functional factors and to deny the perfection of which it is capable. These relations cast a spotlight on leaps of knowledge, such as in language, labor, or science, for which there may be very thin analogies in the crust of ontology. I have tried to show, briefly, that in a science like particle physics, the real character of its research may be grasped only by the binary oppositions that permeate its own practice. Through these, we delve into the society inside science (and relinquish coarse, billiard-ball understandings of society as some extraneous entity adjacent to science with which it is said to "interact") and grasp the profound puzzle of how a group of people finds harmony with nature on the pivot of sharp separations.

But such an analysis can only begin if we take cognizance of Ingold's point of departure: that anthropology must rise above the simplistic demands of description espoused by ethnography. Mere description yields no insight into the task of explaining concepts, interpreting contradictions, or understanding how classifications work. Ingold has rendered us a genuine service by seeking to advance and shift the terms of our discourse; and if anthropology is "a quest for education" (Ingold 2014: 388), it is in the manner of Platonic expansion: we discover knowledge in the shadow of truth, and bring it to life. That some of us are alert to Ingold's renewal is precisely what I mean by anthropology being an experimental mode, where no thought is denied its conditionality, and no practice is allowed to proceed unexamined divested from the yardstick of truth.

Acknowledgments

I would like to thank Tim Ingold, who helped during the writing of this chapter with his generous clarifications and comments provided via emails. I am also indebted to the Max Planck Institute for Religious and Ethnic Diversity, Göttingen, and Irfan Ahmad. I wish to acknowledge the Wenner-Gren Foundation's dissertation grant, without which the research at CERN could not have been undertaken. Last but not least, my teachers at the University of California, Berkeley, have provided outstanding support and encouragement throughout the years for which I express my heartfelt gratitude.

Arpita Roy received her doctorate in Anthropology in 2011 at the University of California, Berkeley, where she taught as a Lecturer for two years thereafter. Her doctoral dissertation was an ethnographic study of physics and physicists at the Large Hadron Collider particle accelerator at CERN in Geneva, Switzerland. She has received postdoctoral research fellowships at the Laboratoire d'Anthropologie Sociale, Paris, followed by the Max Planck Institute for the Study of Religious and Ethnic Diversity, Göttingen, Germany. She is presently at the University of Michigan, Ann Arbor. Her publications have appeared, among others, in *Cultural Anthropology*, *Dialectical Anthropology*, and *HAU: Journal of Ethnographic Theory*.

References

Biagioli, Mario, ed. 1999. *The Science Studies Reader*. New York: Routledge.
Bourdieu, Pierre. 1977. *Outline of a Theory of Practice*. Translated by Richard Nice. Cambridge: Cambridge University Press.
Clifford, James, and George E. Marcus, eds. 1986. *Writing Culture: The Poetics and Politics of Ethnography*. Berkeley: University of California Press.
Descola, Philippe. 2013. *Beyond Nature and Culture*. Chicago: University of Chicago Press.
Douglas, Mary. 1986. *How Institutions Think*. Syracuse: New York University Press.
Durkheim, Émile. 1965 [1915]. *The Elementary Forms of the Religious Life*. Translated by Joseph Ward Swain. New York: The Free Press
Foucault, Michel. 1980. *Power/Knowledge: Selected Interviews and Other Writings 1972–1977*. New York: Pantheon.
Gellner, Ernest. 1974. *Legitimation of Belief*. Cambridge, UK: Cambridge University Press.
———. 1992. *Postmodernism, Reason and Religion*. London: Routledge.
Goody, Jack. 1995. *The Expansive Moment: The Rise of Social Anthropology in Britain and Africa, 1918–1970*. Cambridge, UK: Cambridge University Press.
Ingold, Tim. 2008. "Anthropology Is *Not* Ethnography." *Proceedings of the British Academy* 154: 69–92.
———. 2014. "That's Enough about Ethnography!" *HAU: Journal of Ethnographic Theory* 4, no. 1: 383–95.

———. 2016. "From Science to Art and Back Again: The Pendulum of an Anthropologist." *ANUAC* 5, no. 1: 5–23.

———. 2017. "Anthropology contra Ethnography." *HAU: Journal of Ethnographic Theory* 7, no. 1: 21–26.

———. 2018. *Anthropology and/as Education*. Abington: Routledge.

Latour, Bruno. 2004. *Politics of Nature: How to Bring the Sciences into Democracy*. Cambridge, MA: Harvard University Press.

Malinowski, Bronislaw. 1922. *Argonauts of the Western Pacific: An Account of Native Enterprise and Adventure in the Archipelagoes of Melanesian New Guinea*. New York: Dutton.

Marcus, George E. 2013. "Experimental Forms for the Expression of Norms in the Ethnography of the Contemporary." *HAU: Journal of Ethnographic Theory* 3, no. 2: 197–217.

Marx, Karl. 1964. *Pre-capitalist Economic Formations*. Translated by Jack Cohen. London: Lawrence & Wishart.

Miller, Daniel. 2013. "Commentary: Opportunism, Perspective and Insight." *Social Anthropology* 21, no. 2: 226–29.

Needham, Rodney, ed. 1973. *Right & Left: Essays on Dual Symbolic Classification*. Chicago: University of Chicago Press.

Plato. 1957. *Plato's Theory of Knowledge: The Theaetetus and the Sophist of Plato*. Translated with a running commentary by Francis M. Cornford. New York: Liberal Arts Press.

———. 1977. *Plato's Phaedo*. Translated by G. M. A. Grube. Indianapolis: Hackett Publishing.

Rabinow, Paul. 1996. *Essays on the Anthropology of Reason*. Princeton: Princeton University Press.

Roy, Arpita. 2017. "Signatura rerum: Semiotics of the Sub-nuclear." *Signs and Society* 5, no. S1: 77–99. http://dx.doi.org/ 10.1086/690087.

Russell, Bertrand. 1958. *A Critical Exposition of the Philosophy of Leibniz*. London: George Allen & Unwin.

Sahlins, Marshall. 1976. *Culture and Practical Reason*. Chicago: University of Chicago Press.

Santayana, George. 1925. "Dewey's Naturalistic Metaphysics." *The Journal of Philosophy* 22, no. 25: 673–88.

Snow, Charles P. 1964. *Two Cultures: And a Second Look*. Cambridge, MA: Cambridge University Press.

Thompson, D'Arcy Wentworth. 1961. *On Growth and Form*. Cambridge, MA: Cambridge University Press.

Uberoi, J. P. S. 2019. *Mind and Society: From Indian Studies to General Sociology*, edited by Khalid Tyabji. Oxford: Oxford University Press.

Chapter 3

GRAPHIC DESIGNS

ON CONSTELLATIONAL WRITING, OR A BENJAMINIAN RESPONSE TO INGOLD'S CRITIQUE OF ETHNOGRAPHY

Jeremy F. Walton

Introduction: Writing across the Gap

Times of crisis are also frequently times of heightened productivity. The creative destruction of old gods is a catalyst for the destructive creation of unanticipated perspectives, as horizons open and new vistas appear (Harvey 1991: 16). And so the observation that anthropology is undergoing a time of crisis is not so much an alarm as an invitation to further excavations and linkages. Anthropology's recent crises have centered on the relationship between poststructuralist and "ethnographic" theory (da Col and Graeber 2011; Mazzarella 2017), but conceptual panic has also channeled into methodological polemics. Tim Ingold's (2008, 2014, 2017) scorched-earth campaign against ethnography's status as the signature method of anthropology is among the most uncompromising methodological interventions of recent years. We have assembled in this volume to weigh its insights, and, perhaps, to rescue an infant or two from the gray water.

Ingold's critique of ethnography is inseparable from his overarching ambition to reframe anthropology as a practice of collaborative engagement, an endeavor that aspires to mutual education, edification, attention, and attentiveness (2014: 389). He summons fellow anthropologists "to join in correspondence with those with whom we learn or among whom we study, in a movement that goes forward rather than back in time. Herein lies the educational purpose, dynamic, and potential of anthropology" (2014: 90). In order to achieve this anthropological dynamism, ethnography must be jettisoned, shed like a desiccated, confining skin. Why? Because ethnography puts the cart before the proverbial horse: it misconstrues the formative, protean encounters that yield anthropological knowledge as faits accomplis. Ethnography entails "a temporal distortion that contrives to render the aftermath of our meetings with people as their anterior condition . . . in effect, to cast encounters as ethnographic is to consign the incipient—the about-to-happen in unfolding relationships—to the temporal past of the already over" (2014: 386).[1] Anthropology, from Ingold's perspective, coalesces in the uncircumscribed plenitude of *present* action and interaction, while ethnography is both conducted and written in the *past* tense (see Eisenlohr's contribution to this volume for a counterargument). Ethnography alchemically transforms encounters and "correspondences" into objects and data that become the means to extrinsic, dubious documentary ends (2014).

As it happens, I am highly sympathetic to the disciplinary reorientation that Ingold advocates. Furthermore, I would contend—hopefully with his assent—that policing disciplinary boundaries by chasing one's own methodological tail is far less vital, or interesting, than pioneering new modes of interactive, collaborative knowledge. That said, Ingold's broadside against ethnography entails a lacuna that I welcome as an incitement to further discourse. Ingold criticizes the manner in which ethnography obscures the gap between research and writing by rendering the former a condition of, rather than for, the latter. Ethnography instrumentalizes and objectifies the "correspondences" that yield collaborative anthropological knowledge; on that much we agree (see Ladwig's meditation on "dark anthropology" in this volume for a contrasting perspective). Yet the gap between contexts of collaborative research and the modes of analysis and synthesis that sediment in various forms of writing—field notes, research articles, monographs—persists. How might we write across this gap? That is to say, how might we bridge the spatial and temporal distinction between protean anthropological (not ethnographic!) participation/observation and the discursive, institutional, and—above all—professional imperatives that saturate and structure our discipline?

Unfortunately, Ingold has not supplemented his polemic against ethnography with a constructive response to this urgent question. We may concur that ethnography—"*writing about the people*" (Ingold 2014: 385—emphasis in original)—impoverishes anthropology, but if not ethnography, what sort of -graphy should we practice? From the unassailable position of a full professorship, it is relatively uncomplicated to proclaim that "the steps of participant observation, like those of life itself, are contingent on the circumstances, and *advance toward no end*" (2014: 390—emphasis mine). But what should anthropologists in more straitened professional circumstances—PhD students, adjuncts, postdocs, assistant professors prior to tenure—make of this claim at a time when the injunction to "publish or perish" has become a sorry neoliberal mantra for the social sciences and humanities generally? Most anthropologists are under great pressure to "advance toward end(s)"—that is, to treat contexts of research as means to professional aims. To ignore this stringency is naive at best and a form of complicity at worst. Anthropologists must write *something*. If not ethnography, then what?

I suspect that Ingold has a battery of responses to these queries at hand, and I look forward to learning and benefitting from them. For the time being, however, I would like to broach one possible resolution to the dilemmas and detriments of ethnography that he has diagnosed. One of his most trenchant criticisms, in my estimation, centers on the "temporal distortion" (2014: 386) between research and writing that ethnography necessitates. Clearly, avoiding the inherent pitfalls of ethnography demands acknowledgment and theorization of the temporal and spatial gap between research and writing *in the act of writing itself*. And this, in turn, obliges anthropologists to design a new graphic form—a genre for which there is not yet a name.

Walter Benjamin offers inspiration in this effort. Benjamin's critique of historiography (1968) anticipates many aspects of Ingold's critique of ethnography. Yet, unlike Ingold, Benjamin also breaks the ground for a path leading beyond the mischief created by the "temporal distortions" of historiography (and, mutatis mutandis, ethnography). After rehearsing his critique of historiography, I draw on Benjamin's myriad writings to broach a new graphic form, "constellational writing," which has emerged from and is suited to my research. I base this graphic form on a method that I call "textured historicity" (Walton 2019a; see also Walton 2016). I then pioneer this genre in reference to a longstanding site of my research: the New Mosque in Thessaloniki, Greece.

The Critique of Historiography

Benjamin's critique of historiography—the mode of knowledge of the past entailed by historicism, and the genres of history writing that stem from this image of the past—has achieved worthy notoriety in recent decades, in tandem with a broader appraisal and appreciation of Benjamin as a titanic "off modern" thinker (Boym 2001: xvi; see also Walton 2019b) who presaged many of the signature interventions of postmodernism and poststructuralism. His epigrammatic "Theses on the Philosophy of History" adumbrates this critique of historicism vividly:

> Historicism contents itself with establishing a causal connection between various moments in history. But no fact that is a cause is for that very reason historical. It became historical posthumously, as it were, through events that may be separated from it by thousands of years. A historian who takes this as his point of departure stops telling the sequence of events like the beads of a rosary. *Instead, he grasps the constellation which his own era has formed with a definite earlier one.* (1968: 263—emphasis mine)

The lamentable corollaries of historicism are an ideology of teleological progress and an image of "homogeneous, empty time" (1968: 261), both of which Benjamin indefatigably rejects.[2]

Against the evacuated image of time and the past that pervades historicism, Benjamin envisions a radical synthesis of the present and the past, a collision best captured by the German term *Jetztzeit* ("now-time"): "History is the subject of a structure whose site is not homogeneous, empty time, but time filled by the presence of the now [*Jetztzeit*]" (1968: 261). As Irfan Ahmad (2019) points out in another context, this premium on the present is a hallmark feature of modernist historicity in general (see also Ahmad's introduction to this volume). For Benjamin, however, *Jetztzeit*—a concept that echoes the Christian theological and mystical notion of kairos, the "critical moment," and which is also known as "messianic time"—undermines the progressive, homogeneous temporality of modernity. In another celebrated passage, Benjamin describes the infusion of temporalities that animates *Jetztzeit* as a "flash": "To articulate the past historically does not mean to recognize it 'the way it really was.' It means to seize hold of a memory as it flashes up at a moment of danger" (1968: 255). The allegorical figure of this flashing moment of danger is the famous Angel of History, Paul Klee's Angelus Novus, whose "face is turned toward the past. Where we perceive a chain of events, he sees one single catastrophe which keeps piling wreckage upon wreckage and hurls it in front of his feet" (1968: 257).

Despite contrasts in tone—Ingold does not approach Benjamin's messianic apocalypticism—the critiques of ethnography and (historicist) historiography resonate with each other. Both Ingold and Benjamin inveigh against the "temporal distortions" that stem from the imputation of a causal logic of progression to the past in relation to the present. For Ingold, the rub of the matter is the "ethnographizing" recruitment of moments of correspondence in research—definitive situations of "becoming" (2014: 389)—to an a posteriori logic of "being" that "shifts from engagement to reportage, from the co-imagining of possible futures to the characterization of what is already past" (392). Similarly, for Benjamin, the culpability of historicism resides in its imputation of fixity to the past. To adapt the phenomenological language that Ingold invokes, Benjamin insists that the past is always a matter of becoming, rather than being: "Every image of the past that is not recognized by the present as one of its own concerns threatens to disappear irretrievably" (1968: 255). Or, put another way, the past is only such on the basis of the "constellation" (1968: 263) that it forms in relation to the present in the flashing moment of *Jetztzeit*.

As with Ingold, Benjamin's polemics are more explicit than the remedies he proffers. Nonetheless, his oeuvre stands proudly as an exemplar of the effort "to brush history against the grain" (1968: 258). In particular, *The Arcades Project* (2002), his omnibus opus, epitomizes antihistoricist writing about the past. *The Arcades Project* marshals a startling reading of the built environment and legacies of nineteenth-century Paris as an archive of early capitalist modernity and its constitutive social forms (see also Harvey 2003; Walton 2019b). Benjamin insists that this chronicle only matters because Paris of the nineteenth century is a past that configures, and is reconfigured by, the present in which he writes. Fittingly, the genre of *The Arcades Project* might be described as "constellational" in the manner in which it situates the past and the present in relation to each other.

Over the remainder of this chapter, I advocate and illustrate just this sort of "constellational" writing as a counterethnographic genre in Ingold's sense. In several recent essays (Walton 2019a; see also Walton 2016), I have proposed a counterethnographic method to correspond to this counterethnographic practice of writing, what I call "textured historicity": a "mode of scholarship and knowledge [that] emphasizes the distinctive, embodied encounter between the subject in the present and the objects that convey the past in the present" (Walton 2019a: 357).[3] Before proceeding to a "constellational" rendering of Thessaloniki's New Mosque, it is necessary to acquire a more thorough immersion in the method of textured historicity with assistance from Benjamin's concept of dialectical thinking.

Dialectical Thinking, Textured Historicity, Constellational Writing

Dreams are a key metaphor through which Benjamin illustrates his antihistoricist theory of time, the past, and the present. An epigraph in his essay "Paris, Capital of the Nineteenth Century"—a condensation of the sundry concerns in *The Arcades Project*—is a quotation from the historian Jules Michelet: "*Chaque époque rêve la suivante*" ("Every era dreams its successor") (Benjamin 2007: 148). With Michelet's motto as his beacon, Benjamin "wakefully" interprets the oneiric visions of nineteenth-century Paris: "From this epoch stem the arcades and interiors, the exhibitions and panoramas. They are the residues of a dream world. The realization of dream elements in waking is the textbook example of dialectical thinking" (2007: 162). From Benjamin's vantage, the iron cathedrals of Paris' nineteenth-century arcades are embodiments of the modern interpolation of industry and architecture, which will only reach an apotheosis in the subsequent century. The nineteenth century "dreamed" these elements; dialectical thinking in the twentieth century treats them "wakefully" (see also Buck-Morss 1991).

"Dialectical thinking" captures Benjamin's antihistoricist method in a single phrase. For Benjamin, each present moment must be comprehended dialectically as a "past future." That is to say, if each era "dreams" its own future, then each present moment is also a former future "dreamt" by a previous era, when that era was itself present. *In the past, this present was the future (in a dream).* Simultaneously, each current era projects—dreams—its own futures. Which implies that each present is also a "future past" (see also Kosseleck 2004; Huyssen 2003). *In the future, this present will be past (that which once dreamt). So, the present is a former future in relation to myriad pasts and a coming past in relation to multiple futures.* In Benjamin's oneiric vocabulary, each present era is both "wakeful" in relation to the past and "dreaming" in relation to the future. To misconstrue the present as the simple outcome of previous events is to deny and obscure the dialectical condition(ing) of the present: both a "past future" (the dream from which one has awoken) and a "future past" (the dream that has yet to end). Furthermore, because the future is necessarily undetermined, dialectical thinking is resolutely negative (see also Adorno 1973). Contra both Hegel and Marx, no teleological synthesis or fixed, utopian destination structures the dialectical mediation of the present as a past future and future past.

Dialectical thinking is especially potent in relation to what we might call the material historicity of objects—the scars, traces,[4] and patinas (Dawdy 2016) that accompany objects as they mediate between the past and the present. As Susan Buck-Morss shows in her companion to *The Arcades Project*, Benjamin approached such objects *as* ideas; in doing so, he staunchly refused the high-modern dichotomy between ideal and real, conceptual and material: "Corsets, feather dusters, red and green-colored combs, old photographs, souvenir replicas of the Venus di Milo, collar buttons to shirts long since discarded—these battered historical survivors from the dawn of industrial culture . . . *were* the philosophical ideas, as a constellation of concrete, historical referents" (Buck-Morss 1991: 4—emphasis in original). Here, we return to the motif of textured historicity that I foreshadowed above. Textured historicity expresses a form of knowledge that coalesces through dialectical thinking in relation to the material historicity of objects. The *textured* aspect of this mode of knowledge production emphasizes the distinctive, embodied encounter between and coconstitution of subjects in the present and objects that convey the past in the present (Walton 2019a).[5] Textures—rough, gritty, smooth, porous, variegated—emerge at the site and surface of this encounter. The subject of textured historicity embraces the present, but not on its own terms. She insists that objects, discourses, and material culture in the present achieve meaning dialectically as facets of a past future and a future past.

With antique feather dusters and wrought iron architectural details, we may seem to have ventured far afield from the bedrock concerns of anthropology. Ingold's critique of ethnography is not a call to abandon intersubjective engagement for the social life of things (Appadurai 1988), after all. I should therefore clarify that I am not asserting disciplinary precedence for dialectical thinking and textured historicity. Rather—to return to the principal intervention of this chapter—I have lingered over Benjamin's antihistoricist comprehension of time and objects for two reasons: first, because it resonates with Ingold's critique of the temporal distortions and teleological thrust of ethnography, and, second, because Benjamin's mode of writing might inspire a different form of "-graphy," a genre that foregrounds the temporal and spatial contrasts between research and writing, rather than indenturing the former to the latter.[6] With a nod to Benjamin's notion of the constellations formed by the past and the present, I call this genre "constellational writing." *The Arcades Project* is a primer in constellational writing. Rather than imposing a teleological narrative of causality and continuity on his vast archive of material, Benjamin presents an assemblage of reflections and refractions that render Parisian pasts present in a kaleidoscopic fashion.

Thessaloniki's New Mosque and Its Constellations

As a whole, the city of Thessaloniki is uniquely suited to the negative dialectics of textured historicity and constellational writing (see Walton 2017: xi–xv). In a remarkable study, historian Mark Mazower (2004) has unearthed many of the subterranean histories of this "city of ghosts"—a thriving port for half a millennium under Ottoman rule until it was conquered in 1912 by the Greek army during the First Balkan War and passed to Greek sovereignty. The following decades witnessed the departure of the city's Muslims and subsequent arrival of Ottoman Greek Orthodox Christians during the population exchanges between Greece and newly independent Turkey mandated by the Treaty of Lausanne in 1923 (Mazower 2004: 311ff.) and the decimation of the city's thriving Jewish community in the Holocaust, a result of the Nazi occupation during World War II (2004: 392ff.). In a span of less than fifty years, Thessaloniki witnessed a turbulent, violent demographic and physical transformation that reduced the Ottoman past of the city to a ghostly mirage.

One of the communities of Ottoman Salonika that was effectively obliterated during the early twentieth century had been an unparalleled embodiment of the city's history as a forge of religious and ethnic intersections and hybridity. The *dönme* (Turkish for "turned"), or *Ma'min* (Arabic for "believers"), as they called themselves, were a syncretic religious community that publicly professed Islam yet retained devotion for the millennial figure Sabbatai Zevi, a Sephardic Jew from the city of Izmir who proclaimed himself the Messiah in the mid-seventeenth century (Baer 2010; see also Mazower 2004: 72–76; Neyzi 2002; Sisman 2015; Walton 2016: 520–21). Despite the insularity, endogamy, and relative secrecy of the community, the *dönme* of Salonika thrived during the late Ottoman period of liberalizing reforms known as the *Tanzimat* and achieved prominent status within the merchant bourgeoisie of the city (Baer 2010: 86). As Muslims in a legal sense, the *dönme* were obliged to relocate to Turkey during the population exchange of 1923 (Baer 2010: 141ff.), where their distinction was quickly absorbed by the powerful new solvent of ethnolinguistic Turkish nationalism. With the exception of a handful

Figure 3.1. The new mosque in Thessaloniki, Greece. © Jeremy F. Walton.

of aging Turkish citizens, there are no *dönme* today, certainly not in Thessaloniki. Nonetheless, material testaments to the erstwhile affluence of the *dönme* persist in Thessaloniki's neighborhoods of Agia Triada and Analipsi (the former Ottoman district of Hamidiye), including several lavish mansions and, above all, the New Mosque (Turkish: *Yeni Cami*; Greek: *Geni Tzami*).

I have conducted research related to the New Mosque intermittently since 2016, and will continue to do so in the context of my broader project on the legacies, memories, and forms of amnesia that orient Thessaloniki's Ottoman past today. In an earlier essay (Walton 2016), I explicitly raised the dilemma that the New Mosque and the *dönme* entail for "ethnography" (though not in relation to Ingold's arguments): "How might one conduct an 'ethnography' of . . . a former mosque which no longer functions, or is even remembered, as such?" (515). My point here was that there are very few people with whom an anthropologist might speak about the New Mosque, but Ingold's critique of ethnography is equally pertinent: How might one approach a site such as the New Mosque in a manner that seeks new modes of correspondence with its multiple, divergent, and even contradictory pasts? In what follows, I offer a "constellational" chronicle of the New Mosque (see Figure 3.1) as a possible response to this question.[7]

2014

It is a sweltering late summer day on the Thermaic Gulf. My wife and I arrive in Thessaloniki for a wedding after a marathon overland voyage by train and coach from Zagreb via Belgrade and Skopje. Two days after the nuptial festivities, we set out by foot through the dusty streets of Agia Triada in search of the New Mosque; as we walk, I summarize the history of the *dönme* and the city. Signs for the New Mosque are scarce, but I recall the name of the street on which it is located: *Archeologikou Mousiou*, a testament to the four decades during which the former mosque functioned as the city's Archaeological Museum. Still, we wander aimlessly through narrow side streets and down culs-de-sac for some time before encountering the site. Once spotted, there is no mistaking it—the delicate, eclectic structure, designed by Sicilian architect Vitaliano Poselli (*the* "starchitect" of fin-de-siècle Salonika), incorporates Art Nouveau and Neo-Moorish elements and contrasts sharply with the surrounding architecture of drab, boxy midcentury apartment buildings. The imposing iron gate to the mosque's garden is open, as is the door to the building itself, but we are the sole visitors. A crawl of tortoises orbits the mosque, navigating the discarded marble tombstones that litter the garden. The air is cooler inside, and we pause for a respite. Sheets of butcher paper, presumably detritus from a recent art exhibition, cover much of the floor and walls, but the *mihrab*, designating the direction of Mecca, remains visible. No information about the building, site, or its history is visible.

1925

A clutch of day laborers mills about the courtyard of the shuttered building. On the street outside, sculptures, statues, sarcophagi, and unidentifiable artifacts rest on makeshift palettes. The task for which the laborers have been hired is straightforward: transfer the collection of the city's nascent Archaeological Museum into its new home, the former mosque that has gathered dust since the departure of the final members of its community in 1923 due to the population exchange. Many of the workers were also on the move in 1923—Greek Orthodox Christians from the Pontus, Cappadocia, villages outside of Smyrna and Bursa, they were uprooted from homes and communities by new, abstract powers of states and nations, only to arrive in a city that was, in many ways, more familiar than they had expected. Several of the men glance at the Arabic inscription above the entrance of the new museum. They cannot read it, but they recognize it, and they realize that this space, too, was recently not what it has now become.

2013

The young men and women from Komotini (Turkish: *Gümülcine*), a provincial city in Thrace, Greece's eastern-most province, are not paying close attention to the ceremony for which they have traveled to Thessaloniki—they know that the most important event, the communal prayer (*namaz*), is yet to come. Yiannis Boutaris, the popular, recently elected mayor, praises the gathering as a recapitulation of Thessaloniki's rich, multiethnic, multireligious past (Batı Trakya Haber Ajansı 2013). Beside him, the Turkish consul general and the Greek coordinator for minority affairs in Thrace and the Aegean Islands complete the official tableau. The teenagers are Muslim-Turkish Greek citizens from Thrace, descendants of one of the few communities (along with Constantinople's Greeks) exempted from the population exchanges of 1923. They study at Komotini's Hayriye Madrassa (*Medrese-i Hayriye*), where they learn a version of Sunni-Hanafi Islam dictated and legitimized by Turkey's Directorate of Religious Affairs (see Walton 2017: 53ff.). They are well prepared for the communal prayer to come, the first officially sanctioned Muslim religious service in Thessaloniki since 1923. But many of them are eager for the program to end so that they can explore the city at leisure. As they form rows in order to perform the prayer inside the elegant building, do they imagine how different the rituals performed in this space a century ago might have been?

1902

On an impeccable early autumn morning, crowds swell around the new addition to the Hamidiye district, the preferred residential neighborhood for turn-of-the-century Salonika's Muslim bourgeoisie. This is a coming-out ceremony, in a sense: with a prominent addition to the cityscape, the traditionally insular *Ma'min* announce a new, cosmopolitan dispensation (Sisman 2015). Hacı Mehmet Hayri Pasha, a high-ranking member of the Ottoman Third Army, member of the Yakubi branch of the *dönme*, and principal donor for the mosque (Neumeier 2013) welcomes the crowd. A military orchestra then breaks into the Ottoman anthem of the era, the Hamidiye March (Neumeier 2013). Trumpets and snare drums compete with the rasp of the *zurna*, an Anatolian woodwind; this instrumental juxtaposition in the march echoes the curious arrangement of Western European and Ottoman political and aesthetic forms that coincide during the reign of Sultan Abdul Hamid II.[8] In the joyous atmosphere, the future of the mosque, its community, and Ottoman Salonika as a whole seems bright.

2017

The doors of the exhibition space are open, and visitors in pairs and small groups shuffle in and out on the first evening of the Thessaloniki Biennale. The theme for 2017—embraced enthusiastically by Mayor Boutaris—is "Shared Sacred Sites," and the New Mosque is one of the three exhibition venues. Nowadays, the mosque is owned by the Greek Ministry of Culture and administered by Thessaloniki's Municipal Art Gallery, which schedules art openings, symposia, and other events in the space. In the main hall, art lovers encounter canvasses and sculptures related to the theme of the Biennale. The highlight is a tripartite installation near the center of the main gallery by the Greek-French artist Lydia Dambassina. The following words adorn three marble slabs: "Where is this from? Is this from a Jewish tomb? Or from a Muslim tomb?" Most visitors greet Dambassina's piece with somber appreciation for the morbid histories that she evokes: abandoned Jewish and Muslim tombstones, relics of the Ottoman period and indexes of communal absence, are not difficult to uncover in the city of ghosts. Yet not all Thessalonians share such appreciation. Several months after the start of the Biennale, one of the main posters announcing "Shared Sacred Sites" is defaced by graffiti (Walton and Mahadev 2019: 81). Blue spray paint blots out the Star of David and crescent moon that adorned the poster, leaving only a third symbol, the cross, unmarred.

Conclusion

The preceding paragraphs assemble one constellation of moments in the biography of the New Mosque. Others are imaginable, particularly in relation to future moments that have yet to pass. In keeping with the imperatives of *Jetztzeit*, I have endeavored to write each moment in the present tense. By treating each moment as both a "past future" and a "future past," I have sought to illustrate how the method of textured historicity and the genre of constellational writing might avoid the "temporal distortions" that plague historiography and ethnography as both research methods and modes of writing.

Constellations in the Benjaminian sense bear strong affinities to the "correspondences" that Ingold proposes (2014: 90) as both the means and the ends of anthropology. The difference between the two lies in questions of temporality and subjectivity. Ingold's correspondences, as I understand them, are primarily rooted in the shared time and space of encounters among anthropologists and their interlocutors. The open-ended correspondences among subjects that emerge from such encounters yield unpredictable transformations and reformations of selves and others. Benjamin's constellations, by contrast, are not principally concerned with intersubjective metamorphoses. Rather, they highlight the open-endedness of time itself, the ways in which pasts, presents, and futures are constantly drawn into reciprocal relationship with one another.

Nonetheless, the distinction between the intersubjective and the intertemporal, between Ingold's correspondences and Benjamin's constellations, only extends so far. Constellations inculcate new correspondences, especially in cities haunted by multiple pasts. Thessaloniki illustrates this vividly. It was a city of refugees in the 1910s and 1920s, as the Ottoman Empire crumbled; in the wake of wars in Afghanistan, Iraq, and, above all, Syria, it is a city of refugees again today. Memories and legacies of one era of turmoil and tension filter into the present to offer support to newcomers whose plight is, after all, not so new (see Rexhepi forthcoming). In efforts to correspond with one another in the present, both lifelong and recent Thessalonians establish new constellations among neglected pasts and desired futures. Sites such as the New Mosque, and the pasts that they embody, offer the possibility of unanticipated intersubjective correspondences, as artists, activists, refugees, and passers-by contemplate the history of the building and its lessons from, and for, a time of displacement and discord.

***

In conclusion, a few preemptive comments may help to temper possible allergic reactions to my argument and exposition. I expect that many anthropologists will object that my constellational writing and the research that supports it are not "properly" anthropological at all. Such an evaluation hinges ultimately on one's commitment to the purity of disciplines and methods. I confess that I am not highly committed to such pure (puritan?) ideals, and I suspect that Ingold would concur. More to the point, however, is that I write in a diagnostic rather than prescriptive mood. Textured historicity and constellational writing may or may not resonate with other anthropologists, historians, and students of the past in the present. Regardless, we remain sorely in need of new genres of writing that allow research to aspirate in unanticipated ways.

Like other contributors to this volume—in particular, Eisenlohr and Ladwig—I do not agree with all the blame that Ingold lays at the feet of ethnography—surely more powerful, structural forces than this are at work in "preventing our discipline from having the kind of impact in the world that it deserves and the world so desperately needs" (2014: 383). Revanchist neoliberal positivism, with its objectification, quantification, and "scientization" of scholarly knowledge, extends far beyond ethnography. Anthropologists' misguided methods are not the only, or even primary, mufflers of anthropology's public voice. On the other hand, I fervidly second Ingold's advocacy of a processual anthropology of correspondence and mutual becoming that is open to multiple ends. One of these ends will continue to be -graphic, if not *ethno*graphic. My design in this essay has been to pioneer just such a new -graphic writing. At minimum, such a mode of writing must remain attentive to the multiple possible constellations that maintain among a plurality of temporal moments: those of research, writing, and readership, as well the prehistories and as-yet deferred futures that envelope each and all of them.

Acknowledgments

I would like to thank Irfan Ahmad for his sage guidance throughout the writing process, Piro Rexhepi for inspiring new perspectives on Salonika, and Karin Doolan for accompanying me with keen insights on this, and other, research peregrinations.

Jeremy F. Walton received his PhD in Anthropology from the University of Chicago in 2009. Dr. Walton's first book, *Muslim Civil Society and the Politics of Religious Freedom in Turkey* (Oxford University Press, 2017), is an ethnography of Muslim NGOs, state institutions, and secularism in contemporary Turkey. He designed and leads "Empires of Memory: The Cultural Politics of Historicity in Former Habsburg and Ottoman Cities," an interdisciplinary, multisited project on post-imperial memory in post-Habsburg and post-Ottoman realms, at the Max Planck Institute for the Study of Religious and Ethnic Diversity. In 2019, he guest edited a special issue of the journal *History and Anthropology* on "Ambivalent Legacies: Political Cultures of Memory and Amnesia in Former Habsburg and Ottoman Lands."

Notes

1. Ingold's critique of the temporal distortions of ethnography resonates with Roland Barthes's provocative claim that photography necessarily renders its subjects "already dead" (1981: 77; see also Walton 2020).
2. In his influential "provincialization" of Europe, Dipesh Chakrabarty summons an analogous critique of historicism, "the mode of thinking

[which] tells us that in order to understand the nature of anything in this world we must see it as an historically developing entity, that is, first, as an individual and unique whole . . . and, second, as something that develops over time" (2000: 23). See also Tambar (2014: 43).
3. In an earlier context (Walton 2016: 515), I referred to this method as "disciplined historicity." Since that publication, I have come to prefer the phrase "textured historicity," both because it avoids the inevitable Foucauldian associations that the term "discipline" now summons and because the motif of texture foregrounds the encounter between and mutual formation of subjects and objects, rather than the auto-tutorial practice of the subject herself.
4. Ingold himself has written provocatively about traces as one of the two overarching categories of lines (the other he dubs "threads"): "The trace is any enduring mark left in or on a solid surface by a continuous movement" (2007: 43). For a critique of the concept of the trace, see Fennell (2018).
5. Even more strongly, we might say that textured historicity directs attention to the reciprocal constitution of historical subjects and historical objects. Michel-Rolph Trouillot grasps this dialectical process of mutual constitution with acuity: "The collective subjects who supposedly remember did not exist as such at the time of the events they claim to remember. Rather, their constitution as subjects goes hand in hand with the continuous creation of the past. As such, they do not succeed the past: they are its contemporaries" (1995: 16). Charles Stewart echoes this point in a recent review article on historicity and anthropology: "The historian, or any other historical subject, constitutes history through thought, and possibly research and writing, but at the same time this historian is also constituted by historical events in the course of life and through living within frameworks generated in the deeper past" (2016: 80).
6. Although a departure from the main current of this chapter, it is worth noting that Benjamin and Ingold share a fascination with the act of walking and the figure of the *flâneur* as potential antagonists to teleological thought. Benjamin embodies the figure of the *flâneur* most evocatively in his "Berlin Chronicle." For those walkers able to "lose" themselves in the city, "signboards and street names, passers-by, roofs, kiosks, or bars . . . speak . . . like a cracking twig under his feet in the forest, like the startling call of a bittern in the distance" (2007: 8). Ingold, in a coauthored introduction to a volume on walking, gestures to Benjamin's figure of the *flâneur*: "A wanderer who impresses the byways of the city with his feet, the flâneur finds in its passing details an endless source of fascination. The character he performs, as Benjamin observes, is that of the detective. With his eyes and ears open and alert to any fortuitous but revealing incident, his interest in every little clue to the myriad lives around him resembles that of the small child on his way to school" (Ingold and Vergunst 2008: 15). Both Benjamin and Ingold insist that the act of walking cultivates attentiveness to what Ingold

elsewhere calls the "temporality of the landscape" (1993). I have relied on the meditative techniques of the *flâneur* in my own work as well (see Walton 2017: 174–76).
7. Beyond Benjamin's clear influence on "constellational writing," I also draw on a technique pioneered by historian Edhem Eldem that aspires to vivify the historian's archive by means of "risky narratives of 're-creation' of the human environment of the time, despite the inevitable risk of retrospective projections into a poorly documented mental world of the past" (1999: 142). I should also note that Emily Neumeier's (2013) sensitive essay on the New Mosque's various iterations anticipates my rendering here in multiple respects.
8. For the curious, several renditions of the Hamidiye March are available on YouTube. For instance, see https://www.youtube.com/watch?v=j7Zt3xRwCNo.

References

Adorno, Theodor. 1973 [1966]. *Negative Dialectics*. Translated by E. B. Ashton. New York: Routledge.

Ahmad, Irfan. 2019. "Reply to Anidjar, Fernando, Lawrence and Moumtaz." *Critical Research in Religion* 7, no. 2: 199–207.

Appadurai, Arjun, ed. 1988. *The Social Life of Things: Commodities in Cultural Perspective*. Cambridge, UK: Cambridge University Press.

Baer, Marc. 2010. *The Dönme: Jewish Converts, Muslim Revolutionaries, and Secular Turks*. Stanford: Stanford University Press.

Barthes, Roland. 1981. *Camera Lucida: Reflections on Photography*. Translated by Richard Howard. New York: Hill and Wang.

Batı Trakya Haber Ajansı. 2013. "Selanik'teki Yeni Camii'de 90 yıl sonra namaz kılındı." *Batı Trakya Online*. https://www.batitrakya.org/bati-trakya-haber/selanikteki-yeni-camiide-90-yil-sonra-namaz-kilindi.html.

Benjamin, Walter. 1968. *Illuminations: Essays and Reflections*. Translated by Harry Zohn. New York: Schocken.

———. 2002. *The Arcades Project*. Translated by Howard Eiland and Kevin McLaughlin. Cambridge, MA: The Belknap Press of Harvard University.

———. 2007 [1978]. *Reflections: Essays, Aphorisms, Autobiographical Writings*. Translated by Edmund Jephcott. New York: Schocken Books.

Boym, Svetlana. 2001. *The Future of Nostalgia*. New York: Basic Books.

Buck-Morss, Susan. 1991. *The Dialectics of Seeing: Walter Benjamin and the Arcades Project*. Cambridge, MA: MIT Press.

Chakrabarty, Dipesh. 2000. *Provincializing Europe: Postcolonial Thought and Historical Difference*. Princeton: Princeton University Press.

da Col, Giovanni, and David Graeber. 2011. "Forward: The Return of Ethnographic Theory." *Hau: Journal of Ethnographic Theory* 1, no. 1: vi–xxxv. https://www.haujournal.org/index.php/hau/article/view/hau1.1.001/50.

Dawdy, Shannon. 2016. *Patina: A Profane Archaeology*. Chicago: University of Chicago Press.
Eldem, Edhem. 1999. "Istanbul: From Imperial to Peripheralized Capital." In *The Ottoman City between East and West*, coauthored by Edhem Eldem, Daniel Goffman, and Bruce Masters, 135–206. Cambridge, UK: Cambridge University Press.
Fennell, Catherine. 2018. "Beyond the Trace." *Postcolonial Studies* 21, no. 4: 520–24.
Harvey, David. 1991. *The Condition of Postmodernity: An Enquiry into the Origins of Cultural Change*. Malden, MA: Wiley-Blackwell.
———. 2003. *Paris, Capital of Modernity*. New York: Routledge.
Huyssen, Andreas. 2003. *Present Pasts: Urban Palimpsests and the Politics of Cultural Memory*. Stanford: Stanford University Press.
Ingold, Tim. 1993. "The Temporality of the Landscape." *World Archaeology* 25, no. 2: 152–74.
———. 2007. *Lines: A Brief History*. London: Routledge.
———. 2008. "Anthropology Is *Not* Ethnography." Radcliffe-Brown Lecture in Social Anthropology. *Proceedings of the British Academy* 154: 69–92.
———. 2014. "That's Enough about Ethnography!" *Hau: Journal of Ethnographic Theory* 4, no. 1: 383–95.
———. 2017. "Anthropology contra Ethnography." *Hau: Journal of Ethnographic Theory* 7, no. 1: 21–26.
Ingold, Tim, and Jo Lee Vergunst. 2008. "Introduction." In *Ways of Walking: Ethnography and Practice on Foot*, edited by Ingold and Vergunst, 1–19. New York: Routledge.
Kosseleck, Reinhardt. 2004. *Futures Past: On the Semantics of Historical Time*. Translated by Keith Tribe. New York: Columbia University Press.
Mazower, Mark. 2004. *Salonica, City of Ghosts: Christians, Muslims and Jews, 1430–1950*. New York: Vintage Books/Random House.
Mazzarella, William. 2017. *The Mana of Mass Society*. Chicago: University of Chicago Press.
Neumeier, Emily. 2013. "From Dönme to Biennale: The 'New Mosque' in Thessaloniki." *Ottoman History Podcast*, 13 April. Accessed 17 May 2018. http://www.ottomanhistorypodcast.com/2013/12/from-donme-to-biennale-new-mosque-in.html.
Neyzi, Leyla. 2002. "Sabbateanism, Identity, and Subjectivity in Turkey." *Comparative Studies in Society and History* 44, no. 1: 137–58.
Rexhepi, Piro. Forthcoming. "Cruising Borders in Salonika." *Feminist Review*.
Sisman, Cengiz. 2015. *The Burden of Silence: Sabbatai Sevi and the Evolution of the Ottoman Turkish Dönmes*. New York: Oxford University Press.
Stewart, Charles. 2016. "Historicity and Anthropology." *Annual Review of Anthropology* 45: 79–94.
Tambar, Kabir. 2014. *The Reckoning of Pluralism: Political Belonging and the Demands of History in Turkey*. Stanford: Stanford University Press.
Trouillot, Michel Rolph. 1995. *Silencing the Past: Power and the Production of History*. Boston: Beacon Press.

Walton, Jeremy F. 2016. "Geographies of Revival and Erasure: Neo-Ottoman Sites of Memory in Istanbul, Thessaloniki, and Budapest." *Die Welt Des Islams* 56: 510–32.

———. 2017. *Muslim Civil Society and the Politics of Religious Freedom in Turkey*. New York: Oxford University Press.

———. 2019a. "Introduction: Textured Historicity and the Ambivalence of Imperial Legacies." *History and Anthropology* 30, no. 4: 353–65.

———. 2019b. "*Metrosophy*: Rereading Walter Benjamin in Light of *Religion After Religion*." In *All Religion Is Inter-Religion: Essays in Honor of Steven M. Wasserstrom*, edited by Kambiz GhaneaBassiri and Paul Robertson. London: Bloomsbury Academic.

———. 2020. "Already Dead? Of Tombstones, Empire and Photography." In *Sharpening the Haze: Visual Essays on Imperial History and Memory*, edited by Giulia Carabelli, Miloš Jovanović, Annika Kirbis, and Jeremy F. Walton, 26–41. London: Ubiquity Press.

Walton, Jeremy F., and Neena Mahadev. 2019. "Special Section: Siting Pluralism. Introduction: Religious Plurality, Interreligious Pluralism, and Spatialities of Religious Difference." *Religion and Society: Advances in Research* 10: 81–91.

Chapter 4

NON-CORRESPONDENCE IN FIELDWORK

DEATH, DARK ETHNOGRAPHY, AND THE NEED FOR TEMPORAL ALIENATION

Patrice Ladwig

In discussions surrounding the practicalities and ethics of fieldwork, anthropologists are supposed to fulfill a plethora of roles. As participant observers, we should be engaged, responsible, and attentive. We should care for our informants and stand in a relationship of reciprocity and collaboration with them. In Tim Ingold's exploration of the distinction between ethnography and anthropology, one also finds a specific variation of this ideal. Participant observation and fieldwork are intrinsic for connecting to and establishing relationships with people and things. Drawing on his concept of correspondence, he elaborates: "This brings me back to participant observation. I have already mentioned that participant observation is key to the practice of anthropology, and underwrites the generosity of its approach to attending and responding. It is a way, as I would like to put it, of *corresponding* with people" (Ingold 2017a: 23—emphasis in original). In my reading, correspondence for Ingold does not imply producing an exact match or simulacrum for the things and actions happening around us; rather, it means attending to and establishing correspondence with people such that they become integral to participant observation. Ingold has developed the latter notion with some complexity in several of his writings, and he uses a variety of descriptions and metaphors for it, often drawing on artistic productions.[1] For him, participant observation is a form of "living attentionally with others" (Ingold 2014: 389), and it should be understood "not as ethnographic, but as educational" (2014: 392). Equally central to this is his warning against converting participant observation into objectification: "The great mistake is to confuse observation and objectification. To observe, in itself, is not to objectify. It is to notice what people are saying and doing, to watch and listen, and to respond in your own practice. That is to say, observation is a way of participating attentively, and is for this reason a way of learning" (Ingold 2017a: 23).

With reference to Timothy Jenkins (1994), Ingold proposes that participant observation is rather a series of apprenticeships, a form of education and a way of learning. On a basic level, I find this approach to participant observation very appealing. Correspondence and nonobjectification can be read as novel ways of collapsing the distance between participant observer and the people and things with whom anthropologists work. In another context, he uses the phrase "labour of love" (Ingold 2018: 6) to describe the reciprocal relations of gratitude evolving through being in correspondence. We do not deal with observation as an extractive, objectifying enterprise. To be in correspondence and not to objectify, then, can be read as specific ways of establishing *connections* that enable us to *care* for the things and the people with whom we work. Philosophical works that employ Ingold's notions, such as Reinhard Knodt's (2017: 16; 43) recent publication, also emphasize that a philosophy of correspondences is one that does not foreground fetishes of postmodern thinking such as difference, border drawing, and fractioned, incommensurable identities. Rather, correspondence thinking is constituted by continuously drawing connections, and by letting them unfold in and with another in atmospheres (see Macho 2017).

One the one hand, these imperatives to connect and exchange with the people and things we work with can be understood as reactions to the critiques anthropology and its fieldwork practices were subject to in the context of their colonial origins (Asad 1973) and their extractive enterprise of data collection (Robben and Sluka 2007: 17–19). On the other hand, this implies that being willing to, but not being able to, adhere to these standards is often sensed as a failure to properly connect with people in the field. Or, philosophically speaking, it can be considered as a form of alienation, as "a kind of dysfunctional relation (for example, an unnatural separation or hostility) between entities" (Leopold 2007: 68). But is this urge to connect, to correspond, to love, and to call for the abandonment of objectification and detachment a stance that overcompensates many of the postmodern critiques? Can this imperative to connect and exchange also become problematic in itself because disconnection and alienation here get an exclusively negative image?

In a recent volume with the telling title *Fieldwork Is Not What It Used to Be*, James Faubion asks us to rethink this emphasis on connecting. For him, the point is not that good anthropology is, and has always been, about connecting to people and things, and it is not about the discovery of the diversity and multiplicity of these connections. For him, "more emphatically, the point is that only connecting is neither in fact or in principle anthropologically adequate" (Faubion 2009: 145). How intensely, when, and with whom should we connect? When Ingold refers to objects and explores correspondences in the context of weaving (2000), I find his way of rethinking what observation implies very appealing and, indeed, very enlightening. However, in situations where participant observation is far away from its ideal circumstances, and when our observing and work with people are embedded in rather negative conditions, the rules of the game can change. Under conditions of severe power asymmetries, marginalization, or especially when conducting "fieldwork under fire" (Nordstrom and Robben 1995) that entails considerable risk, corresponding, connecting, and nonobjectification can quickly reach their limits.

In this chapter, I want to discuss one such fieldwork context, and relate it to Ingold's notions of correspondence, attentionality, and nonobjectification. I claim that this understanding of fieldwork has a humanistic and poetic appeal that nevertheless implies a certain absoluteness and radicalism, which, I propose, derive from certain theological baggage and holistic idealism of Ingold's work. I take a project I was involved in from 2007 to 2009 on Buddhist death rituals as a starting point for my reflections. In the course of the fieldwork I carried out, I had to do a fair bit of what I will label with reference to Sherry Ortner (2016) as dark ethnography. Attending many funerals, and working for several weeks with morticians in crematoria in Laos and Thailand, I increasingly felt affected by death pollution and encountered situations in which I felt I had to disconnect from the people and things around me. I turned my attention away from certain people and things, and increasingly objectified my work by intentionally alienating myself from the field. Without necessarily unpacking a whole body of literature on the concept of alienation and its links to objectification,[2] I want to propose that (temporal) alienation and calls for "participant objectivation" (Bourdieu 2002) are not only coping mechanisms, but can actually become fieldwork strategies in the context of dark anthropology. I argue that while being out of correspondence and performing objectification may at first sight seem like betraying a holistic approach to participant observation, it can also be considered from a positive perspective. I therefore propose that we should not see alienation as a negative state of separation, but as an opening for the fault lines and cracks that develop when trying (and failing) to be ethical in real life participant observation. Alienation, as both social condition and experience during fieldwork, can therefore indeed facilitate positive potentials.[3]

Correspondences, Attentionality, and Dark Ethnography

The suggestion to take "anthropology as a practice of education" is central to Ingold's proposal about the renewal of anthropology as a discipline. As previously mentioned, he urges anthropologists to construe participant observation as a practice of establishing correspondences, which he understands as a continuous coupling of movements between the anthropologist's perception and that of others. In his reflections on walking, Ingold employs a musical metaphor (referring to Alfred Schütz) for defining correspondence in more detailed ways. He proposes that the players in a string quartet and other musicians "are not exchanging musical ideas—they are not interacting in that sense—but are rather moving along together, listening as they play, and playing as they listen, at every moment sharing in each others 'vivid presence'" (Ingold 2013: 106). Participant observation is therefore not simply interaction, but an immersion and coupling of movements. Extending this coupling to an affective dimension, Ingold refers to the work of the architect and design theorist Lars Spuybroek, who urges us to analyze "what things feel when they shape each other" (Spuybroek 2011: 9). Ingold interprets this as "a form of feeling-knowing that operates in the interstices of things" (2013: 108).

Fieldwork for Ingold is about interventions, questions, and responses—about "living attentively with others" (2014: 389). He elaborates:

> Surely participant observation, if nothing else, is just such a practice. It is one that calls upon the novice anthropologist to *attend*: to attend to what others are doing or saying and to what is going on around and about; to follow along where others go and to do their bidding, whatever this might entail and wherever it might take you. This can be unnerving, and entail considerable existential risk. (Ingold 2014: 389)

Ingold's proposal is persuasive for some areas of anthropology that give space to aesthetics, or have poetic potentials such as anthropological–philosophical excursions on landscapes and craftsmanship. I am on the one hand deeply impressed by these empathetic and abstract reflections, but on the other hand I am also surprised that there is little place for dissonance and failure in his account. The last sentence of the quote above clearly acknowledges that Ingold also has a sense for more difficult fieldwork situations (see also Roy's contribution in this volume); but in my opinion, this can also signal the limits of correspondence-thinking and attentionality. When the unnerving experiences one can endure during fieldwork and the risks involved get too much, can it be better to be not in correspondence, and to alienate oneself and resort to objectification and nonempathetic ways of doing research?

I want to discuss these questions with some excursions into the realities of what Sherry Ortner has labeled dark anthropology. She defines this as an "anthropology that emphasizes the harsh and brutal dimensions of human experience, and the structural and historical conditions that produce them" (Ortner 2016: 49–50). According to Ortner, in the 1980s and 1990s, a Foucault-inspired theory apparatus was employed to analyze and critique the unfolding effects of global neoliberalism.[4] This focus on power and its effects provoked a "marked increase in anthropological work looking at experiences of violence and cruelty" (Kelly 2013: 213). In a similar vein, reflections on fieldwork carried out under extreme, or at least difficult, conditions have in recent years increasingly entered discussions on what can be expected of anthropologists in terms of fieldwork methods and ethical standards. Works now considered modern classics (Daniel 1996; Scheper-Hughes 1993; Das 1990)[5] showed that anthropologists can work under circumstances such as war, revolution, poverty, and actually reach out to a wider public by bringing these topics to the open. But what became equally obvious was that many of the methods and ethical standards developed in more classical and less conflictual fieldwork settings were rather inadequate for such works. Many fieldwork trainings still seem to take ideal field conditions as the norm.[6] Key terms such as "reciprocity," "collaboration," and "partnership"—or "correspondence" and "attentionality" to use Ingold's terms—that now describe anthropology's approach in the field are important, but are usually only used as positive and connecting features. To what extent do they have to be modified when shifting to dark ethnography? Or, are correspondence, attentionality, and nonobjectification useful here, and what do the limits of their applicability reveal about their theoretical grounding?

Crematoria and Death Pollution

The following ethnographic snippets draw on my work on Buddhist funerals and crematoria. In some sense, they can only in a restricted sense be described as dark anthropology as defined by Ortner, as the phenomena researched in this project were not necessarily linked to neoliberalism, which she outlines as a crucial element for the increase of such studies (Ortner 2016; but also see Laidlaw 2016). However, many perceptions of and ways of dealing with death might also be quite specific for modernity. The privatization and outsourcing of death that has been controversially discussed for decades by historians and anthropologists alike could be analyzed in such a framework.[7] However, one could also consider the anthropology of death as the universal and classic topic of dark anthropology beyond neoliberalism. Despite huge variations, death pollution is almost universal due to the corpse being considered an "object of horror and dread" (Hertz 1960: 12) in most societies. Its contaminating effects can also be traced to the violence of separation inherent in death. What Parry (1994: 216) postulates for Hinduism, where pollution is "also brought about by—one might say purposeful, even violent—the separation of bodies" might, therefore, have wider implications beyond India.

In the rural and, to a lesser extent, urban areas of my field sites in Laos and Thailand, funeral rites have remained a public affair. The wake for the deceased is still widely practiced, and corpses are regularly visible for children and adults alike in houses and on funeral pyres (Ladwig and Williams 2012). When taking up my first postdoc position in a project on Buddhist funeral cultures in 2008, I initially gave little thought to the dark aspects of the work ahead of me. Attending and filming many cremations, and interviewing family members, monks, and morticians on death matters, were on some level much easier than initially anticipated, as the families we visited and the morticians with whom we worked in crematoria openly welcomed us. They surely did not perceive me as a suffering and bereavement voyeur. However, the work I carried out in crematoria in northern Thailand at times proved to be difficult, as the effects I came to identify as pollution began only to gradually manifest themselves over time.[8] I got increasingly stressed out over the course of two months and felt unanticipated effects from my research.

Despite not being a Buddhist, and initially not sharing concepts of death pollution and impurity with the people in the field, I started to feel polluted after my working days in the crematorium. The feelings of bodily and mental uncleanliness and a sort of weariness became so strong that toward the end of the fieldwork, I was reluctant to continue my work. I concluded that I had received an overdose of death. Pollution, according to Mary Douglas (2002), is a result of the contact or presence of an anomaly, a break in the flow of things that resists classification and endangers the community. Pollution, as an "interplay between form and formlessness" (2002: 150), had affected not only me, but the morticians who were responsible for the cremations and the final handling of corpses also suffered under pollution. The morticians' jobs socially marginalized them—especially the older ones repeatedly mentioned that in the past, and to some extent still today, people avoided them. In their work and ritual practices, they clearly acknowledged the dangers of death pollution. They had to deal with several spirits that were located on the cremation ground; and in a complex series of offerings, they had to ask them for permission to perform their work, and thereby placate them (see Figure 4.1). The crematoria workers also employed preventive measures: they all had protective tattoos (*sak lay*, in the form of a Sanskrit *yantra*) and employed magical spells (*katha*) when opening coffins (see Figure 4.2).[9] The words in Thai and Lao to describe funerals and cremations also attest to this: *ngan amongkhun* describes all sequences of funeral rites and signifies "inauspicious event." I theoretically knew the cosmology of death pollution, but I wasn't prepared for sensing it. After working there for some weeks, what in Pali Buddhist texts is called *kilesa* (defilements) and *asubha* (ugly, loathsome, impure) started to make sense for me. The monks and morticians also offered me help and urged me to employ local ritual technologies. For example, I started to use the buckets prepared by Buddhist monks containing blessed water (*nam sompoi*). But trying to be in correspondence in that sense and following the practices of people I worked with did not really change my condition.

While in the first weeks I naively saw my fieldwork as equivalent to more neutral topics, I realized later that I could not simply pretend I was working on a "normal" topic. Due to time constraints in terms of fieldwork and assistance and the nature of collective project work, I could not simply take a break; I had to keep on going. But how? In some sort of intuitive manner, I started to ignore more and more things that affected me negatively. I voluntarily decreased my subjective and emotional investment, and partially closed myself off by avoiding certain sights (corpses), sounds, smells, interview topics (death and emotions), and people (close relatives and partners of the deceased). This was difficult because we were welcomed and hosted in such generous ways. I did not want to insult and dismiss the people

Figure 4.1. Worker of a local crematorium, presenting offerings to spirits, Thailand. © Patrice Ladwig.

with whom we worked, but I also needed to find a way to distance myself without actually leaving the field. In other words, I needed *less* correspondence and needed to alienate myself from the events and people surrounding me. I had to "make a thing belong to another," as one translation of the Latin word *alienare* suggests (see Jay 2018). In not being able to respond, I experienced what Melvin Seeman defines as one of the crucial forms of alienation, namely powerlessness in which "the expectancy or probability held by the individual that his own behavior cannot determine the occurrence of the outcomes, or reinforcements, he seeks" (Seeman 1959: 786). However, having been educated with a sense of fieldwork and participant observation that emphasized attention and immersion—here taken as variants of what Ingold describes as correspondence and attentionality—I felt a sense of defeat, and that I was betraying my interlocutors. Participant observation as an empathetic practice became a burden because things could not be handled anymore in the way I desired it. The ideal settings often taken for granted when speaking of connecting and corresponding or reciprocity and attentionality were clearly not there. How caring and attentive can one really be when doing such a fieldwork, I asked myself.

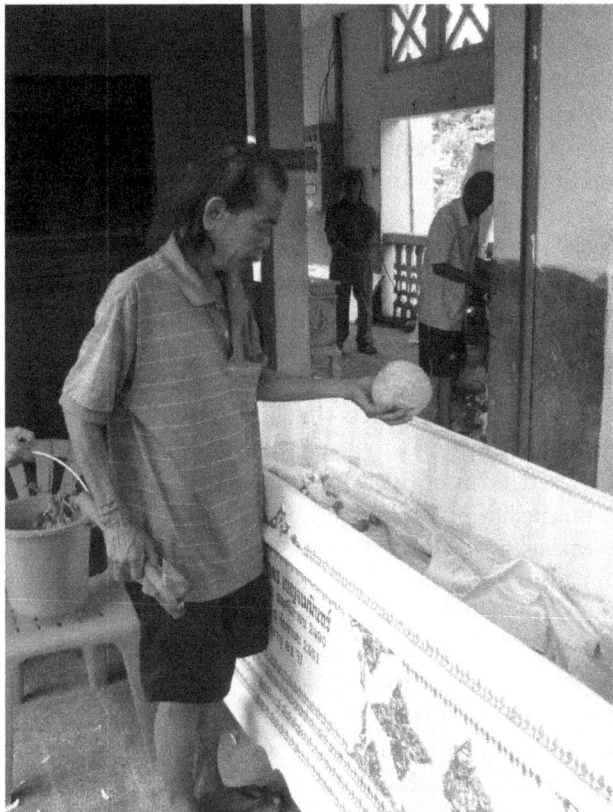

Figure 4.2. Mortician (*sappaloe*) in front of an open coffin, Thailand. Photo by the author. © Patrice Ladwig.

In order to link my pollution case with the holistic nature of Ingold's correspondence and attentionality thinking, some aspects deserve closer examination here. Acknowledging that "the notion of correspondence, admittedly, comes with a certain amount of theological baggage," he mentions the mystic Emmanuel Swedenborg, and his notions of harmony and mutuality (Ingold 2013: 107–8). He obviously does not simply take over these mystical teachings, but the central position of harmony and musical metaphors in Ingold's writings at least suggests a certain affinity to them. He adds more theological baggage to his conceptual apparatus when he states that "correspondence, whether with people or with other things, is a labor of love, of giving back what we owe to the human and non-human beings with which and with whom we share our world, for our own existence and formation" (Ingold 2018: 5). The links between humans, nonhumans, and their surroundings are outlined when Ingold discusses Lars Spuybroek's meditations on stones and plants that are arranged in certain patterns. He quotes Spuybroek's reflection on the spectator's position in relation to that pattern: "I am with the stones and plant immediately, fitting in with them" (Spuybroek 2011: 152).

Although the absence of (partially obsessive) discussions in anthropology on power from Ingold's work is also refreshing in my view, it is at the same time one of it greatest flaws. Participant observation for him seems to take place in a space devoid of cracks, differences, and interests of conflict. Or, as Patrick Eisenlor phrases it in his contribution in this volume, Ingold sidelines "the incommensurabilities, disjunctures, and even conflicts that are often necessary parts of field research in anthropology." Instead, we seem to move in Leibniz system of prestabilized harmony where monads can interact with each other, but only on the basis of an already given, godly plan for the best of all possible worlds (Leibniz 1720: §§80–87). Or, when putting it somewhat ironically, do we find ourselves in a poetic, power-free corner of Habermas's public sphere, where equality and love enable everyone to participate in communicative action (Habermas 1981)? Things just seem to fall into their place and answer to each other in correspondence. Like in the performance of a string quartet, participant observation as correspondence always seems to work out when things and people connect, fit to each other, and acknowledge each other's gratitude for existence. My point is not that Ingold's notions resemble naive idealism, as he certainly has a sense for the difficulties of certain types of fieldwork and topics (see Ingold 2014: 389). But what very much shines through here is an ideal vision of the field that mobilizes great and partially theologically infused terms that, however, on a practical level must remain vague. Andrew Shyrock has also recognized this. When, for example, Ingold is asked in an interview to comment on the potentially negative sides of fieldwork, he—very much like a theologian who has remained in the ivory tower and not worked in the slum of the liberation theologian—affirms abstract notions, and thereby evades the question.[10] I think that his evasion and the limits of his notions when applied in dark ethnographic cases derive from these theologically inspired and harmony oriented undercurrents of theorizing, which leave no space for ambivalence, partiality, and fragmentation. Given anthropology's shift to dark topics in recent decades (à la Sherry Ortner), Patrick Eisenlohr (this volume) congruently attests that "Ingold's vision of anthropological fieldwork is remarkably untimely."

So what happens when one enters a field where there is no prestabilized harmony, where the musicians of a string quartet play out of tune, where the fieldworker falls into a situation that is marked by dissonance and conflict, and where the labor of love is eclipsed by less favorable conditions? Many classical accounts of fieldwork represent the anthropologist as undergoing a rite of passage, and as someone who emerges triumphantly after periods of difficulty and hardship. Although this superhuman image has come under heavy critique, it has now been substituted (or at least supplemented) by a thorough ethicizing of fieldwork. The fieldworker is not so much anymore a survivor of hardship and difficulties who gains a sort of higher conscience through overcoming an existentialist shock,[11] but rather someone who behaves professionally and fulfills the ethical standards not only demanded by his interlocuters, but also by a variety of other institutions and clients.[12] Jeffrey Sluka states that fieldworkers "now seem to be confused about who our 'clients' are—those studied, ourselves, funders and sponsors, the public? And, if all four, do we have ethical obligations to them all?" (Sluka 2007: 272). The anthropologist is now supposed to become an ethical and professional superhuman who always responds to the needs of the people with whom she works, but at the same time—without contradictions—must be able to care for herself, satisfy funding bodies, and produce research that is based on a fieldwork experience marked by immersion and reciprocity. I do not want to suggest that Ingold demands any of this when he calls for correspondences and nonobjectification, but there are crucial parallels to be found, as both ethical codes and his correspondence thinking seem to rely on a rather idealized notion of the field.

Where is the place for cracks, contradiction, and dissonance beyond correspondence as ideal and research ethics as a new manifestation of an imagined ideal behavior? Philippe Bourgeois's critique of anthropological research ethics in my opinion offers a good counterpoint to the abstraction that codes of research ethics imply and to Ingold's seemingly conflict- and power-free notion of correspondence. Bourgeois (1995: 288) states that the ethics of anthropological research "are too complicated and important to be reduced to unambiguous absolutes." These complexities and complications often only become visible when entering field sites that deviate from the norm. Therefore, empirical research must take into account "internal inconsistencies and ultimate ethical poverty" (1995: 288) of certain situations and actors, including the sometimes clueless participant observer. Bourgeois himself has published an important piece on dark ethnography dealing with crack dealers and notions of respect in East Harlem (Bourgeois 1995). Getting the trust of and establishing long-term relations with the street-dealers and criminals with whom Bourgeois worked was by no means easy. It demanded a lot of improvisation, disguise, and enduring a certain level of humiliation and even violence (Bourgeois 1995: 19ff. and 30ff., for example). This kind of participatory research cannot be neatly subsumed under an ethical code, or under Ingold's correspondence thinking. Like in other cases of dark ethnography, the initial conditions can only be dealt with when one is willing to accept inconsistencies, improvisations, and by admitting a certain level of ethical poverty of the researcher's position in face of the complexity of the research situation. Or, when linked to alienation and estrangement, one probably has to accept that it is not possible to be in control and in correspondence all the time, and "that man does not experience himself as the acting agent in his grasp of the world," as Erich Fromm (1961: 44) put it in his interpretation of Marx's theory of alienation.

Improvisation and Objectification

Under "normal" conditions in the field, the ethics of reciprocity between fieldworker and the people with whom anthropologists work can be considered one of the main pillars of the anthropologist's work. What could Bourgeois's reference to "internal inconsistencies and ultimate ethical poverty" imply when we move away from these contexts? Codes of ethics for anthropologists have now become standard in the audit-world of academia. These codes of conduct are perhaps necessary and important. But they are also of rather limited use on a practical, everyday level. Like Kantian deontological ethics or the Christian command of love, these ethics are necessary foundations of the ideal that, however, are not designed for giving detailed, practical guidance in all situations. Kovats-Bernat (2002: 2—emphasis mine) observes:

> The problem with such an approach is that it assumes ideal field circumstances for interacting with informants (i.e., stability, trust, quietude, security, freedom from fear) and presupposes the ethnographer's position of control. But what one discovers when working in dangerous fields is that these conditions rarely exist, *forcing anthropologists to innovate new tactics and techniques for getting needed data* while at the same time minimizing attendant risks that are virtually unanticipated by most ethnographic methods.

What, then, can be done of if one gets overpowered by the negativity of dark ethnography? Or, transferred to my fieldwork situations in the death ritual project I described above, how could I continue doing fieldwork in a project that provided a rather strict timeframe, but which in some ways had become unbearable for me because I had received a polluting overdose of death? This is the moment, according to Kovats-Bernat, when one has to start to improvise and invent new tactics and rethink ways for getting data that might perhaps be less ethical or correspondence oriented than we might usually expect.

The most important strategies for me were to increase the grade of objectification in my work and to focus on the potential outputs of the project. I saw the work I was doing as documentary and as if I was already writing up at a desk. I remained a participant, but I marginalized this role in favor of observation as objectification. In other words, I shifted toward abstraction in the dialectics of involvement and detachment: "Detachment is necessary to construct the abstract reality: a network of social relations including the rules and how they function—not necessary real to the people studied" (Powdermaker 1966: 9; see also Robben and Sluka 2007). By focusing on the abstraction of death matters and data collection with a reduced emotional investment, I thereby tried to move away from the reality I encountered in the field. For Ingold, this strategy is what he describes as "'tangentialism,'" in which "our meeting is but a glance that shears away from the uncomfortable business of mixing our own endeavors too closely with the lives and times of those with whom our research has brought us into contact" (Ingold 2017b: 80). For him, "correspondence and tangentialism are precise opposites" (2017b: 80).

This stance, which Ingold also labels as the "cowardice of scholars" (Ingold 2017b: 80), is, in cases beyond my rather moderate pollution problem, actually an imperative that can secure the position of the researcher. In more tricky fieldwork situations, being in correspondence can actually become a real problem. Take Ton Robben's reflections on what he calls "ethnographic seduction" in the context of his work on the dirty war in 1970s Argentina: interviewing both victims and perpetrators, he recognized during his fieldwork that the good rhetoric of members of the military, and the testimonies of victims became means of seduction that disabled his ethnographic gaze (Robben 1995). Too much attention, care, and love can, therefore, become a trap. Robben's situation can also be linked to another, positive form of alienation that Georg Simmel (1950) alludes to in *The Stranger*. For Simmel, "objectivity may also be defined as freedom: the objective individual is bound by no commitments which could prejudice his perception, understanding, and evaluation of the given" (Simmel 1950: 405). The stranger, through his ambiguous position and detachment from local networks, can, according to Simmel, actually take on roles that demand objectivity and cannot be fulfilled by someone who is immersed into the locale.[13]

In Ingold's philosophy of correspondences, there is a firm rejection of the stance that participation and observation can be disconnected. Objectification is something natural scientists, not anthropologists, do. Recalling Michael Jackson's (1989) reflections on the topic, he affirms that observation cannot produce objective data: "Nothing could be further from the truth. For to observe is not to objectify; it is to attend to persons and things, to learn from them, and to follow in precept and practice" (Ingold 2014: 387). For me, Ingold's fervent rejection of objectification echoes some postmodern critiques of anthropology that postulated that objectification is a form of violence. But in difference to these approaches, for Ingold, objectification also destroys a certain form of holism, of oneness. He considers partiality and assemblage as detrimental to correspondence thinking. He is therefore "reluctant to refer to the gatherings of social life as assemblies, or as incidents of 'assemblage'" (Ingold 2016: 13). It therefore comes as no surprise that when Ingold (2000) discusses the role of objects such as baskets and so forth, he focuses on skill, immersion, and correspondence, but not on their features as a commodity *and* a cultural product with a certain biography, as Kopytoff (1986) does.

Not only with Ingold has objectification acquired mostly negative connotations in recent decades; it has also become associated with processes of dehumanization in contexts of slavery, the position of women in advertisement and the porn industry, and so forth. Although Marxist notions of objectification are undoubtedly complex, Marx takes it as one of the defining features of modernity. While previous historical epochs were imagined by Marx as being marked by the rule of persons over persons, capitalist society becomes one in which things come to rule over persons. As a fieldworker objectifies in the act of producing data, he becomes alienated from himself and from the people and things with which he works. The fieldworker—like the factory worker in Marx's account of alienation from the act of production—"does not feel content but unhappy, does not develop freely his physical and mental energy but mortifies his body and ruins his mind. The worker therefore only feels himself outside his work, and in his work feels outside himself" (Marx 1959: 274). When understood as a negative act, alienation turns observation into a "hostile act that reduces our subjects to mere 'objects' of our scientific gaze" (Robben and Sluka 2007: 18). But is this feeling of being outside one's work necessarily a negative phenomenon that is externally imposed on us and makes us unhappy, as Marx suggests? I think that in some cases, the fact that "labor is external to the worker" (Marx 1959: 74) can actually be a desired state of affairs.

Pierre Bourdieu, who has coined the phrase "participant objectivation" (Bourdieu 2002), also holds a positive stance toward objectification—what I here call alienation. He asserts that one does not have to choose between participant observation and the objectivism of the gaze from afar, and thereby rejects the postmodern navel gazing that has haunted anthropology since the *Writing Culture* turn (see also Aishima, this volume). In his thinking, knowledge is always embodied "in a practical mode" (Bourdieu 2002: 288) that is not necessarily apparent either to the anthropologists or to the persons and things under observation. Therefore, objectivation as a form of objectification can be said to always demand a certain distancing that I illustrate with the term "alienation."[14] In the situation in which I found myself in Thailand, alienation as objectification actually became a new tactic and a technique for gathering data under difficult conditions. In his reflections on the imperative to connect during fieldwork, Faubion (2009: 146) actually suggests that "a good dose of alienation from the ordinary course of social and cultural life is also useful" for dealing with the practicalities of fieldwork.

Conclusion

In Ingold's theorizing of correspondences, I overwhelmingly see string quartets that play harmonic music. However musician Frank Zappa once noted with reference to the creation and destruction of harmonies in the process of composing that "any composition (or improvisation) which remains consistent and 'regular' throughout is, for me, equivalent to watching a movie with only 'good guys' in it" (Zappa 1990: 289). As we all know, fieldwork in general, and especially those involving dark topics, very often feature bad guys and negative emotions. James Faubion's (2009: 146) pragmatic suggestion that "the fieldworker does well to have a considerable thickness of skin—if not an incapacity to recognize social disapproval, then at least a generous gift of indifference," might here be one among many answers.

However, one should not overlook how the holism of correspondence thinking, just like some aspects of ethical codes for research, puts a huge burden on the shoulders of fieldworkers. Although Ingold's ideas about correspondence and attentionality clearly stand in a humanistic tradition, their idealism and theologically infused grounding can actually have negative effects. To dramatize here a little bit by using Ingold's vocabulary, leaving correspondence and retreating into the cowardice of tangentialism is a betrayal of the labor of love and, therefore, one's interlocutors. Therefore, alienating oneself from the field can only produce feelings of deficiency and guilt. In the complex and ambivalent context of dark ethnography, this becomes a weight under which the participant observer *must* collapse. But the standards set by Ingold's correspondence thinking are even in normal ethnographic contexts not very suitable for preparing graduate students for fieldwork. Even outside of dark anthropology, the overwhelming majority of researchers in earlier stages of their career actually develop a deep sense of failure while doing fieldwork.[15] Immersion is often understood in a too totalizing way, and a bit of sociological distancing in the sense of Bourdieu (2002) would help to minimize these feelings of failure.

I do not want to suggest that we should completely turn away from striving for holism and correspondence or practicing fieldwork as an ethical enterprise. I merely want to point out that the holism of correspondence can also take on oppressive features when it reigns in all spheres. What I find interesting in contexts of dark anthropology beyond ideal circumstances are the cracks, fault lines, and folds that become part of the process of establishing correspondences. I therefore suggest that correspondence thinking must be transformed so that "internal inconsistencies and ultimate ethical poverty" (Bourgois 2007: 288) can become part of it without necessarily giving up its ideals. Similar to Christopher Kovats-Bernat (2002: 6), who sees "the reflexivity of contemporary ethnography as an honesty about the limitations of our vision," I propose that allowing for more improvisation and freedom of movement of the participant observer would already be a first step. To allow for temporary objectifying movements in and out of correspondence, a further theoretization of when and under which circumstances one can employ alienation and objectification as a strategy of fieldwork was presented as a possibility to keep on working in a polluted context of dark ethnography. In this sense, "objectivity is by no means non-participation . . . but a positive and specific kind of participation" (Simmel 1950: 404) that leaves room for roles that cannot be taken when being immersed or in correspondence. Alienation would here neither be a "painful obstacle to feeling whole or at one with the world" (Jay 2018) nor a failure to be in correspondence with a whole. Its overcoming would also not be an "achievement of self-transparency, authenticity, personal integrity and solidarity" (Jay 2018), as the anthropologist-as-hero model suggests. It would just be pragmatic, realistic strategy that recognizes that the work anthropologists do is always a necessarily flawed act of translation that is ridden with inconsistencies. Ethical standards for fieldwork are important for orientation, even when they are unattainable. But the gap that opens up between ideals and their unattainability should also be recognized as a space not only of failure, but also as one where the ethics of fieldwork and participant observation unfold.

Acknowledgments

Thanks to all project participants at the University of Bristol (especially Rita Langer) who shared the joys and dreads of Buddhist death with me in the course of the, at times, rather morbid research process. Our research in Chiang Mai was generously supported by Professor Apinya Fuengfusakul, Nawin Sopapum, and Suebsakun Kidnukorn. Thanks also to the staff working in the local crematoria of Chiang Mai who allowed me to gain an understanding of their peculiar, but at the same time quotidian, work and tasks there. Finally, thanks to Irfan Ahmad for his careful reading of my chapter and his inspiring comments.

Patrice Ladwig studied Social Anthropology and Sociology, and obtained his PhD from the University of Cambridge. His work focuses on the anthropology of Buddhism (Laos and Thailand), death and funeral cultures, colonialism, the link of religion to communist movements, and general social theory. He currently works at the Max Planck Institute for the Study of Religious and Ethnic Diversity, Göttingen, and carries out research on economic modernization, religion, and ethics in the context of the Max Planck Cambridge Centre for the Study of Ethics, Human Economy and Social Change. Among other numerous publications, he is the coeditor of *Buddhist Funeral Cultures of Southeast Asia and China* (Cambridge University Press, 2012) and *States of Imitation: Mimetic Governmentality and Colonial Rule* (Berghahn, 2020).

Notes

1. I return to aspects of and metaphors for correspondence and associated notions later.
2. When alienation "can be described as a form of separation—a separation that is considered undesirable from some point of view" (Geyer 2001: 388), this already hints to the negative history of the concept. Raymond Williams has explored similar shifts in the meaning of alienation and estrangement, which he links to Rousseau. In this version, "man estranged from his *original* (often historically primitive) nature and man estranged from his *essential* (inherent and permanent) nature" (Williams 1976: 34—emphasis in original).
3. Geyer attests that while alienation usually signifies an undesired separation, he notes that the "literature about the possible positive functions of alienation is very sparse indeed" (Geyer 2001: 388). Below, I explore these positive potentials with reference to some recent theories of alienation, but also with reference to Georg Simmel's (1950) account of the stranger.
4. For the pros and cons of this argumentation, see the special section of *HAU* (2016) devoted to this theme.
5. For an overview, see the excellent annotated bibliography *Conducting Field Research in Context of Violent Conflict*, by Nathalie Gasser (2006).
6. See Amy Pollard's (2009) survey "Field of Screams." To me, her findings suggest that in terms of training, methodology, and fieldwork ethics, the discipline still very much clings to rather idealistic notions of the field in which conflict, risk, and failure are merely side effects.
7. See, for example, Laqueur's (2015) critique of Philippe Ariès (1976), one of the strongest proponents of the death suppression thesis. Perhaps much of the darkness modern society associates with death is a product of a specific historical experience and development, which scholars like Philippe Ariès have described as a silencing and marginalization of death.
8. For more detailed ethnography and (Buddhist) concepts of pollution in Laos and Thailand and their links with Hindu ones, see Ladwig (2018).
9. All terms deriving from Lao or Thai are in italics and have no specific marker. Words from other non-European languages will be indicated.
10. Shyrock comments here on the interview conducted by MacDougall (2016). He states: "Whenever she invites him to comment on practicalities—how to prepare for fieldwork; how to avoid doing bad ethnography; how to deal with trauma—he heads to higher ground or he implies that anthropology is just like the rest of life, which it's clearly not" (Shyrock 2016).
11. The model of the anthropologist who is initiated in the field, and through the encounter with existential crisis and painful experiences grows and matures, is skillfully dismantled by Carolyn Nordstrom (1995: 149). She asserts that an understanding of crisis and dangers during fieldwork are

not lurking possibilities of existential enlightenment, "but brutally inescapable facts" one remembers and has to deal with.
12. Peter Pels (1999) already described this professionalization of anthropology through the implementation of new ethical codes. He argued that this professionalization also had to be understood as a form of corporatization that was supposed to provide technical and moral quality control like in any company.
13. Simmel (1950: 404), for example, refers to Italian cities, which "call their judges from the outside, because no native was free from entanglement in family and party interests."
14. Bourdieu does not employ alienation as a term, but invokes a kind of sociological distancing that has obviously less radical implications than my use of it. However, in my opinion, it can be considered a mild form of alienation. In Bourdieu's theory of practice, "participant objectivation undertakes to explore not the 'lived experience' of the knowing subject but the social conditions of possibility—and therefore the effects and limits—of that experience and, more precisely, of the act of objectivation itself" (Bourdieu 2002: 282).
15. The outcomes of the work with researchers who were interviewed by Pollard (2009) about emotions in the field and their experiences of failure and insufficiency also correspond to my own experience, and that of many graduate students and young postdocs to whom I talked: a majority felt that their first long-term fieldwork was marked by failure and insufficient immersion, burdening them with guilt.

References

Ariès, Philippe. 1976. *Western Attitudes Toward Death*. London: Marion Boyers.
Asad, Talal. 1973. *Anthropology and the Colonial Encounter*. Ithaca: Cornell University Press.
Bourdieu, Pierre. 2002. "Participant Objectivation." *Journal of the Royal Anthropological Institute* 9, no. 2: 281–94.
Bourgeois, Philippe. 1995. *In Search of Respect: Selling Crack in El Barrio*. Cambridge, UK: Cambridge University Press.
Bourgois, Philippe. 2007. "Confronting the Ethics of Ethnography: Lessons from Fieldwork in Central America." In *Ethnographic Fieldwork: An Anthropological Reader*, edited by Antonius Robben and Jeffrey Sluka, 288–97. Malden: Wiley-Blackwell.
Daniel, Valentine E. 1996. *Charred Lullabies: Chapters in an Anthropography of Violence*. Princeton: Princeton University Press.
Das, Veena. 1990. "Introduction: Communities, Riots, Survivors—The South Asian Experience." In *Mirrors of Violence: Communities, Riots and Survivors in South Asia*, edited by Veena Das, 1–36. Delhi: Oxford University Press.

Douglas, Mary. 2002. *Purity and Danger: An Analysis of the Concepts of Pollution and Taboo*. London: Routledge.
Faubion, James. 2009. "The Ethics of Fieldwork as an Ethics of Connectivity, or The Good Anthropologist (Isn't What She Used to Be)." In *Fieldwork Is Not What It Used to Be: Learning Anthropology's Method in a Time of Transition*, edited by James D. Faubion and George E. Marcus, 145–66. Ithaca: Cornell University Press.
Fromm, Erich. 1961. *Marx's Concept of Man*. New York: F. Ungar Publishing.
Gasser, Nathalie. 2006. *Conducting Field Research in Context of Violent Conflict: An Annotated Bibliography*. Bern: Swiss Peace.
Geyer, Felix. 2001. "Alienation, Sociology of." In *International Encyclopedia of the Social and Behavioral Sciences*, edited by Neil Smelser and Paul Baltes, 388–92. Oxford: Elsevier.
Habermas, Jürgen. 1981. *Theorie des kommunikativen Handelns. Bd. 1: Handlungsrationalität und gesellschaftliche Rationalisierung* [Theory of Communicative Action. Vol. 1: Reason and the Rationalization of Society]. Frankfurt am Main: Suhrkamp.
Hertz, Robert. 1960. "A Contribution to the Study of the Collective Representation of Death." In *Death and the Right Hand*, edited by Rodney Needham and Claudia Needham, 27–86. New York: Free Press.
Ingold, Tim. 2000. "On Weaving a Basket." In *The Perception of the Environment: Essays on Livelihood, Dwelling and Skill*, edited by Tim Ingold, 339–48. London: Routledge.
———. 2008. "Anthropology Is Not Ethnography." *Proceedings of the British Academy* 154: 69–92.
———. 2013. *Making: Anthropology, Archaeology, Art and Architecture*. New York: Routledge.
———. 2014. "That's Enough about Ethnography!" *HAU: Journal of Ethnographic Theory* 4, no. 1: 383–95.
———. 2016. "On Human Correspondence." *Journal of the Royal Anthropological Institute* 23, no. 1: 9–27.
———. 2017a. "Anthropology contra Ethnography." *HAU: Journal of Ethnographic Theory* 7, no. 1: 21–26.
———. 2017b. *Correspondences. Knowing from the Inside*. University of Aberdeen. https://knowingfromtheinside.org/files/correspondences.pdf.
———. 2018. "Art and Anthropology for a Living World." Paper presented at École des Arts, Paris, May 2018. http://chaire-arts-sciences.org/wp-content/uploads/2018/05/Art-and-Anthropology-for-a-Living-World-DEF.pdf.
Jackson, Michael. 1989. *Paths Toward a Clearing: Radical Empiricism and Ethnographic Inquiry*. Bloomington: Indiana University Press.
Jay, Martin. 2018. "A History of Alienation." *Aeon*. 14 March 2018. https://aeon.co/essays/inthe-1950s-everybody-cool-was-a-little-alienated-what-changed.
Jenkins, Timothy. 1994. "Fieldwork and the Perception of Everyday Life." *Man* 29, no. 2: 433–55.

Kelly, Tobias. 2013. "A Life Less Miserable?" *HAU: Journal of Ethnographic Theory* 3, no. 1: 213–16.
Knodt, Reinhard. 2017. *Der Atemkreis der Dinge—Einübung in die Philosophie der Korrespondenz* [The Breathing Circle of Things—Introduction to a Philosophy of Correpondences]. Frankfurt: Herder.
Kopytoff, Igor. 1986. "The Cultural Biography of Things: Commoditization as Process." In *The Social Life of Things: Commodities in Cultural Perspective*, edited by Arjun Appadurai, 65–91. Cambridge, UK: Cambridge University Press.
Kovats-Bernat, Christopher. 2002. "Negotiating Dangerous Fields: Pragmatic Strategies for Fieldwork amid Violence and Terror." *American Anthropologist* 104, no. 2: 208–22.
Ladwig, Patrice. 2018. *Between Death Pollution and Modern Biopolitics: Crematoria, Morticians and Buddhist Ritual in Chiang Mai, northern Thailand* (unpublished conference paper). The Sociopolitical Life of Death, University of Nijmegen, 1 November 2018.
Ladwig, Patrice, and Paul Williams. 2012. "Introduction." In *Buddhist Funeral Cultures of Southeast Asia and China*, edited by Paul Williams and Patrice Ladwig, 1–21. Cambridge, UK: Cambridge University Press.
Laidlaw, James. 2016. "Through a Glass, Darkly." *HAU: Journal of Ethnographic Theory* 6, no. 1: 47–73.
Laqueur, Thomas. 2015. *The Work of the Dead: A Cultural History of Mortal Remains*. Princeton: Princeton University Press.
Leibniz, Gottfried Wilhelm. 1720 [1714]. *Lehr-Sätze über die Monadologie* [Theorems on Monadology]. Frankfurt.
Leopold, David. 2007. *The Young Karl Marx: German Philosophy, Modern Politics, and Human Flourishing*. Cambridge, UK: Cambridge University Press
MacDougall, Susan. 2016. "Enough about Ethnography: An Interview with Tim Ingold." *Dialogues. Cultural Anthropology Website*. 5 April 2016. https://culanth.org/fieldsights/841-enough-about-ethnography-an-interview-with-tim-ingold.
Macho, Thomas. 2017. *Rezension zu: Der Atemkreis der Dinge—Einübung in die Philosophie der Korrespondenz* [Review of the Breathing Cirlcle of Things—Introduction to a Philosophy of Correpondences]. http://www.reinhard-knodt.de/?page_id=6.
Marx, Karl. 1959. "Estranged Labor." In *Economic and Philosophical Manuscripts of 1844*. Translated by Martin Mulligan. Moscow: Progress Publishers. https://www.marxists.org/archive/marx/works/1844/manuscripts/labour.htm.
Nordstrom, Carolyn. 1995. "War on the Front Lines." In *Fieldwork under Fire: Contemporary Studies of Violence and Survival*, edited by Carolyn Nordstrom and Antonius Robben, 129–52. Berkeley: University of California Press.
Nordstrom, Carolyn, and Antonius Robben. 1995. "Introduction: The Anthropology of Violence and Ethnography of Violence and Sociopolitical Conflict." In *Fieldwork under Fire: Contemporary Studies of Violence and*

Survival, edited by Carolyn Nordstrom and Antonius Robben, 1–23. Berkeley: University of California Press.

Ortner, Sherry. 2016. "*Dark Anthropology* and Its Others: Theory Since the Eighties" *HAU: Journal of Ethnographic Theory* 6, no, 1: 47–73.

Parry, Jonathan. 1994. *Death in Benares*. Cambridge, UK: Cambridge University Press.

Pels, Peter. 1999. "Professions of Duplexity: A Prehistory of Ethical Codes in Anthropology." *Current Anthropology* 40, no. 2: 101–14.

Pollard, Amy. 2009. "*Field of Screams:* Difficulty and Ethnographic Fieldwork." *Anthropology Matters* 11, no. 2: 1–24.

Powdermaker, Hortense. 1966. *Stranger and Friend: The Way of an Anthropologist*. London: Seeker and Warburg.

Robben, Antonius. 1995. "The Politics of Truth and Emotion among Victims and Perpetrators of Violence." In *Fieldwork under Fire: Contemporary Studies of Violence and Survival*, edited by Carolyn Nordstrom and Antonius Robben, 81–203. Berkeley: University of California Press.

Robben, Antonius, and Jeffrey Sluka. 2007. "Fieldwork in Cultural Anthropology." In *Ethnographic Fieldwork: An Anthropological Reader*, edited by Antonius Robben and Jeffrey Sluka, 1–28. Malden: Wiley-Blackwell.

Scheper-Hughes, Nancy. 1993 [1989]. *Death without Weeping: The Violence of Everyday Life in Brazil*. Berkeley: University of California Press.

Seeman, Melvin. 1959. "On the Meaning of Alienation." *American Sociological Review* 24, no. 6: 783–91.

Shryock, Andrew. 2016. "Ethnography: Provocation. Correspondences." *Cultural Anthropology*. 3 May 2016. https://culanth.org/fieldsights/871-ethnography-provocation.

Simmel, Georg. 1950. "The Stranger." In *The Sociology of Georg Simmel*, edited by Kurt Wolff, 402–8. New York: Free Press.

Sluka, Jeffrey. 2007. "Fieldwork Ethics." In *Ethnographic Fieldwork: An Anthropological Reader*, edited by Antonius Robben and Jeffrey Sluka, 271–75. Malden: Wiley-Blackwell.

Spuybroek, Lars. 2011. *The Sympathy of Things: Ruskin and the Ecology of Design*. Rotterdam: Nai Publishers.

Williams, Raymond. 1976. *Keywords: A Vocabulary of Culture and Society*. New York: Oxford University Press.

Zappa, Frank, with Peter Occhiogrosso. 1990. *The Real Frank Zappa Book*. New York: Simon and Schuster.

Chapter 5

COMMITMENT, CORRESPONDENCE, AND FIELDWORK AS NONVOLITIONAL DWELLING

A WEBERIAN CRITIQUE

Patrick Eisenlohr

In a series of recent interventions, Tim Ingold (2008; 2011: 229–43; 2014; 2017a) argues against using the term "ethnographic" for our encounters with people and for the fieldwork in which these encounters take place. To him, such encounters are not intrinsically ethnographic; rather, he holds that this is

> a judgment that is cast upon them through retrospective conversion of the learning, remembering and note-taking which they call forth into pretexts for something else altogether. This ulterior purpose, concealed from the people whom you covertly register as informants, is documentary. It is this that turns your experience, your memory and your notes into material— sometimes spun quasi-scientifically as "data"—upon which you subsequently hope to draw in the project of offering an account. (Ingold 2014: 386)

Nevertheless, I think it is necessary to understand our encounters with people in the field as ethnographic, because they are of a special kind. To give a preliminary answer to Ingold's question about what could possibly distinguish an encounter that is ethnographic from one that is not (Ingold 2014: 386), it is my contention that our knowledge interests and institutional, ethical, and professional commitments as anthropologists structure encounters with our interlocutors not only during fieldwork, but also do so even beforehand. It makes a big difference whether somebody engages in participant observation in order to do anthropology (engaging in ethnographic fieldwork) or whether one does participant observation as an activist, or even as a guerilla who seeks to "learn from the people" from a Maoist perspective (Shah 2017), as an advertiser seeking access to markets, as a spy, a missionary, a writer or long-term tourist, or a journalist. This distinction is the major difference between ethnographic fieldwork and participant observation that serves other ends. For all its sophistication, Ingold's intervention does not allow for this crucial and necessary differentiation. An ethnographic encounter is a particular "frame" in a Batesonian and Goffmanian sense (Bateson 1972; Goffman 1974), a certain definition of what kind of situation and action this is supposed to be.

For this reason, as anthropologists conducting fieldwork, our practical goals are also bound to be different from the practical goals many of our respondents pursue as we encounter them—and the same also often applies to our ideological commitments and those that inform the actions of our respondents. Ingold suggests that it is common for anthropologists to conceal such interests and commitments and to pursue the actual purposes of our research covertly (Ingold 2014: 386). He draws an image of ethnographic fieldwork as the mere recording and description of single cases that are then fed into a posterior comparative endeavor called anthropology. This to me seems a distortion of what anthropologists do. It is against the ethical standards of anthropology to engage in undercover and undeclared research, concealing from one's interlocutors that the anthropologist will work what she learns in her encounters with interlocutors into written scholarly texts, within ethical limits. Some anthropologists have indeed violated these standards by secretly conducting intelligence work alongside their ethnographic pursuits, using the latter as a cover for the former (Price 2016). It has, however been much less common for anthropologists to conceal their roles as ethnographers and to make their interlocutors believe that they are actually long-term tourists, activists, marketing researchers, fiction writers, or guerillas, or are there in some other role, disavowing their profession as ethnographers with academic knowledge interests. Those anthropologists who have violated the ethical standards of the discipline have rarely kept secret their roles as ethnographers, but remained silent about their other problematic, nonethnographic pursuits, instead of the other way around. As an anthropologist, my understanding of properly conducted fieldwork is that it involves being clear and open about one's academic knowledge interests as they can easily go into different directions from those concerns and commitments that inform our respondents' actions in our encounters with them. Such academic knowledge interests are of course also very different from our own concerns and everyday commitments as anthropologists when we are not engaged in ethnographic research.

Even though the relationships between anthropologists and their interlocutors that emerge from such divergences of interests and commitments are often highly complex, Ingold argues that we need to strive for a kind of processual nonseparation from our respondents and their activities. This is what he points to when he stresses the necessity of an "ontological commitment" (Ingold 2014: 387) and the quasi-musical "correspondence" between the participant observer and the people with whom she works.

> Launched in the current of real time, participant observation couples the forward movement of one's own perception and action with the movements of others, much as melodic lines are coupled in musical counterpoint. For this coupling of movements that, as they proceed, continually answer to one another, I have adopted the term *correspondence* (Ingold 2013: 105–8). By this I do not mean the endeavor to come up with some exact match or simulacrum for what we find in the happenings going on around us. It has nothing to do with representation or description. It is rather about answering to these happenings with interventions, questions and responses of our own—or in other words, about living *attentionally* with others. Participant observation is a practice of correspondence in this sense. (Ingold 2014: 389—emphasis in original)

For Ingold, anthropologists and their interlocutors are also part of the same "meshwork":

> Like the voices of choral music, whose harmony lies in their alternating tension and resolution, the entwined lines of the meshwork join with one another, and in so doing, possess an inner feel for each other and are not simply linked by external contiguity. I shall adopt the term sympathy to refer to this feel. As the design theorist Lars Spuybroek explains, sympathy is a "living with" rather than a "looking at," a form of feeling-knowing that operates in the interstices of things. It is, Spuybroek writes, "what things feel when they shape each other" (Spuybroek 2016: xvii). (Ingold 2017b: 12)

As the cited passages indicate, Ingold suggests that achieving such correspondence and searching for the kind of holistic truth anthropology strives for are closely connected. This, to me, seems problematic for two reasons. First, Ingoldian correspondence and ontological commitment do not sufficiently distinguish between ethnographic fieldwork in the tradition of anthropology and the multiple other kinds of participant observation oriented to different, even opposed, ends, thereby glossing over their decisive differences. Second, it downplays the potential and even sometimes necessary differences in interests and goals between ethnographers and their respondents. Describing field research, as Ingold does, as a quasi-musical coupling of movements that continually answer to each other runs the danger of sidelining the incommensurabilities, disjunctures, and even conflicts that are often necessary parts of field research in anthropology.[1] These also include power differentials between respondents and ethnographers that in the formative days of anthropology typically favored the anthropologist but nowadays can turn out either way. To deny the influence of a prior intellectual and professional commitment on one's partaking in the "currents of everyday life" (Ingold 2014: 386) not only raises the risk of dangerous romanticism, but above all means deluding oneself.

Time and Attention

What Ingold denounces as an "ulterior purpose" (2014: 386), which is only applied to the encounters with people after they have unfolded—meaning our specific intellectual and institutional interests are often not fully shared by our respondents—does in fact profoundly structure our encounters with people, not only ex post facto. Our purposes affect our anthropological endeavors from the very outset, even before such encounters begin. This has little to do with a "temporal distortion" or "schizochronia," alluding to an imaginary organic temporal oneness as a tacit standard (see also Jeremy Walton's related critique in this volume). It is, unlike Ingold (2014: 386) suggests, also unrelated to Fabian's (1983) allochrony (the denial of temporal coevalness to the people anthropologists write about). If we follow Ingold's call to engage in correspondence "launched in the current of real time" (Ingold 2014: 389)—and his view that to practice anthropology is to "restore the world to presence, to attend and respond. It is to move forward in real time, not to stop the clock in order to look back" (Ingold 2017b: 24)—we must also be involved in what I call the prospective shaping of ethnography. Phenomenology has taught us that a shared "now" of presence in the current of "real time" is never simply given but is instead the product of constantly intersecting retentions and protentions, and can never be separated from them. In anthropological fieldwork, our professional goals and commitments are a nonnegligible part of the anticipations and memories that are involved in the very production of presence and the now of "real time" in the encounters we are experiencing.[2]

We ethnographers are certainly often "caught up in the currents of everyday life" (Ingold 2014: 386), but never quite in the same way, because these currents are not what brought the ethnographer to the field. Anthropologists in their role as ethnographers seek encounters with people in the field because of academic knowledge interests, a rather rarified multigenerational pursuit tied to particular fundamental questions about the nature of social life and its institutional frames. I do not want to suggest that anthropologists cannot through their field experience also pursue other projects alongside the goals of their profession. Also, in the course of time, anthropologists may and often do develop personal friendships with their interlocutors, establishing human bonds that transcend the entire research enterprise. Anthropology, however, is a devotion to a particular intellectual tradition. Its analytical goals are frequently different from our own and our respondent's other everyday goals and projects. They also result in prospective shaping of our encounters, instead of a "retrospective conversion of our learning" (Ingold 2014: 386), because they inform and color our encounters in the field beforehand and as they unfold. They are the main reason for us to be there and to encounter people in the field.

Certainly, anthropology has certain inbuilt, foundational, and necessary values, without which the pursuit of anthropology would not make sense. These are the notions that every way of life has, in principle, an intrinsic value, and that no way of life, broadly understood, is a priori superior to others.[3] Therefore, anthropology needs to strive to make the world more accepting of diversity, and there are situations, such as coming face-to-face with genocide and ethnic cleansing, where the foundational values of anthropology and activism completely overlap. However, most situations anthropologists encounter in fieldwork are far more complex and ambiguous; and in such situations, there will always be a gap between the partisanship of activism and the search for holistic truth.

To me, Ingold's argument for living with others "attentionally" as opposed to living with others intentionally (Ingold 2014: 389; 2017b: 18–19) also raises questions. By the latter, he means what anthropologists do when they partake in the currents of everyday life with other people, but then use that participation for an ulterior purpose, namely ethnography. In order for this distinction to work, Ingold needs to clearly separate intentions in the sense of a questionable orientation to ulterior goals beyond the act of attending to someone from the more pervasive intentionality of the fieldworker. From a phenomenological perspective, intentionality, which vastly exceeds conscious acts of volition that are just one among several of its manifestations, is involved in any sort of act or relating-to, including cognitions. This also includes acts of attention—or for that matter, a processual understanding of human action as "becomings" engaged in "humaning" (Ingold 2014: 389). I welcome Ingold's shift toward forms of attention that do not emerge from conscious volition or are not otherwise consciously directed by a subject. "The key quality that makes a movement attentional lies in its resonance with the movements of the things to which it attends—in its going along with them" (Ingold 2017b: 19). Such nonsubjective movements and forms of attention belong to the most consequential dimensions of social life, and any rich fieldwork experience is full of them. I myself have found the neo-phenomenological analytic of atmospheres (Böhme 1995; Schmitz 2014) useful to think about these forms of attention (Eisenlohr 2018). It is probably no coincidence that Ingold and others resort to the sonic metaphor of resonance in their description, as such forms of attention often involve bodily felt suggestions of movement that do not emerge from subjective volition. But however powerful and central such suprasubjective forms of attention are for social life, including participant observation, they do not make the commitments that distinguish ethnographic research from other kinds of fieldwork less significant. Commitment, a rather conscious act of volition, is indeed the key term here. The intellectual, ethical, and institutional commitments that shape ethnographic fieldwork before it has even begun are much more the substance of a Weberian vocation rather than resembling becomings—Deleuzian or otherwise. Therefore, it is in my view impossible to excise the clearly volitional dimensions that separate ethnographic fieldwork from the multiple other kinds of participant observation directed to rather different goals. Anthropology stands and falls with such commitments, because doing anthropology is a calling.

The Problem of Doing Research with People Who Pursue Projects You Reject

As an admittedly old-fashioned example for the kind of traditional, intellectual, and institutional commitments that may structure our interactions as anthropologists in the field before they even begin, consider this "emeritus rant of the day," a Facebook post by Marshall Sahlins of 31 August 2017:

> What happened to Anthropology as the encompassing human science, the comparative study of the human condition? Why is a century of the first hand ethnography of cultural diversity now ignored in the training and work of anthropologists? Why are graduate students in the discipline ignorant of African segmentary lineages, New Guinea Highlands pig feasts, Naga head-hunting, the kula trade, matrilateral cross cousin marriage, Southeast Asian galactic polities, Fijian cannibalism, Plains Indian warfare, Amazonian animism, Inuit kinship relations, Polynesian mana, Ndembu social dramas, the installation of Shilluk kings or Swazi kings, Azande witchcraft, Kwakiutl potlatches, Australian Aboriginal section systems, Aztec human sacrifice, Siberian shamanism, Ojibwa ontology, the League of the Iroquois, the caste system of India, Inner Asian nomadism, the hau of the Maori gift, the religion of the Ifugao, etc. etc. *We are the custodians of this knowledge*, and we are content to let it be forgotten. Where else in the university are these things to be taught, or is it that they are not worthy of scholarly contemplation, and should just be confined to the dustbin of intellectual history?
>
> Maybe in a few hundred years, if the human species survives the dark ages of planetary degradation, there will be a cultural renaissance driven by the discovery of some buried or flooded libraries filled with astonishing memoirs of human achievement. (Sahlins, 31 August 2017, quoted in da Col 2017: ii–iii—emphasis mine)

I do not necessarily subscribe to all of this as the core mission for us as anthropologists. But here is the point: the pursuit of such intellectual commitments, whether those listed by Sahlins or a slightly different set, may bring us in Ingoldian correspondence with many of our interlocutors, but not necessarily all of them. Especially interlocutors with activist commitments may sometimes pursue rather different goals than the intellectual commitments that are the reason for anthropology to exist. In discussing correspondence, Ingold makes clear that he does not intend the term to mean sameness and that its mutual responding leaves room for disagreement between the anthropologist and her interlocutors. But in the practice of anthropological fieldwork, there are many examples of tensions, disagreements, and even the breakdown of relationships between anthropologists and informants. Even allowing for differences and disagreements, describing all these in terms of the resonances of Ingoldian correspondence and meshworks would be a stretch, an overestimating of commensurabilities (see also Ladwig's critique in this volume), as well as a sidelining of impersonal logical relations of rupture, contradiction, and separation in fieldwork that can be central to understanding other worlds, as argued by Arpita Roy, this volume. At the very least, these ideas of what participant observation in anthropology is or should be downplay the divergences and disjunctures between anthropologists and their interlocutors that arise as a result to their commitment to different projects. In his explication of "agencing" as one of the key dimensions of correspondence, Ingold writes, "[I]n the correspondence of agencing, then, there are no volitional subjects, no 'I's or 'you's to place before any action" (Ingold 2017b: 17). If fieldwork is, as Ingold writes, a practice of correspondence, then fieldwork can be, to take one of Ingold's examples, like a walk, when you are not the intentional subject doing the walking but when the walking walks you, as a "dwelling in habit" (Ingold 2017b: 16). But is it justified to take such modes of nonvolitional agencing as the condition of participant observation, indeed social life per se, and declare volitional subjectivity an illusion, as Ingold appears to do when he describes participant observation as a practice of correspondence? For many, such experiences of being walked by the walk in resonance with others are moments of a special kind and cannot serve as a general description of what participant observation is or should be. Ethnographers and their interlocutors cannot constantly be joined in dwelling together, responding to each other, as Ingold argues, out of habit and care in non-volitional terms (Ingold 2017b: 10–11, 20–21). Because they may be committed to different projects, they are sooner or later likely to exit out of Ingoldian correspondence, facing each other as subjects whose volitions are at odds with each other. Fieldwork as a nonvolitional flow in dwelling with others can never be an exhaustive description of participant observation. While such correspondence is desirable in many ways, can yield unique insights, and may recur in fieldwork, it does not come to terms with power, conflict, and incommensurable commitments between volitional actors. As a general vision of participant observation, it is therefore out of this world, a world where actors also manipulate and overpower others, treating them as means to other ends.

While disjunctures between the anthropologist's projects and values and those of people she encounters in the field may imperil correspondence, relationships of correspondence may in turn also emerge in contexts unrelated to anthropology as a project. Following Ingold, it is entirely possible not just to imagine anthropologists, but also others who engage in participant observation, such as missionaries, activists, spies, or guerrillas, to enter into meshwork and practices of correspondence with people in the field, which again raises the question of the fundamentally different projects and values to which these types of fieldworkers are committed. It appears that there is no necessary relationship between fieldwork as correspondence in Tim Ingold's terms and the values and knowledge interests that are fundamental to anthropology, not just as a discipline but also as a calling.

Let us return to Sahlins's self-described "rant" quoted above and take an example from it that I was confronted with in my fieldwork in Mauritius concerning caste. This issue necessarily led to a divergence between my academic commitments and the commitments of several of my Mauritian interlocutors. Caste is not supposed to exist in Mauritius, and if its existence is grudgingly acknowledged, there is a local near-consensus that caste in Mauritius has no legitimacy any more. Nevertheless it is undeniable that caste continues to structure entire areas of social life, and not only among Mauritian Hindus; it also has, via Hindu political dominance, a considerable influence on the political system of the entire country (see also Claveyrolas 2017: 159–86). Researchers who directly address the issue of caste in Mauritius are likely to incur the ire of politically well-connected Hindu activists who want to discourage discussion of a subject that, as they see it, fosters division in a "Hindu community" and challenges its boundaries. In contrast, such activists regard unifying such a community and the defense of its boundaries as among their most urgent goals. In that respect, having among other subjects also discussed caste among Hindu Mauritians (Eisenlohr 2006: 66–110, 222, 278, 292–93), I have been much luckier than other ethnographers of Mauritius engaging with the subject. These include Burton Benedict, whose ethnography on Indo-Mauritians—the first anthropological monograph on Mauritius based on field research in the late 1950s in which he documented nonvegetarian, low-caste rituals (Benedict 1961)—was banned in Mauritius. More recently, Suzanne Chazan-Gillig and Pavitranand Ramhota's ethnography on Mauritian Hinduism (Chazan-Gillig and Ramhota 2009) became subject to a factual embargo in Mauritius, because following activist pressure, the Mauritian academic institution that copublished the work refused to distribute it in Mauritius, keeping the two hundred copies sent from France and destined to be sold in Mauritius under lock.[4]

Every society has a *Lebenslüge*, a life-structuring lie, or several of them: issues that have a constitutive importance for society but are often denied in "real life." It hardly needs to be mentioned that this insight has been behind the birth of modern social science, which since its beginnings has been devoted to the analysis of latent but highly consequential social processes and mechanisms that largely unfold outside the awareness and volition of individual human actors, whether from Durkheimian, Marxist, or Weberian perspectives. The anthropological search for a holistic truth also needs to uncover such latent issues or processes, even if that results in a divergence from the wishes and aspirations of some of our interlocutors in the field and imperils our resonant correspondence with them. Especially during the first half year of my dissertation fieldwork in Mauritius in 1997–98, I encountered a number of Hindutva activists in Mauritius who wrongly assumed that my research on what in Mauritius are officially but misleadingly labeled the "ancestral cultures" and "ancestral languages" of Hindu Mauritians and my knowledge of Hindi implied support for their Hindu nationalist worldview. A few of them tried to instrumentalize me as a foreign academic in order to lend legitimacy to their cause. One was a politically very well-connected public figure who had to be handled with great care. Not only were my own politics at odds with this particular powerful interlocutor, having others perceive me as aligned with her projects and politics would also have been detrimental to the research I wanted to do, as it would likely have antagonized other interlocutors with whom I was eager to engage. I felt I had no choice but to completely withdraw from this unwanted embrace.

That is to say, our projects as anthropologists can be compatible with those of others, but also sometimes not. As much as I was devoted to understanding Hindutva activists on their own terms as far as possible, the Ingoldian call for correspondence and ontological commitment as a way to engage with them would not have seemed plausible to me. Instead, my experience with Hindutva activists in Mauritius raised the themes of noncorrespondence, uncertainty, and the unraveling of relationships in social life, often because actors sought to overpower others. These fundamentals of sociality can also strike in interactions with interlocutors in the field, wherever located. And my encounter with Mauritian Hindu nationalist activists was not yet really of the kind of ethnography Sindre Bangstad has called "doing research on people we don't (necessarily) like" (Bangstad 2017), here referring not only to the ethnography of right-wing populism, but also to encounters with informants one truly resents. As much as I rejected their politics, and their attempts to instrumentalize my research for their cause, these particular Mauritian Hindu nationalists were all pleasant and generous interlocutors and even gracious hosts in my encounters with them, an experience that can be disturbing in a different way. These were most charming and helpful people who had never been personally implicated in any acts of violence but nevertheless said things that made me cringe and who were connected to networks of unsavory people in India. If it was implausible for me to live my interactions with these Mauritian Hindu nationalist activists according to Ingold's call for correspondence and ontological commitment, it would be entirely impossible, if not absurd, in the face of truly malevolent informants who actively pursue dangerous and reprehensible projects. I would, for example, not be able to inhabit an ontological commitment or live in resonant correspondence while doing research on, say, neo-Nazis in my own German society. Such interlocutors also often have distinct ideas about the people with whom one should study and learn from that are incompatible with any anthropological perspective, a point related to Irfan Ahmad's critique in this volume. While this might be an extreme example, it is certain that anthropological field research on right-wing populist and ethno-nationalist movements worldwide involves similar challenges, and that Ingoldian correspondence and ontological commitment would be rather unhelpful categories to describe many of the relationships between anthropologists and their informants in such movements. In such settings, it is easily imaginable that, for example, activists of a certain persuasion would be in relationships of correspondence and ontological commitment with the people they work with in the field in ways that would be difficult for an anthropologist.

Resonance and Its Disavowal

There is another widespread condition that anthropologists face in the contemporary world that, in my view, make it very difficult, if not impossible, to stick to the notions of anthropological fieldwork that Ingold advocates. Ingold's vision of anthropological fieldwork is remarkably untimely. It is more evocative of Heidegger's doubtlessly idealized Black Forest craftspeople and farmers almost a century ago than contemporary settings in a globalized world where we all partake in public spheres with long-distance ramifications to a much greater extent and where we are, therefore, inevitably confronted with the themes of sociability among strangers and impersonal forms of address. We conduct fieldwork in settings that are also thoroughly mediated by discourse, images, sounds, and ideologies that do not emerge from these settings or their flows of everyday life and are furthermore relatively independent from the local contexts in which they are taken up. Such settings are thus difficult to imagine, mainly in terms of a "meshwork" of entanglements between the anthropologists and her interlocutors that, expanding on Ingold's use of the sonic metaphor of resonance (Ingold 2017b: 19; see also Ingold 2011: 178), would yield a kind of correspondence that resembles what William Mazzarella has called mimetic resonance. Mazzarella identifies the term with Peter Sloterdijk's sonic metaphor of constitutive resonance (Sloterdijk 2011): "Constitutive resonance suggests a relation of mutual becoming rather than causal determination" (Mazzarella 2017: 5). Ingold insists that meshworks have loose ends and can be potentially spun further indefinitely. But here, the question of scale comes in, putting in question the usefulness of the meshwork metaphor. I think it is safe to assume that the great majority of anthropologists who conduct fieldwork today do so in settings that partake in different scales of circulation, up to the global, and are rather removed from the more pastoral settings of resonant correspondence with one's interlocutors. But this particular condition of most field sites today taken aside, that they are part of public spheres and shot through with its attendant media practices with global ramifications, ethnographic fieldwork can as a matter of principle never only be about the kind of ontological commitment and correspondence that deserves to be called mimetic or constitutive resonance. As Mazzarella has put it, "One of the most remarkable things about the anthropological approach—participant observation—is the way it turns constitutive encounter into method, ambivalently both affirming and disavowing mimetic resonance" (Mazzarella 2017: 21). Tim Ingold's rejection of the term "ethnographic" is motivated by the affirmation of such resonance, while overlooking the need for its simultaneous disavowal. Even if such resonance is not sameness, it aims for a kind of nonseparation between an anthropologist and her interlocutors that recalls somatic attunement. However, anthropology is also about confronting the field with categories such as comparative concepts and languages that do not emerge from it. An exclusive stress on correspondence, ontological commitment, and constitutive resonance in field research would evacuate the need for anthropology; there would just be an organic wholeness.

Comparison

Tim Ingold's suggestion that anthropologists are still committed to an understanding of comparison as the search for nomothetic universals paints an inaccurate picture of anthropologists' actual engagements with comparison and universals. Ingold agrees that anthropology is fundamentally comparative, "because for any path life might take, it could have taken other paths" (Ingold 2017a: 22). In a similar vein, he has made a case for anthropology as comparative in the following terms: "The endeavour [anthropology] is essentially comparative, but what it compares are not bounded objects or entities but ways of being. It is the constant awareness of alternative ways of being, and of the ever-present possibility of 'flipping' from one to another, that defines the anthropological attitude. It lies in what I would call the 'sideways glance'" (Ingold 2008: 84). Tim Ingold, therefore, does not reject comparison as such but thinks that such comparison should not involve the relating of our encounters in the field to broader comparative categories and themes. Ingold furthermore claims that anthropologists who consider their empirical method to be ethnography unwittingly commit to a logic of merely collecting empirical data for subsequent theoretical generalizations (Ingold 2014: 390–91). I think this is a misrepresentation of what most anthropologists do, and not just because theorizing shapes ethnographic fieldwork long before it begins. It is also questionable to assume, like Ingold does, that when anthropologists take their interactions in the field to be ethnography they become engaged in a search for generalizations as objective laws or structures of the sort that structural functionalists such as Radcliffe-Brown were after. The distinction, going back to Max Weber, between universals as ideal types versus real types is crucial here (Weber 1949: 90).[5] As I see it, addressing the broader questions to which anthropology attends is impossible without more general comparative categories and notions understood as hypothetical ideal types, not objective universals, and to abandon them would amount to giving up the discipline as a whole. Identifying comparison on the basis of ethnography with positivist data-collecting and the subsequent building of real type generalizations on their basis is a caricature of comparativist scholarship that has little to do with the sophisticated and self-reflexive forms of comparison anthropologists have engaged in.

In his latest intervention in the debate on ethnography, Ingold writes that ethnography is logically dependent on the distinction between idiographic and nomothetic sciences (Windelband 1980), and that understanding participant observation as ethnography commits one to this distinction (Ingold 2017a: 22; see also Ingold 2008). Because it has been shown long ago that this distinction is impossible to uphold, I find implausible Ingold's suggestion that in calling what they do ethnography many anthropologists have been oblivious of the untenability of the idiographic–nomothetic distinction. Against those that take ethnography to be mainly idiographic, anthropologists have long known that there is no such thing as a pure, singular description free from more general assumptions and theories. This is not just because anthropologists produce their accounts in a narrow range of languages, English being by far the most powerful among them, and their categories, thereby depending on the semiotic types built into them. Max Weber taught us more than a century ago that value judgments are responsible for the selection of a particular scholarly issue, and that such judgments do not just emerge from the social processes we study, but also result from prior theories, knowledge interests, and other broader assumptions that are themselves historical (Weber 1949). Such value judgments are also responsible for the more generalized ideal types we inevitably draw on in our descriptions. The latter are also the result of our knowledge interests—that is, value judgments of what anthropologists find significant and relevant in the infinite flux of life (unlike Marxists and structural-functionalists, who believe in real types). It is important to note that a processual ontology like the one Ingold favors in his anthropological writings is not incompatible with ideal types as tentative universals, only with the Marxist and structural-functionalist assumption of universals as real types, arrived at through nomothetic sifting through units of "data" or "case studies." Ingold denounces the search for universals through comparison, because "any such universals, however, are abstractions of our own, and as Whitehead was the first to point out, it is a fallacy to imagine that they are concretely instantiated in the world as a substrate for human variation" (Ingold 2008: 90). However, only the assumption of real types, not of ideal types, is subject to what Ingold, following Whitehead, has denounced as the "fallacy of misplaced concreteness" (Whitehead 1938: 66, cited in Ingold 2008: 90). Also, through hermeneutic theory, we have long known that any interpretative act draws on prior judgments, assumptions, generalizations, and theories of what we are confronted with, and that these are a necessary precondition for any interpretative rapprochement, let alone a fusion of horizons (Gadamer 1975). I welcome Ingold's call to overcome the idiographic-nomothetic distinction, but there are not many anthropologists who would conceive their work along such lines today, nor does calling what they do ethnography commit anthropologists to this distinction in any way.

If there is one thing that would rob anthropology of relevance and a public voice it would be the dismissal of broader comparative themes central to an understanding of the contemporary world, such as nationalism, religion, extreme forms of social inequality, "populism," changes in media-driven public spheres, sustainability, and so on. The challenge for anthropology is not to get rid of these ideal-typical categories, but to retheorize them in a way that goes beyond the European origins of several of these terms. Anthropologists necessarily and unavoidably bring these broader themes and the knowledge interests tied to them to the ethnographic encounter. Having become global categories through the colonial encounter, themes such as the nation, religion, ethnolinguistic identity, and the public sphere have in any case long become part of the lifeworlds of our interlocutors, wherever they may be. Indeed, the activists among them often engage in nationalization and religionization in ways that make the gaps between their and anthropologists' commitments glaringly apparent. Turning away from such ideal types and comparative themes and denouncing them as alienating universals in the name of a resonant oneness with one's respondents in the field and the flows of everyday life in which we encounter them is not just abandoning ethnography but anthropology itself.

Conclusion

In this chapter, I have made a case for distinguishing between participant observation as an ethnographic encounter and participant observation geared toward multiple different, nonanthropological ends. I have argued that anthropology is a calling that requires volitional commitment to particular values and knowledge interests that shape fieldwork long before it begins and give it its ethnographic character. The commitments and interests tied to anthropological fieldwork often sharply diverge from the commitments and interests that drive the participant observation of the activist, the guerilla, the spy, the market researcher, or the long-term tourist. Maintaining this distinction is crucial, and using the term "ethnographic" to point to the specificity of anthropological fieldwork is important. The professional commitments of anthropologists often provide a fruitful basis for working together with interlocutors in the field. They also sometimes bring us into conflict with the goals and commitments of some of our interlocutors who may for example pursue activist projects that the anthropologist is bound to reject. Understanding fieldwork as quasi-musical correspondence and nonvolitional dwelling with others as Tim Ingold does is unhelpful for coming to terms with such conflicts of interests and commitments in the field. Not just anthropologists, but also missionaries, spies, activists, journalists, and guerrillas can enter into Ingoldian meshwork and correspondence with people while doing fieldwork. However, this cutting of correspondence across professional roles does not make the divergence in values and knowledge interests that separate the anthropologist's work from those of others less relevant. If anything, it makes such differences more salient and important. Ingold's understanding of participant observation as meshwork and dwelling in correspondence is also remote from the realities and scales of field sites in the contemporary world where the anthropologists and her interlocutors very often partake in public spheres with their anonymous form of address and global circulation of images and discourse. Finally, I have argued that unlike Ingold suggests, understanding fieldwork as ethnographic does in no way commit anthropologists to the reduction of fieldwork encounters to "data" to be fed into the nomothetic search for universals. As a comparative discipline, anthropology necessarily involves drawing on concepts and categories with universal pretensions. Rather than searching for nomothetic real types such as universal laws and structures as structural-functionalists and Marxists used to do, many anthropologists' theorizing cannot be captured with the ideographic–nomothetic opposition. Instead, it seems that nowadays many anthropologists follow a Weberian understanding of social science. Having abandoned the search for timeless and holistic explanatory models, they approach the comparative concepts that their discipline necessarily depends upon with hermeneutic sensibilities, treating them as provisional, ideal-typical universals that are themselves historical.

Acknowledgments

I thank Irfan Ahmad for organizing the discussion from which this chapter emerged and for his helpful critical comments on my contribution. I also benefited from Birgit Abels's close readings of the chapter. Further, I am also indebted to all my other participants in the discussion, in particular Patrice Ladwig, Nathaniel Roberts, Arpita Roy, Peter van der Veer, and Jeremy Walton, for their astute observations and feedback.

Patrick Eisenlohr is professor of Anthropology and chair of Society and Culture in Modern India at the University of Göttingen. He obtained a PhD from the University of Chicago and previously held positions at Utrecht University, Washington University in St. Louis, and New York University. He is the author of *Little India: Diaspora, Time and Ethnolinguistic Belonging in Hindu Mauritius* (University of California Press, 2006) and *Sounding Islam: Voice, Media, and Sonic Atmospheres in an Indian Ocean World* (University of California Press, 2018). He has worked on a range of issues in the anthropology of media, linguistic anthropology, and sound studies, especially on the sonic dimensions of religion, media and religion, language, and citizenship.

Notes

1. In a related vein, in this volume Hatsuki Aishima addresses similar disjunctures and divergences while teaching anthropology to members of communities with whom anthropologists study.
2. Ingold actually argues along related lines in his reflections on longing as a key dimension of correspondence. According to him, longing "brings together the activities of remembering and imagining. Both are ways of presencing: remembering presences the past; imagining presences the future" (Ingold 2017b: 21). But in participant observation understood as Ingoldian correspondence, why should this presencing as remembering and imagining exclude the anthropologist's professional formation and commitments?
3. At this point, there is an overlap between the intellectual commitments of anthropology and its responsibilities in the world. In a recent exchange about Ingold's provocations on ethnography, Daniel Miller wrote that "anthropology has greater responsibilities to the world that just its own intellectual conceit" (Miller 2017: 30). However, at the core, the foundational values of anthropology, its intellectual commitments, and its responsibility in the world are one and the same.
4. "Dr Suzanne Chazan-Gillig, anthropologue: A Maurice, les castes sont toujours un sujet tabou," *Week-End*, 16 July 2017. No explanation was given by the Mahatma Gandhi Institute for the nondistribution of the book in Mauritius, and it is difficult to ascertain what the actual reasons for the factual embargo were. Given that the book went into the details of the highly sensitive issue of the nexus of caste, ritual, and politics in Mauritius, it seems rather likely that the book's treatment of this subject motivated its factual nonrelease by the copublishing Mauritian institute. The book's release in France was unimpeded. In the meantime, the book's factual embargo appears to have ended and it has begun to circulate in Mauritius as well.
5. "An ideal type is formed by the one-sided accentuation of one or more points of view and by the synthesis of a great many diffuse, discrete, more or less present and occasionally absent concrete individual phenomena, which are arranged according to those one-sidedly emphasized viewpoints into a unified analytical construct (*Gedankenbild*). In its conceptual purity, this mental construct (*Gedankenbild*) cannot be found empirically anywhere in reality. It is a utopia" (Weber 1949: 90).

References

Bangstad, Sindre. 2017. "Doing Fieldwork among People We Don't (Necessarily) Like." *Anthropology News* 58, no. 4: e238–43.

Bateson, Gregory. 1972. *Steps to an Ecology of Mind*. Chicago: University of Chicago Press.

Benedict, Burton. 1961. *Indians in a Plural Society: A Report on Mauritius*. London: Her Majesty's Stationary Office.
Böhme, Gernot. 1995. *Atmosphäre: Essays zur neuen Ästhetik*. Frankfurt: Suhrkamp.
Chazan-Gillig, Suzanne, and Pavitranand Ramhota. 2009. *L'hindouisme mauricien dans la mondialisation: Cultes populaires et religion savante*. Marseille: IRD.
Claveyrolas, Mathieu. 2017. *Quand l'hindouisme est créole: Plantation et indianité à l'île Maurice*. Paris: Éditions de l'École des hautes études en sciences sociales.
da Col, Giovanni. 2017. "Of rants, shortcuts, and revolutions." *Hau: Journal of Ethnographic Theory* 7, no. 2: i–viii.
Eisenlohr, Patrick. 2006. *Little India: Diaspora, Time and Ethnolinguistic Belonging in Hindu Mauritius*. Berkeley: University of California Press.
———. 2018. *Sounding Islam: Voice, Media, and Sonic Atmospheres in an Indian Ocean World*. Oakland: University of California Press.
Fabian, Johannes. 1983. *Time and the Other: How Anthropology Makes Its Object*. New York: Columbia University Press.
Gadamer, Hans-Georg. 1975 [1960]. *Truth and Method*. New York: Seabury Press.
Goffman, Erving. 1974. *Frame Analysis: An Essay in the Organization of Experience*. New York: Harper & Row.
Ingold, Tim. 2008. "Anthropology Is *Not* Ethnography." *Proceedings of the British Academy* 154: 64–92.
———. 2011. *Being Alive: Essays on Movement, Knowledge and Description*. London: Routledge.
———. 2014. "That's Enough about Ethnography!" *Hau: Journal of Ethnographic Theory* 4, no. 1: 383–95.
———. 2017a. "Anthropology contra Ethnography." *Hau: Journal of Ethnographic Theory* 7, no. 1: 21–26.
———. 2017b. "On Human Correspondence." *Journal of the Royal Anthropological Institute* 23: 9–27.
Mazzarella, William. 2017. *The Mana of Mass Society*. Chicago: University of Chicago Press.
Miller, Daniel. 2017. "Anthropology Is the Discipline but the Goal Is Ethnography." *Hau: Journal of Ethnographic Theory* 7, no. 1: 27–31.
Price, David. 2016. *Cold War Anthropology: The CIA, the Pentagon, and the Growth of Dual-Use Anthropology*. Durham: Duke University Press.
Schmitz, Hermann. 2014. *Atmosphären*. Freiburg: Alber.
Shah, Alpa. 2017. "Ethnography? Participant Observation, a Potentially Revolutionary Praxis." *Hau: Journal of Ethnographic Theory* 7, no. 1: 27–31.
Sloterdijk, Peter. 2011 [1998]. *Spheres*. Vol. 1: *Bubbles-Microspherology*. Minneapolis: University of Minnesota Press.
Weber, Max. 1949 [1904–17]. *The Methodology of the Social Sciences*. Translated and edited by Edward A. Shils and Henry A. Finch. Glencoe, IL: Free Press.

Whitehead, Alfred North. 1938 [1926]. *Science and the Modern World*. Harmondsworth: Penguin.
Windelband, Wilhelm. 1980 [1894]. "Rectorial Address, Strasbourg, 1894." *History and Theory* 19, no. 2: 169–85. (English translation of Wilhelm Windelband, *Geschichte und Naturwissenschaft*, Rede zum Antritt des Rektorats der Kaiser-Wilhelms-Universität Straßburg, gehalten am 1. Mai 1894. https://edoc.hu-berlin.de/handle/18452/1097.)

Chapter 6

A NEW HOLISTIC ANTHROPOLOGY WITH POLITICS IN

Irfan Ahmad

I welcome Ingold's (2014) intervention "That Is Enough about Ethnography," which is connected to his two earlier publications (2008a, 2008b) as well as a sequel that appeared in 2017. Together, these writings enable us to examine some of the well-established assumptions anthropologists hold about their discipline. My engagement with Ingold amounts to neither a full-scale embrace nor a dismissal of his thought-provoking position. Drawing on my fieldwork on the interface amongst terrorism, media, political theory, and international relations (IR), I offer an immanent critique emerging from my on-going project (see note 14) to develop an anthropology of terrorism. Despite the momentous worldwide impact of the "global war on terror" on human and ecological lives and the choice to define "terrorism"[1] as prime enemy of the New World Order (NWO), an anthropology of terrorism, proper to itself, is yet to arrive (see below).

The Argument

Refreshing as I find Ingold's position enunciated in his many writings (2008a; 2008b; 2014; 2017), I critique them for effacing politics and IR. Integral to this effacement is the term "the people," which he uses without accounting for its theoretical baggage and wider implications. Tracing the trajectory of anthropology's subject matter from "the primitive," "race," "tribe," "the native," "culture," and so on to "the people," I ask how replacing earlier terms with "people" is useful.

The category of "the people," let me stress, is central to Ingold's writings noted above, as it is to his very definition of anthropology as "philosophy with the people in" (1994: xvii).[2] Bringing the political and IR in also entails a reformulated holism, which has historically been central to anthropology. I propose a new notion of holism at the confluence of politics, IR, and other fields. Both these issues are linked to the conceptualization of anthropology concerned not so much with what Ingold calls "the real" but, as I suggest, with "the true." My critique in the pages ahead, I hope, sharpens the debate on the role and salience of anthropology in the past as well as in the future, an objective that crucially informs Ingold's intervention.

Ingold's aim is to secure "the kind of impact in the world" anthropology "deserves" and "the world so desperately needs" (2014: 383–84). This will remain unmet, he observes, as long as a conflation persists between anthropology and ethnography, on one hand, and ethnography/fieldwork and participant observation (PO), on the other. His article diagnoses this double conflation, also upheld by practitioners of other disciplines, to rescue anthropology "under threats."[3] He undoes the conflation by suggesting that "the ethnographer writes up; the anthropologist—a correspondent observer at large—does his or her thinking in the world" (2014: 391). As stated in the Introduction to this volume, in questioning this conflation, Ingold offers a much-needed corrective and reminder. My focus here is on other aspects of his writings.

My first contention is that anthropology cannot continue to remain obsessed with "others" as it did with nonelites (Nader 1974; Gusterson 1997). "The objective of ethnography," writes Ingold (2008b: 69; 2014: 386), is "to describe the lives of people other than ourselves." Not only should we study "ourselves," but we must also ask how a population becomes "other" in relation to "us." Ingold takes the term "people" as given, eliding thereby the vital question of who constitute the people and if there is a people in the first place. Questions such as these are, however, essential to political theory and IR. In describing PO as attending "to what others are doing or saying and to what is going on around or about," he assumes others are nonelites and accessible. But what if anthropologists study terrorists (state and nonstate), counterterrorists, or intelligence operatives who work secretly (e.g., see Masco 2014)? How about the military and business elites, factories that produce weapons and their scientists, or executive barons of gigantic corporations, the income of whom may exceed the income of many poor countries combined (Allen 2004: 1)? What about those conditions when even "veranda anthropology" is impossible?

Malinowski's (1948: 122–23) much-cited admonition of observation from the "veranda of the missionary compound, Government station, or planter's bungalow" and his call to "go out into the villages, and see the natives at work" is taken as illustrative of model fieldworks. The premise that anthropology studies nonelites remains unexamined. To go past Malinowski, what about fieldwork with military elites, counterterrorists, and intelligence officials when an ordinary anthropologist cannot even get to the barbed iron gates, let alone veranda, of the hyper-guarded compounds where power elites work or reside? That is, can there be anthropology of a phenomenon where there is no, what Hortense Powdermaker (1966: 285, 287)—an American student of Malinowski—termed, "small community" and "physical proximity" as precondition for and constitutive of anthropology and its participant observation?

My second argument is that for anthropology to be a telling voice beyond its departmental silo, it must begin to practice a new holism—not the kind of yore and nearly hushed by Ingold, but a reformulated one that disavows spatial immediacy as much as disciplinary parochialism. If the goal is to understand the world, not just humans, the parameters of that world are not limited by the territorial space of community and society (or their local subunits), both of which stand synonymous with nation–states (Bauman 1973; Giddens 1990). Nor are they exhausted by anthropology's endeavors to the exclusion of other disciplines. Holism, I propose, is translocal—what Comaroff and Comaroff (2003) christen as on "an awkward scale." It is equally multidisciplinary—or indisciplinary, if you will. The inquiry emanating from the reformulated holism undertakes studies "not within a village or a nation-state but within the globe [i.e., interstate and international system]" (Burawoy 2000: 29). It assigns priority, not primacy, to the political. Neither holism—Ingold (2008b: 81) uses it only once in its orthodox sense—nor politics with IR at its fulcrum, however, figure in Ingold's text.

It follows that the suggested holism cannot be disciplinary: sociological imagination (Mills 1959) or anthropological imagination (Dimen-Schein 1977). Lest anthropology resign itself to oblivion, it has to harness a public imagination aimed not only to illuminate what Ingold calls "real life" but instead to arrive at "the true." And this is my third argument. Drawing on Fassin (2014), I suggest that the real ought to be differentiated from the true. The point clearly is not to dislodge the real from the true but to view them in a dialectical interrelationship.

This chapter is divided into four sections. Discussing their neglect, it underlines how politics and IR are important to any anthropological inquiry. From there, it proceeds to show how "the people" as a term is highly contested. The first two sections make this argument. The second argument in the third section demonstrates the need for a reformulated holism with politics, IR, and multidisciplinarity as its lynchpins. Without this notion of holism, so goes the contention, there cannot be a robust anthropology of terrorism or of "Islamic terrorism." The final section dwells on the third argument about the dialectical interrelationship between the real and the true. I conclude with a summary of the chapter to reinforce its key contentions.

Anthropology, Politics, IR

To overcome the conundrum anthropology faces, it is to Radcliffe-Brown that Ingold (re)turns, and whom Ingold appears to equate with a hero in his prose (2008b: 70–79, 90). A section of his article is titled "In Defence of Radcliffe-Brown," who saw ethnography and anthropology as radically distinct.[4] Ethnography describes the particular, whereas anthropology pursues generalizations. For Radcliffe-Brown, anthropology was a nomothetic and theoretical discipline, as opposed to an ideographic one (e.g., history). To regain anthropology's voice, Ingold maintains, is to restore its nomothetic goal. Politics and the state, however, are absent from Ingold's texts. This absence is due probably to two factors. First, from its inception, the discipline has been largely indifferent to politics, which is evident, inter alia, in the division of anthropology into four fields—physical/biological, archaeological, linguistic, and sociocultural—where the political is starkly absent (see Figure 6.1; for more on this, see Ahmad 2018). Second, it seems to be the legacy of Radcliffe-Brown, who laid "the foundations of . . . social anthropology" and whom Ingold defends. Disinterested in, if not hostile to, the state in the 1940s, when political anthropology began in Africa under British imperialism, it spoke of politics, not the state. Indeed, Radcliffe-Brown (1940: xxiii) dismissed the state as a "fiction of the philosophers."[5] Though as a subdiscipline, political anthropology gave attention to politics and the government and also studied, as Fuller and Harriss (2001) note, princely polities (e.g., Geertz 1980)—until recently it remained uninterested in the modern state (Ahmad 2009a; Gledhill 2000; Kurtz 2001; Spencer 2001). Though Evans-Pritchard and Geertz shared a vision of anthropology

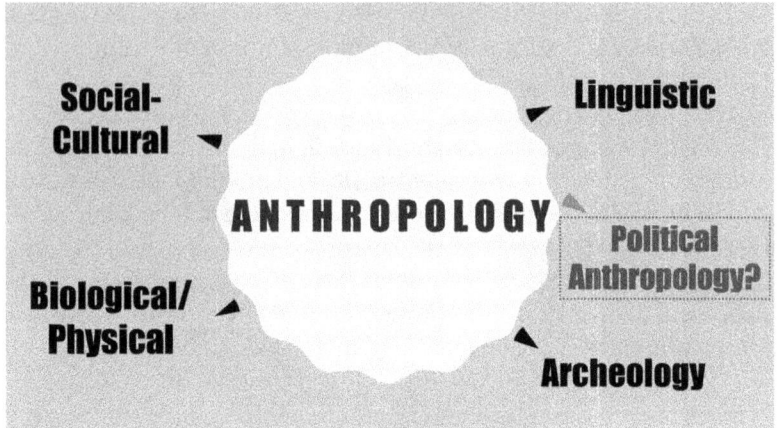

Figure 6.1. Absent political anthropology in four-field anthropology. © Irfan Ahmad.

as a humanistic discipline (against Radcliffe-Brown's as a science), both effaced politics. Evans-Pritchard did not record the terror bombings the British undertook in Sudan to subdue the Nuer (Mukherjee 2009: 26). Geertz placed the 1966 massacre of half a million Indonesians by the state in a mere footnote (Nader 2011: 213).

A key factor behind the absence of the state in anthropology was its focus on stateless societies like the Nuer, which Evans-Pritchard theorized as acephalous (Lewellen 2003: 30).[6] It follows that anthropology's concern was the non-West—variously called primitive, savage, simple societies, and so on.[7] The most common phrase was perhaps "other cultures"; Beattie (1964) titled his textbook *Other Cultures*. For my purpose, what is significant is the tacit supposition about the boundedness of "other cultures" and the scale on which they were methodologically mapped. A cultural exploration presupposed a territory. I suggest that the conjunction of the conceptual and the territorial was central to holism, a disciplinary distinction anthropology was then proud of, spanning the theoretical rivalry among functionalism, structural functionalism, and the interpretative turn (Parkin 2007). Though noting that no community is isolated and its relations spread the world over, Radcliffe-Brown demarcated the spatiality of social structure—"unit entities," he called them. By taking "any convenient locality of a suitable size, we can study the structural system as it appears," and we can "observe, describe, and compare the systems of social structure of as many localities as we wish" (1952: 193). Malinowski expressed the conjunction of locality with holism as follows:

the whole area of tribal culture in all its aspects has to be gone over in research. The consistency, the law and order which obtain within each aspect make also for joining them into *one coherent whole*....

An Ethnographer who sets out to study only religion, or only technology, or only social organization cuts out an artificial field for inquiry, and he will be seriously handicapped in his work. (Malinowski 1922: 11—emphasis added)

The famous *Notes and Queries in Anthropology* likewise stressed investigating connections "with the social structure, the economic system, religion, language, and technology" (CRAI: 1954: 38). Notice that in this holism or "methodological collectivism" (Vincent 1990: 57), neither Malinowski nor *Notes and Queries* mentioned politics, let alone IR. What I want to argue is that anthropology's holism was territorial as much as disciplinary—territorial in terms of any convenient locality of a suitable size and disciplinary in that there was hardly a need for political scientists (or scholars of politics as the discipline is named so by some practitioners and departments), geographers, economists, or others. In Malinowski's quote above, the whole area of tribal culture substitutes as a whole. They were seen as the same, it seemed.

We are face-to-face with a puzzle. Precisely at a moment when the world and its international relations were being organized as a system of nation–states, which became the master unit of everything, including social structure and culture, not only did anthropology keep IR[8] and politics out of its ambit, its scale of investigation was also hugely skewed. Even when culture qua culture—local, ethnic, regional, or otherwise—mattered only vis-à-vis "national culture," anthropology kept IR and nationalism at bay. Social structure was likewise construed within nation–states, even though both social structure and culture were fundamental to IR, especially in its "area studies," where many anthropologists worked (Weber 2010: 11; Dirks 2015). Anthropologists—from Kluckhohn (Almond 1950: 277) and Margaret Mead (Mukherjee 2009: 27) to Montgomery McFate, a key architect of "human terrain systems" linked to global war on terror (Gonzalez 2007; Kelly, Jauregui, Mitchell, and Walton 2010; Price 2011)—also worked for the state, in times of warfare too. In 1953, Mead and Rhoda Métraux produced a manual titled *The Study of Culture at a Distance*. In it, Mead made no secret of the "political applications" of anthropological knowledge:

The approach described in this Manual has been used for a variety of political purposes: to implement particular governmental programs within a country, to facilitate relationships with allies, to guide relationships with partisan groups in countries under enemy control, to

> assists in estimating enemy strengths and weaknesses, and to provide a rationale for the preparation of documents at the international level. All these uses involve diagnosing the cultural regularities in the behavior of a particular group or groups of people that are relevant to the proposed action—whether this be the dissemination of propaganda statement, issuing an order against fraternization, a threat of a certain type of reprisal, an introduction of new international regulation, or a like matter. (Mead 2000: 441)

What Mead showed was the taken-for-granted premise of the international order, for which anthropologists worked, but a robust analysis of that order remained outside of anthropology's horizon. Such is the international context to account for works anthropology undertook to produce "national character," "national personalities," and "national identities" (Fabian 1983: 46–52; Silverman 2005: 295–96), and, to cite van der Veer (2016: 31, 159n20), even "the macro sociological form of ethnic profiling." Borneman (1998: 29) thus describes American anthropology as "foreign policy"—a premise echoed by political scientist Gabriel Almond (1950: 277), who stressed anthropology's utility for international politics.

The affinity between anthropology and IR is manifest in a confluence between the "national interest" of the state and studies of "national culture" by anthropologists. The anthropological search for "national character" and "national personalities" echoes national interest. Geertz's *Islam Observed* is no exception. He argued that though Indonesia and Morocco were both Muslim, they had contrasting "historical personages" and "national archetype[s]," marked respectively by syncretism, quietism, inwardness, patience, poise, and aestheticism on one hand, and puritanism, zeal, fervor, impetuosity, toughness, moralism, populism, and obsessive self-assertion on the other (1968: 54). Hans Morgenthau, a German American and the founder of post-World War II realist theory in IR (Kaufman 2006: 24), mostly remains foreign to anthropological texts. It was he who, during the early years of the Cold War, formulated the idea of "national interest," later to become the universal tenet of international politics.[9] Connected to the German notion of *Lebensinteressen* (life interests), the term underwent many incarnations between 1948 and 1954, when it was purged of any morality to become a principle of "political realism." By then a *Wirklicheitswissenchaftler*, a "scholar of reality" (Frei 2016: 45, 40), Morgenthau redefined national interest simply as power and foreign policy as "the precondition for national greatness and survival" (Navari 2016: 53, 49). Nation, culture, and state fused into a single entity to become national interest, the furtherance of which got hooked to the glory of state power.

Does "the People" Exist?

Given the centrality of modern states and politics in shaping and determining human lives, as the preceding discussion demonstrates, Ingold's definition of ethnography as description of "the lives of people" or "encounter(s) with people" needs to be examined. Until 1950 or so, anthropologists did not use the category or term "people." Marcel Mauss (2009: 11, 13, 7, 112—emphasis added) described ethnography as "the detailed observation of a tribe." Ethnography's equation with tribes or "the natives" was so unquestionable that in the *Manual of Ethnography*, whose scope was "limited to societies inhabiting the French colonies and to societies of the same level," Mauss urged ethnographers not to call what they studied people: "The words *peuple* or *peuplade* 'people' are best avoided; the word 'tribe' is preferable."[10] Malinowski held the same view. The passage cited above from *Argonauts of the Western Pacific* about holism shows how "tribe" was central to anthropology. Malinowski concluded the programmatic chapter of the same book by outlining one of the goals of "ethnographic fieldwork" as "the organization of the tribe, and the anatomy of its culture" (1922: 11; also see Malinowski 1945: 30). How did the subject of anthropology, then, change from "tribe" via "ethnicity"[11] to what Ingold calls "the people"?

In 1948, a fellow anthropologist from North Africa told Ramkrishna Mukherjee (2009: 19) in Paris: "Today we are 'tribals' and the 'anthropologists' study us, but tomorrow we shall attain independence and, then, we shall be 'people' and the 'sociologists' and 'political scientists' will come to study us." My point is not that political scientists or sociologists alone should study "people." Instead, I ask: Is there a people out there and can anthropology simply take people as given to conduct participant observation among them? Or, should it also examine how a people is (un)made or interrupted through practices, inter alia, of political theory and IR?

Margaret Canovan (2005: 2), a scholar of political thought, notes that as a term, "the people" in English and other European languages has a triple meaning: as sovereign, as nation, and as nonelite. In Anglophone discussion, it also means human beings. This meaning, however, remains linked to the first three meanings. The first two meanings—as sovereign and as nation—pertain squarely to politics and IR (Bishai 2007; Carruthers 2001: 56–60). Without going into canonical texts such as Plato's or Aristotle's, as political theorists do (White and Ypi 2017), it is plausible to say that people is not a prior notion—instead, it derives its meaning from the very stuff that constitutes politics and gets identified or decomposed in the course of political contestations, the horizons of which are national and international at once. Canovan (2005: 140) concludes that "the people is undoubtedly one of the least precise and most promiscuous of concepts" and, therefore, it is "quintessentially a political concept." It signifies so many things that for Ernesto Laclau, it became an "empty signifier" (Mudde and Kaltwasser 2017: 9). Furthermore, populism splits people into authentic/real and false. Nigel Farage's celebratory statement after the Brexit verdict that it was the "victory for real people" exemplifies this point (Müller 2016). Ethnic cleansing is also an act of peoplehood aimed at purifying a people believed to have been contaminated by an impure "other" (Mann 2005).

In the early 2010s, I was invited to a conference on Islam. I wanted to present my then new work based on fieldwork with journalists in India and how "reporting" about terrorism in media worked. My aim was to write a short essay on the three big Ts: terrorism, treason, and technology (media). I sent an abstract that began as follows: "In post-9/11 India, scores of individuals (including minors below the age of 18) were arrested, tortured, imprisoned and killed in 'encounters' as 'terrorists.'" I received a reply stating that "the abstract looks as if it could be as concerned with Maoists as with Islam." The advice was to name terrorists as "Muslim." I replaced "individuals" with "Muslims" and it was readily accepted. Clearly, at stake here is the demarcation of the "people." Terrorists cannot be people without a religion, because the Euro-American states have declared a war on terror by instituting an equivalence between terror and Islam (cf. Verkaaik 2013; see below).

Viewed in terms of people who comprise citizens with voting rights in a demarcated territory, terrorists jailed or under trial, however, do not have voting rights in India. So do prisoners of certain categories in some states in the United States (Srivastava 2012). Tocqueville, a major theorist of democracy, viewed prisoners as enemies, a small hostile nation within the nation (Harcourt 2014: 8). This already messy condition gets messier because the concept of the people is linked to nation, nation to community (imagined community, after Anderson 1991), national community to the state, and the state to sovereignty. Woodrow Wilson's (1918) proclamation of the right to national self-determination invoked people, nationality, and nation as near synonyms. Within the nation, however, as people, minorities are separate from the rest of the national community in terms of their differences in language, religion, race, and so on. They are also inferior—as the term "minority" originally implied (Bishai 1998: 172). At stake here is not only the juridical—as in the case of whether or not prisoners are part of the people, for instance—but also the larger political matrix of which the juridical is a at best a symptom, an important one. Let me illustrate this with an example from India.

During my fieldwork with media practitioners in India, I found that the majority of them (and they were from the majority Hindu community) held that there was a definite link between terrorism and Islam (Ahmad 2009b, 2014, 2017b). When asked if Hindus also engaged in terrorism, they regarded this as almost an impossibility. To them, Hinduism (unlike Islam) was a religion uniquely and constitutively predisposed toward peace. If some Hindus took to violence, they did so in reaction and self-defense and hence outside the pale of terrorism. Such an assumption was not simply sociocultural but also legal and operative in interpreting cases of political violence linked to people from the minority and majority communities.

In discussing terrorism, Julia Eckert notes how India's laws on terrorism and their application assume a prior motive and theory of violence. This theory posits that violence by Muslims emanates from religious "fanaticism" and is premeditated. Violence by Hindus, in contrast, is a "natural reaction." Therefore, the former is dealt with under antiterrorism laws, whereas the latter comes under the Indian Penal Code (IPC). To demonstrate this, she referred to the alleged attacks by Muslims on the Sabermati train at Godhra station (known as Godhra train case), which killed fifty-seven Hindus inside a coach in February 2002. As the attackers were nonevidentially taken to be Muslims, they were tried under the new antiterrorism law, POTA (Prevention of Terrorism Act, 2002), whereas the subsequent "retaliatory" violence against Muslims (which killed over two thousand) by Hindus was dealt with under IPC. Eckert (2012: 330—emphasis in original) observed that "there was the perception of a growing double standard in Indian law or of a *dual law* that judged Muslim violence and protest as terrorism and Hindu violence as 'natural reaction' or spontaneous 'outburst.'" Though she did not ground her argument in relation to literature on the "people," it is clear that this legal disparity was equally about defining the "people." The 2013 anti-Muslim violence in Muzaffarnagar in Uttar Pradesh—a preface to the 2014 election—was likewise called a "riot," not terrorism, because most of the attackers were Hindus and most of the victims Muslims (Ahmad 2013).[12]

This prior theory of terrorism is by no means limited to India. In 2011, Anders Behring Breivik killed seventy-seven people in Norway. *The New York Times, Washington Post,* and *The Atlantic* did not wait for any evidence and blamed the massacre on Muslims. *The Sun* described it as "Norway's 9/11" (Ahmad 2015; Ali et al 2011: 1; Bangstad 2014). Norwegian TV began discussing how the attack resembled the Al-Qaeda–style operations (Eriksen 2011). However, once it became known that the terrorist was a white Norwegian, the media scene radically changed. Some began to call Breivik a convert to Islam or a "good disguise" (Nussbaum 2012: 49). Despite the proclamation in the manifesto by Breivik (2011: 1,404) that "I consider myself to be 100 percent Christian" and am a "supporter of a monocultural Christian Europe," media never called him a terrorist, let alone a Christian one. This refusal cannot be captured through brisk, localized empiricism; it needs a historical mapping of the self-definition by the West through secular–religious dualism. Addressing the 1893 World Parliament of Religions in Chicago, Alexander Web remarked:

> If a Mohammedan, Turk, Egyptian, Syrian or African commits a crime the newspaper reports do not tell us that it was committed by Turk, a Egyptian, a Syrian or an African, but by a Mohammedan. If an Irish man, an Italian, a Spaniard or a German commits a crime in the United States we don't say that it was committed by a Catholic, a Methodist or a Baptist, nor even a Christian. (in Gottschalk and Greenberg 2013: 21–22)[13]

Notably, unlike holistic cultural explanations in the case of violence by Muslims, Breivik's was depicted as purely individual.

The stage is now set to go past the limiting, even crippling, notion of anthropological holism to take it to a wider plane, on an awkward scale, as it were. For anthropology to become itself, a reformulated notion of holism is a necessity, not a choice.

Toward a New Holism on an Awkward Scale

As shown above, the equation between terrorism and Islam functioned in both India and Norway in that while the explanatory pivot of political violence by Muslims was primarily religious, the political violence by Hindus and Christians stood evacuated of any religious-cultural factor and was understood mainly as reactive or a matter of individual pathology. That discourses of Islamic terrorism encompass most

Figure 6.2. Heterogeneous singularity about equation between Islam and terrorism. © Irfan Ahmad.

of the world (Asia, Africa, Australia, Europe, North America, Middle East, even South America) is too obvious to repeat. Their translocal and international character are reproduced even in those viewpoints that are seemingly nonhostile to Muslims and which aim to break the innate link between Islam and terrorism (and thereby reinstall it, by no means paradoxically, though). Consider the semantically similar statement made repeatedly by diverse actors ranging from politicians to media outlets and civil society actors across the nation–states as different and distant as Australia, India, Norway, and the United States: "Not all Muslims are terrorists but all terrorists are Muslims" (see Figure 6.2). The heterogeneous singularity of this equation equally figured in the United Nations document (dated 24 December 2015; see United Nations 2015), "United Nations Global Counter-Terrorism Strategy." This equation was starker in the conference on the "prevention of violence extremism," which the United Nations Development Programme (UNDP) organized in 2016 in Oslo. As an invited participant to the conference, I read the UN document (as well as others) circulated by organizers.[14] Can ethnography, largely concerned as it is with the particular in a demarcated site, field, or location, account for the singularity of the equivalence between Islam and terrorism with its heterogeneous articulations in so many different contexts and at so many levels—local, national, regional, international, global[15] (these words are far from obvious to me, however)?

In my view, ethnography in itself cannot explain this unless it properly takes into account the wider forces of politics and IR. As alluded to above, the development of IR and anthropology as more professionalized disciplines in the West took place in the largely shared international political milieu of the early twentieth century. With the institutionalization of nation–states as the "normal" unit of international politics, first as the League of Nations and later as the United Nations after WWII, culture and societies were deeply bound up with this international political order. And the most decisive theory in IR was Realism: "the central tradition in the study of world politics," the rest being no more than "a footnote to Realism" (Dunne and Schmidt 2001: 142). Drawing on the tradition of thinking of Thucydides (460–406 BC), Machiavelli (1469–1527), Thomas Hobbes (1588–1679), and others, at the core of Realism lay the doctrine of raison d'état (reason of state) unconstrained by any morality. The fundamental assumptions informing Realism, as well as its offshoot, Neo-Realism, were those of international anarchy, fear, and enmity (Weber 2010). Carl Schmitt (1996), who viewed politics as instituting the boundary between friend and foe, influenced Morgenthau, just as he influenced Henry Kissinger (Cohen 2004: 4n11).

Such is the backdrop against which to construe the Cold War,[16] during which the Soviet bloc was named as the enemy of the so-called free, democratic Western world (Mamdani 2002). And the enemy was pure evil. In an interview with CNN, a key architect of the CIA and an influential advocate of Realism, diplomat-scholar George Kennan (1904–2005), observed: "We like to have our enemies in the singular, our friends, if you will, multiple. But the enemy must always be a center, he must be totally evil, he must wish all the terrible things that could happen to us—whether [that] made sense from his standpoint or not" (in Zulaika 2009: 136).[17] Kennan made this observation about WWII. The interview itself, however, was conducted in 1996, only years after the inauguration of the so-called New World Order by George Bush Sr.

Elsewhere, I have discussed at length how Islam was identified as a new enemy after the dissolution of the USSR left the US with no enemy (Ahmad 2017b: 123–25). Colin Powell expressed the need for a new enemy categorically: "I am running out of demons. I am running out of enemies" (Waltz 2000: 2). According to political theorist John Keane (1993: 15), "the global demise of communism is producing a new bogey, the demon of Islam, against which there are growing calls for a new political crusade." The object of the crusade, as it unfolded more prominently after 9/11, was Islamic terrorism. It is important to note that terrorism without the prefix Islamic, as anthropologist Joseba Zulaika (2009: 143) writes, had already begun to emerge as an enemy of the West in the closing years of the Cold War.

The nature and mechanisms of international politics discussed above equally obtained footing in India. In 1994, B. N. Jog, a Marathi journalist wedded to Hindutva's violent ethnic ideology, published *Threat of Islam: The Indian Dimensions*. As the title reveals, Islam was depicted as a global threat, while the book focused on its Indian aspects. The same year, police arrested Nisaruddin Ahmad, a student of pharmacy and resident of Gulbarga in the state of Karnataka, while he was on his way to college. Two months later, his brother was also arrested. Dubbed as terrorists, both were accused of taking part in many blasts in trains. The worst forms of custodial violence and torture were meted out to Nisaruddin. The only evidence upon which Nisaruddin was booked was a confession he had made while in custody. He had confessed that he "accepted his role in planting bomb in the compartment of A.P. Express on 06.12.1993." This confession was a ditto copy of another unsigned confession by Nisaruddin (key ground for his release). After a long legal battle lasting twenty-three years, Nisaruddin was released in 2016 (his brother in 2008). Upon his release, Nisaruddin expressed the state-directed trauma and sufferings he went through as follows: "I am free but what you see now is a living corpse" (Jaleel 2016; Alam 2016).

Nisaruddin's case as a terrorist—an Islamic terrorist at that—was neither solitary (there were several others, see Staff 2019) nor unrelated to international politics. Nothing demonstrates this more sharply than the statements of Narendra Modi in a TV debate after 9/11. Currently Prime Minister of India, in 2001 Modi was general secretary of the Bharatiya Janata Party (BJP), then in power and known for its anti-Muslim, ethnic politics. Modi congratulated the Indian media for speaking the "truth" when it used the phrase "Islamic terrorism." He opined that terrorism was innate to Islam (less emphatically also to Christianity), for it did not consider other religions to be true. In his view, "the whole world" had witnessed terrorism "for 1400 years" (since the Prophet Muhammad's time). He saw the post-9/11 era as a battle between "humanity" and "terrorism." Read Modi's exchange with journalist Rajdeep Sardesai:

> Sardesai: Why don't you give one assurance that [when] there will be an election campaign in UP [the largest state] you will not use the incident [9/11] . . . to stir a communal divide, to label every Muslim in this country as . . . an Islamic terrorist?

> Modi: It is a tragic condition in my Indian media that [there is] such a challenge to the humanity and we are talking about footpath politics? What are we doing? . . . When people are talking about the challenge to humanity, we are talking about UP politics.

The humanity in Modi's remarks obviously did not exist as a prior idea. Instead, it was fashioned through the disingenuous rhetoric of terrorism that the BJP put on an international stage to replay Schmittean politics of friend against enemy. Modi's following commennts in the same debate also show how the Indian discourse of terrorism is derived from, as well as constitutive of, international discourses on terrorism:

> See, because of India's initiative in the UN meeting twice, we have made terrorism an issue. Due to this, we have succeeded in dividing the country into two camps: those who are against terrorism and those who are in support of terrorism. I think that the recent incident in America [9/11] will intensify it [the division]. The world is about to be divided (*batnē*) into two parts: those who are in favor of humanity and those who are against humanity. (Modi 2013).

What is striking in the quote above is that Modi's reference to India's initiative in making terrorism an international issue goes well beyond the party line (BJP versus the Congress Party), because it is the initiative of India as a state. No less significant is the dualism in Modi's language that astonishingly resonates with that of Bush Jr. (on which, see Asad 2007; Mamdani 2002). It is by contrasting the ubiquity of the term "Islamic terrorism" and the absence of a corresponding term "Hindu terrorism" that I want to close this section.

While Modi is clear about the validity of the term "Islamic terrorism," he and his party—indeed most Hindus in India, including the "rival" Congress party (Bhardwaj 2018)—are against the very notion of "Hindu terrorism." This is despite the participation of Hindus for an explicitly Hindu cause in several violent cases that led to numerous killings (Ahmed 2008; Jaffrelot and Maheshwari 2011; Raghunath 2014, 2017).[18] Consider the 2018 case of an American fictional spy thriller (a television series) called "Quantico." In it, Priyanka Chopra, a Hindu actress, played the role of an FBI agent, Alex Parrish. Chopra foiled a terror plot by Indians in which, ahead of a summit over Kashmir, they were planning to attack Manhattan and blame it on Pakistan. As proof that the plotters were Indians, Chopra held up the Hindu rosary. So vehement was the protest by Indians in India and in the diaspora that Chopra immediately apologized. So did ABC Studios, the producer of "Quantico." Protesters were angry "for showing India in a negative light" (Staff 2018; Agence France-Presse in Delhi 2018). If read carefully, "India" here means Hindus, because seldom did the same Indians (Hindus) protest when Indian Muslims were arrested on false charges of terrorism and when an equation between Indians whose religion is Islam and terrorism was repeatedly made. It is worth noting that the Indian government too made this equivalence between India and Hindus. After 9/11, when some Indian women were attacked in the United States on the assumption of being Muslims, the Indian embassy issued a note asking them to wear a *biindī* (a colorful dot in the middle of the forehead), a sign associated with Hindu women. That the embassy did not care about Indian Muslim women who did not wear *bindī* is obvious (Chakravartty 2002: 211n4).

Five years before the telecast of "Quantico," in 2013, the National Investigation Agency (NIA), an Indian counterterrorism agency, arrested Khurshid, a Muslim student of science, for his alleged role in a bomb blast during an election rally to be addressed by Modi in Patna. Khurshid was later released because of no evidence of his involvement. After he was set free by the NIA, I met him many times as part of my research on terrorism. In one meeting, he told me that the NIA had seized his mobile phone with 600 contact numbers, of which 250 numbers were of his Hindu friends and contacts. For further investigation, the NIA and police called many numbers of his Muslim contacts but none with a Hindu name.

The need for the kind of holism I have argued for and illustrated in the preceding pages need not be further emphasized. Recall my discussion of Malinowski and Radcliff-Brown and the skewed, unproductive ways in which they conceptualized holism. In the Epilogue to *Stanger and Friend: The Way of an Anthropologist*, Powdermaker (1966: 285, 287–88), a student of Malinowski, reiterated the depoliticized, skewed notion of holism hooked to participant observation as follows: "The participant observation method was forged in the study of small homogeneous societies, in which the anthropologist lived for an extended period of time, participated in them, learned the language, interviewed, and constantly observed." She continued to be so wedded to anthropology's identification/preoccupation with "small community," "physical community," and "physical proximity" that she took their absence in her work on Hollywood as a challenge. Recently, David Parkin (2007: 1–3) edited a volume on holistic anthropology. In its Introduction, he noted two senses of holism: society as a whole and anthropology itself as a holistic discipline. The four-field division of anthropology in America—archaeology, physical anthropology, linguistics, and cultural anthropology—symbolizes the latter. That it is incongruent to speak of division and whole in the same breadth flies past Parkin. That this holism brackets out, among others, politics and IR, does so even more swiftly.

The Real and the True

Most social scientists across the disciplinary divides maintain that their concern is with "social reality." Anthropologists are no different. According to Michael Herzfeld (2017:129), the future of anthropology rests on how it "deals with the problem of reality." In a similar vein, Ingold (2014: 393—emphasis mine) is concerned with reality and real life: "For ethnography, when it turns, is no longer ethnography but the educational correspondence of *real life*."[19] In my view, the goal of anthropology is not only to study that which is real but to arrive at that which is true, so that the separation between the two is decomposed in a simultaneous act where the real corresponds to the true, or the search for the true leads to tracing of new faces of the real, thereby guiding our inquiry to examine those doxa that often pass as the real. Within the context of this chapter's main empirical theme, that shots are fired, bombs explode, buildings are set on fire, people are killed—acts described as terrorism—and individuals are arrested, tortured, and imprisoned as terrorists belong to the real. But is that real also and necessarily the true?

As a first year master's student of sociology, I contributed an article (Ahmad 1995) to a new university journal *Social Reality*, which had received support from sociology professors of Jawaharlal Nehru University, New Delhi. I recall my objection to the editor, a doctoral student: Is sociology also not about reaching the truth and the true? My view was not considered worthy of discussion because of the "reality" of my being a junior student and the editor being a doctoral researcher. Since then, I truly have had an acute sense of discomfort with the idea of reality.

Didier Fassin's intervention about the relationship between reality and truth becomes important to engage with here. He heuristically differentiates between reality and truth. Against the likely equivalence between the two, he posits them as concepts in constant tension: "the real being that which exists or has happened and the true being that which has to be regained from deception and convention" (2014: 41). Anthropologists' task is to "articulate the real and the true . . . in the exploration of life" (2014: 45). The quest for the real and the true at times may mean going past bare and known facts as well as instituting a relation to facts, events, structure, and history unnoticed by the interlocutors.[20] I am inclined to include also those social scientists who miss the connection of which Fassin speaks. Calling the premise that fiction explores truth and anthropology explores reality into question,

Fassin aptly observes that anthropological inquiry into truth articulates "various levels of reality" (48).

I am aware that there is no easy, much less singular, way in which one can ask the question about the real and true in relation to terrorism, not least because this field of study as well as the larger world we all inhabit are heavily securitized to police even what qualifies as a question. It is worth writing, however, that after his arrest, the question that occupied Khurshid throughout was the truth of terrorism. For the blasts in the election rally to be addressed by Modi in 2013 in Patna, why did the police arrest innocents like him but not those who actually organized the explosions? What is the truth (*sach*), he repeatedly asked, behind the terrorist blasts?

Concluding Remarks

If simplified and stated parsimoniously, one of the many conclusions of this chapter may amount to an articulation of anthropology as "political philosophy with 'people' in." The reason I put people within quotation marks is that as a discipline, anthropology historically described its subject matter as the study of tribe, primitive, savage, simple society, and so on—all outside of the West as a conceptual entity. Ingold's replacement of these terms with "the people," therefore, does not solve the problem, because, like earlier terms, "people," too, is highly contested. Above all, "people" as a term belongs squarely to the political, not simply within the nation but also in the realm of international relations (IR). My key argument was that "the people" is not an entity prior to the vortex of politics; rather it becomes (or does not) an entity in the course of contestations the scale of which is by no means local (nor is its nature cultural–social only). Both politics and IR, however, are absent from Ingold's valuable expositions on anthropology and ethnography.

This chapter has also argued for a notion of holism that is unlike Malinowski's and which anthropology has yet to fully recognize. Unlike Radcliffe-Brown's idea, the scale of holism is not "any convenient locality of a suitable size," but the whole of the political field—local, national, regional, international, and global—without which neither society nor culture can be adequately understood. It is equally interdisciplinary, indeed indisciplinary. An anthropology of terrorism entails a reformulated holism at the intersections of politics, IR, and other disciplines.

To this end, I have questioned Ingold's characterization of anthropology as description of "the lives of people other than ourselves." Instead, my contention has been that anthropology can no longer be only about "them" in the same way as it must also study up by examining the power elites who are not as accessible as the ordinary folks are. My insistence on studying "us" and "ourselves"—the explanation of Anders Breivik killing seventy-seven people in Norway served as the primary example—aimed to demonstrate that holism as a concept must not be reserved, as Durkheim meant, for non-Western people alone. Ratifying the distinction between sociology and ethnology, Durkheim (2013: 159) observed: "All the social forms which are observable as distinct and organized in more complex societies [the West; therefore, sociology] are to be found there ["lower societies;" therefore, ethnology] in a state of interpenetration which highlights better their unity" (for more, see Ahmad 2018). Bruno Latour (1993: 7) summed up this premise of anthropology crisply: "For traditional anthropologists there is not—there cannot be, there should not be—an anthropology of the modern world" because unlike among the savages, the social fabric among the modern Westerners is not "seamless" or holistic.

Finally, I have argued that if anthropology has to find its voice beyond the departmental silo, its concern has to be the true and truth (in the plural, see Caputo 2013), not merely reality or real life—for to start and stop at reality is to succumb to power. As a senior advisor to Bush said, "We are an empire now, we create our own reality. And while you are studying that reality—judiciously, as you will—we will act again, creating other new realities, which you can study too, and that is how things will sort out" (Suskind 2004). If scholars of anthropology do not also make truth and true as prime foci of their inquiry, they will largely remain like Morgenthau, who was (rather, he became) a *Wirklicheitswissenchaftler*: a "scholar of reality" with no genuine morality or ethical pursuits.

Acknowledgments

I would like to thank Peter van der Veer, Director of the Max Planck Institute for the Study of Religious & Ethnic Diversity for facilitating the discussion that made this book, and chapter, possible. Arpita Roy provided valuable comments during and after the discussion. Patrice Ladwig and I had many critical conversations on the relations between anthropology and ethnography after the discussion. Jeremy Walton not only read a draft of this chapter with critical insights but also offered his deft editorial suggestions. Along with words, he also often reads the author's mind. I am indebted to all. Errors, if any, are mine.

Irfan Ahmad (PhD in anthropology, University of Amsterdam) is Senior Research Fellow, Max Planck Institute for the Study of Religious & Ethnic Diversity, Göttingen, Germany. Previously, he acted as an associate professor of political anthropology at Australian Catholic University and senior lecturer at Monash University. He is author of *Islamism and Democracy in India* (Princeton University Press, 2009) and *Religion as Critique: Islamic Critical Thinking from Mecca to the Marketplace* (University of North Carolina Press, 2017). Recently, he coedited *The Algebra of Warfare-Welfare* (Oxford University Press, 2019). He has taught at Australian and Dutch universities. Founding coeditor of *Journal of Religious & Political Practice*, he is on editorial boards, inter alia, of *Public Anthropologist* and *South Asia*. In 2018, he wrote the "Renewing Political Anthropology" column for *Anthropology News*. He also contributes to debates in global media.

Notes

1. I take "terrorism" and "Islamic terrorism" as politicized terms, even when used without quotation marks.
2. All page numbers with year of publication but without author's name refer to Ingold's texts.
3. Kapferer (2007), Mahmood (1996), and Sahlins (1999) earlier wrote about such threats.
4. Defending Radcliffe-Brown, "the life-long rival of Malinowski" (Leach 1977: 5–6), may imply an attack on Malinowski. Edmund Leach, who regarded Malinowski as "the greatest and most original of all social anthropologists" remarked that "both in the flesh and in his writings he [Radcliffe-Brown] seemed to me to be something of a fraud" and "nearly all the ethnographic evidence which he cited . . . was borrowed from other people, though sometime the borrowing was unacknowledged."
5. Absence of the political is equally manifest in *Companion Encyclopedia of Anthropology*, edited by Ingold (1994), the three parts of which are titled "humanity," "culture," and "social life." Ann Kingsolver (2001: 4—emphasis added) likewise takes anthropological and academic theories as "the stories we tell ourselves to make sense of life and to determine where we are as we navigate *social space*." The exclusion of the political—is social

space not also political?—is as stark as of the potential in that preoccupation with "where we are" suspends, if not abolishes, where we want to be.
6. On the evolution of the state and stateless societies and anthropology's take on them, see Carneiro (1970), Eriksen (2001), Kottak (2008), Vincent (1990). Hansen and Stepputat (2005, 2001) made the state vital to anthropology. However, their concerns remained largely national and outside of the West.
7. The inside cover flap of *History of Anthropology* by Alfred Haddon, published in 1934, described it as an "authoritative account of . . . the study of primitive man."
8. The key difference between International Politics and IR is this: the former does not see beyond the state, the latter also accounts for the nonstate actors like MNCs and NGOs (Shimko 2010: xvi).
9. Crane Ross (2007), a British diplomat who resigned after the invasion of Iraq, notes how he was trained to see the world in terms of states whose goal it is to secure and aggrandize national interests.
10. Words like "people" and "tribe," Badiou (2013: 22) reminds us, were terminological arms of colonialism: "the imperial colonial camp would prefer to speak of 'tribes' or 'ethnic groups,' if not 'races' and 'savages.' The word 'people' was only suitable for the conquering powers, elated by the conquest itself: 'the French people,' 'the English people,' yes . . . . But the Algerian people, the Vietnamese people? No!"
11. After Mauss and Malinowski, "ethnicity" came into vogue (Wolf 2001: 76–77) to replace "tribe" in textbooks like Eriksen's (2001: 261–74) and Kottak's (2008: 299–325); also see Ahmad (2017c: 36).
12. Politician L. K. Advani described the violent Ayodhya campaign in 1992 that destroyed the Babri mosque in Uttar Pradesh as "the greatest mass movement" of free India (Kanungo 2002: 204). "Mass" refers to people, the "right" kind of people. However, when tens of thousands of Kashmiris take to the streets to voice their just demands, the term "people" or "mass" is withdrawn. Instead, they get branded as "separatists," "militants," a "mob," or the like. This is similar to the Californian police terming protests by the Mexican immigrants in Los Angeles as nothing to do with democracy but as a "threat to law and order" (Hartnett 2011: 2).
13. Withdrawal of the word Christian in explaining Basque nationalism—especially its violent face—is puzzling, even though for its ideologue de Arana-Goiri, the loss of Basque independence was due to decline in religious commitment. Heiberg (1989: 53) put it tersely: "Spain was anti-Basque and anti-Christ."
14. I devote a chapter to that conference in the book manuscript *Terrorism in Question: Toward a New Public Anthropology* (Ahmad undated). It is based on my fieldwork with Indian media practitioners and "terrorists"—one of them an Australian citizen of Egyptian origin released from Guantanamo Bay. I met him in Melbourne. One of the Indian "terrorists" I met was an American citizen of Indian origin imprisoned in India. I met them after their release. I have also written about what it means to be an In-

dian anthropologist from a minoritized position writing about terrorism; see Ahmad (2017a).
15. To Sloterdijk's observation that it is "the people in the West [who] are the only ones who speak of globalization" (in Noordegraaf-Eelens and Schinkel 2011: 188), let me add those aspiring to be the West.
16. As a term, "cold war" is linked to Islam. Spanish in origin, *la guerra fría* (cold war) described medieval relations between Islam and Christendom as neither of war nor of peace (Trumpbour 2003: 107; cf., Heo and Kormina 2019: 3). Interestingly, partisans of the Soviet Union took it as an ideologically inflected term coined and used by the US. In the Soviet discourses, the term "cold war" was rarely used; when used, it was specified as a foreign concept (Heo and Kormina 2019: 3–4).
17. de Abreu (2019) offers a rich anthropological–historical account of the communist threat the Salazar regime in Portugal staged during the cold war.
18. Some have justified using "Hindu terrorism" as a term (see Komireddi 2011). My point is that, like Christian terrorism, it is not part of the regnant political or media vocabulary.
19. Ingold (2017: 23–24) merely refers to the true and the truth. He does not relate them to the real in the ways in which I do here.
20. With much force and lucidity, Graeber (2011: 28) contends even going against informants' own view.

References

Agence France-Presse in Delhi. 2018. "Bollywood Star Apologizes over Hindu Terror Plot Row." *The Guardian*. 10 June.

Ahmad, Irfan. 1995. "Looking for the End of the Tunnel." *Social Reality* 1, no. 2: 64–66.

———. 2009a. "Genealogy of the Islamic State: Reflections on Maududi's Political Thought and Islamism." *Journal of Royal Anthropological Institute* 15: S145–62.

———. 2009b. *Islamism and Democracy in India: Transformation of Jamaat-e-Islami*. Princeton: Princeton University Press.

———. 2013. "Modi as Future Indian PM? Development, Camp and the 'Muslim Vote.'" *OpenDemocracy*. 30 November.

———. 2014. "Kafka in India: Terrorism, Media, Muslims." In *Being Muslims in South Asia*, edited by Robin Jeffrey and Ronojoy Sen, 291–329. New Delhi: Oxford University Press.

———. 2015. "Anthropology/Sociology and International Relations: The Importance of C. Wright Mills." Paper presented at *Australian Anthropological Society Conference*, University of Melbourne.

———. 2017a. "Anthropological Publics, Public Anthropology: An AAA Annual Meeting Roundtable." *HAU: Journal of Ethnographic Theory* 7, no. 1: 491–93.

———. 2017b. "Injustice and the New World Order: An Anthropological Perspective on 'Terrorism' in India." *Critical Studies on Terrorism* 10, no. 1: 115–37.

———. 2017c. *Religion as Critique: Islamic Critical Thinking from Mecca to the Marketplace*. Chapel Hill: University of North Carolina Press.

———. 2018. "On the Absence of the Political in Four-Field Anthropology: Column Renewing Political Anthropology." *Anthropology News*. 8 November.

———. Undated. *Terrorism in Question: Toward a New Public Anthropology*. Book manuscript.

Ahmed, Zubair. 2008. "'Hindu Terrorism' Debate Grips India." BBC News. 21 November. http://news.bbc.co.uk/2/hi/south_asia/7739541.stm.

Alam, Mehtab. 2016. "Who Will Return Our Precious Years, Ask the Wrongfully Incarcerated." *The Wire*. 24 December.

Ali, Wajahat, Eli Clifton, Matthew Duss, Lee Fang, Scott Keyes, and Faiz Shakir. 2011. *Fear, Inc.: The Roots of the Islamophobia Network in America*. Washington, DC: Centre for American Progress.

Allen, Kieran. 2004. *Max Weber: A Critical Introduction*. London: Pluto.

Almond, Gabriel. 1950. "Anthropology, Political Behavior, and International Relations." *World Politics* 2, no. 2: 277–84.

Anderson, Benedict. 1991. *Imagined Communities: Reflections on the Origin and Spread of Nationalism*. Rev. ed. London: Verso.

Asad, Talal. 2007. *On Suicide Bombing*. New York: Columbia University Press.

Badiou, Alain. 2013. "Twenty-Four Notes on the Uses of the Word 'People.'" In *What Is a People?*, edited by Alain Badiou, Pierre Bourdieu, Judith Butler, Georges Didi-Huberman, Sadri Khiari, and Jacques Rancière, 21–31. New York: Columbia University Press.

Bangstad, Sindre. 2014. *Anders Breivik and the Rise of Islamophobia*. London: Zed Books.

Bauman, Zygmunt. 1973. *Culture as Praxis*. London: Routledge and Kegan Paul.

Beattie, John. 1964. *Other Cultures: Aims, Methods, and Achievements in Social Anthropology*. London: Routledge and Kegan Paul.

Bhardwaj, Supriya. 2018. "Rahul to Karnataka Congress: Refrain from Using Terms like Hindu Extremists for BJP, RSS." *India Today*. 14 January. https://www.indiatoday.in/india/story/rahul-to-karnataka-congress-refrain-from-using-terms-like-hindu-extremists-for-bjp-rss-1144734-2018-01-14.

Bilimoria, Purushottama. 2006. "The Pseudo-Secularization of Hindutva and Its Campaign for Uniform Civil Codes." *Nidan: Journal of the Department of Hindu Studies* 18: 1–21.

Bishai, Linda. 1998. "Sovereignty and Minority Rights: Interrelations and Implications." *Global Governance* 4, no. 2: 157–82.

———. 2007. *Forgetting Ourselves: Secession and the (Im)possibility of Territorial Identity*. Lanham, MD: Lexington.

Borneman, John. 1998. *Subversions of International Order: Studies in the Political Anthropology of Culture*. Albany: State University of New York.

Breivik, A. B. 2011. *2083: A European Declaration of Independence*. Available at https://info.publicintelligence.net/AndersBehringBreivikManifesto.pdf.

Burawoy, Michael. 2000. "Introduction: Reaching for the Globe." In *Global Ethnography: Forces, Connections, and Imaginations in a Postmodern World*, edited by Michael Burawoy, et al, 1–40. Berkeley: University of California Press.

Canovan, Margaret. 2005. *People*. Cambridge, UK: Polity.

Caputo, John. 2013. *Truth: Philosophy in Transit*. London: Penguin.

Carneiro, Robert. 1970. "A Theory of the Origin of the State." *Science* 169: 733–738.

Carruthers, Susan. 2001. "International History: 1900–1945." In *The Globalization of World Politics: An Introduction to International Theory*, edited by J. Baylis and S. Smith, 51–73. Oxford: Oxford University Press.

Chakravartty, Paula. 2002. "Translating Terror in India." *Television & New Media* 3, no. 2: 205–12.

Cohen, Jean. 2004. "Whose Sovereignty? Empire Versus International Law." *Ethics & International Affairs* 18, no. 3: 1–24.

Comaroff, Jean, and John Comaroff. 2003. "Ethnography on an Awkward Scale: Postcolonial Anthropology and the Violence of Abstraction." *Ethnography* 4, no. 2: 147–79.

CRAI (Committee of the Royal Anthropological Institution of Great Britain and Ireland). 1954 [1874]. *Notes and Queries on Anthropology*. 6th rev. ed. [rewritten]. London: Routledge & Kegan Paul.

de Abreu, Maria José. 2019. "Medium Theory; Or, 'The War of the Worlds' at Regular Intervals." *Current Anthropology* 60, no. 5: 656–73.

Dimen-Schein, Muriel. 1977. *The Anthropological Imagination*. New York: McGraw-Hill.

Dirks, Nicholas. 2015. *Autobiography of an Archive: A Scholar's Passage to India*. New York: Columbia University Press.

Dunne, Tim, and Brian Schmidt. 2001. "Realism." In *The Globalization of World Politics: An Introduction to International Theory*, edited by J. Baylis and S. Smith, 141–61. Oxford: Oxford University Press.

Durkheim, Emile. 2013 [1982]. *The Rules of Sociological Method and Selected Texts on Sociology and Its Method*. Translated by W. D. Halls and edited by Steven Lukes. 2nd ed. Basingstoke: Palgrave.

Eckert, Julia. 2012. "Theories of Militancy in Practice: Explanations of Muslim Terrorism in India." *Social Science History* 36, no. 3: 321–45.

Eriksen, Thomas. 2001. *Small Places, Large Issues: An Introduction to Social and Cultural Anthropology*. 2nd ed. London: Pluto.

———. 2011. "A Darker Shade of Pale: Cultural Intimacy in an Age of Terrorism." *Anthropology Today* 27, no. 5: 1–2.

Fabian, Johannes. 1983. *Time and the Other: How Anthropology Makes Its Object*. New York: Columbia University Press.

Fassin, Didier. 2014. "True Life, Real Lives: Revisiting the Boundaries Between Ethnography and Fiction." *American Ethnologist* 41, no. 1: 40–55.

Frei, Christoph. 2016. "*Politics among Nations*: Revisiting a Classic." *Ethics & International Affairs* 30, no. 1: 39–46.

Fuller, Chris, and J. Harriss. 2001. "For An Anthropology of the Modern Indian State." In *The Everyday State and Society in Modern India*, edited by C. J. Fuller and Veronique Benei, 1–30. London: Hurst.

Geertz, Clifford. 1968. *Islam Observed: Religious Development in Morocco and Indonesia*. Chicago: University of Chicago Press.

———. 1980. *Negara: The Theatre State in Nineteenth-century Bali*. Princeton: Princeton University Press.

Giddens, Anthony. 1990. *The Consequences of Modernity*. Stanford: Stanford University Press.

Gledhill, John. 2000. *Power and Its Disguises: Anthropological Perspectives on Politics*. 2nd ed. London: Pluto.

Gonzalez, Roberto. 2007. "Towards Mercenary Anthropology? The New US Army Counterinsurgency Manual FM 3-24 and the Military-Anthropology Complex." *Anthropology Today* 23, no. 3: 14–19.

Gottschalk, Peter, and G. Greenberg. 2013. "Common Heritage, Uncommon Fear: Islamophobia in the United States and British India, 1684–1947." In *Islamophobia in America*, edited by C. Ernst, 21–51. New York: Palgrave.

Graeber, David. 2011. *Debt: The First 500 Years*. New York: Melville.

Gusterson, Hugh. 1997. "Methodology: Studying Up Revisited." *PoLAR* 20, no. 1: 114–19.

Haddon, Alfred. 1934. *History of Anthropology*. London: Watts & Co.

Hansen, Thomas Blom, and Finn Stepputat, eds. 2005. *Sovereign Bodies: Citizens, Migrants and States in the Postcolonial World*. Princeton: Princeton University Press.

———. 2001. *States of Imagination: Ethnographic Explorations of the Postcolonial State*. Durham: Duke University Press.

Hanson, Pauline. Hanson's statement tweeted by *Nine News Australia* and retweeted by Shea Barclay. Accessed 6 November 2018. URL no longer available.

Harcourt, Bernard. 2014. "The Invisibility of the Prison in Democratic Theory." *The Good Society* 23, no. 1: 6–16.

Hartnett, Stephen. 2011. "Introduction: Empowerment or Incarceration-Reclaiming Hope and Justice from a Punishing Democracy." In *Challenging the Prison-Industrial Complex*, edited by Stephen Hartnett, 1–12. Urbana: University of Illinois Press.

Heiberg, Marianne. 1989. *The Making of the Basque Nation*. Cambridge, UK: Cambridge University Press.

Heo, Angie, and Jeanne Kormina. 2019. "Introduction: Religion and Borders in (Post-)Cold War Peripheries." *The Journal of Religion* 99, no. 1: 1–17.

Herzfeld, Michael. 2017. "Anthropological Realism in a Scientific Age." *Anthropological Theory* 18, no. 1: 129–50.

Ingold, Tim. 1994. "General Introduction." In *Companion Encyclopedia of Anthropology*, edited by Tim Ingold, xiii–xxii. London: Routledge.
———. 2008a. "Anthropology Is *Not* Ethnography." *British Academy Review* 11: 21–23.
———. 2008b. "Anthropology Is *Not* Ethnography." *Proceedings of the British Academy* 154: 69–92.
———. 2014. "That Is Enough about Ethnography." *Hau: Journal of Ethnographic Theory* 4, no. 1: 383–95.
———. 2017. "Anthropology Contra Ethnography." *Hau: Journal of Ethnographic Theory* 7, no. 1: 21–26.
Jaffrelot, Christophe, and Malvika Maheshwari. 2011. "Paradigm Shifts by the RSS? Lessons from Aseemanand's Confession." *Economic and Political Weekly* 46, no. 4: 42–46.
Jaleel, Muzamil. 2016. "After 23 Years in Jail, I am Free but What You See Now Is a Living Corpse, Says Nisar." *Indian Express*. 30 May. https://indianexpress.com/article/india/india-news-india/babri-masjid-demolition-train-blast-tada-supreme-court-acquitted-in-babri-anniversary-train-blasts-case-nisar-2824883/.
Kanaungo, Pralay. 2002. *RSS's Tryst with Politics: From Hedgewar to Sudarshan*. Delhi: Manohar.
Kapferer, Bruce. 2007. "Anthropology and the Dialectic of Enlightenment: A Discourse on the Definition and Ideals of a Threatened Discipline." *Australian Journal of Anthropology* 18, no. 1: 72–94.
Kaufman, Robert. 2006. "Morgenthau's Unrealistic Realism." *Yale Journal of International Affairs*: 24–38.
Keane, John. 1993. "Power-sharing Islam?" In *Power-sharing Islam?*, edited by Azzam Tamimi, 15–31. London: Liberty for Muslim World Publications.
Kelly, John, Beatrice Jauregui, Sean Mitchell, and Jeremy Walton, eds. 2010. *Anthropology and Global Counterinsurgency*. Chicago: University of Chicago Press.
Kingsolver, Ann. 2001. *NAFTA Stories: Fears and Hopes in Mexico and the United States*. Boulder, CO: Lynne Rienner.
Komireddi, Kapil. 2011. "India Must Face up to Hindu Terrorism." *The Guardian*. 19 January.
Kottak, Conrad. 2008. *Anthropology: The Exploration of Human Diversity*. 12th edition. Boston: McGraw-Hill.
Kurtz, Donald. 2001. *Political Anthropology: Power and Paradigms*. Boulder, CO: Westview Press.
Latour, Bruno. 1993 [1991]. *We Have Never Been Modern*. Translated by Catherine Porter. Cambridge, MA: Harvard University Press.
Leach, Eddmund. 1977. *Custom, Law, and Terrorist Violence*. Edinburgh: Edinburgh University Press.
Lewellen, Ted. 2003. *Political Anthropology: An Introduction*. 3rd ed. Westport, CT: Praeger.
Mahmood, Cynthia. 1996. *Fighting for Faith and Nation: Dialogues with Sikh Militants*. Philadelphia: University of Pennsylvania Press.

Malinowski, Bronislaw. 1922. *Argonauts of the Western Pacific*. Prospect Heights, IL: Waveland Press.

———. 1945. *The Dynamics of Cultural Change*. New Haven: Yale University Press.

———. 1948. *Magic, Science and Religion and Other Essays*. Boston: Beacon.

Mamdani, Mahmood. 2002. "Good Muslim, Bad Muslim: A Political Perspective on Culture and Terrorism." *American Anthropologist* 104, no. 3: 766–75.

Mann, Michael. 2005. *The Dark Side of Democracy: Explaining Ethnic Cleansing*. Cambridge, UK: Cambridge University Press.

Masco, Joseph. 2014. *The Theatre of Operations: National Security Affect from the Cold War to the War on Terror*. Durham: Duke University Press.

Mauss, Marcel. 2007 [1967]. *Manual of Ethnography*. Translated by Dominique Lussier, edited and introduced by N. J. Allen. New York: Berghahn. Books

Mead, Margaret. 2000 [1953]. "Political Applications of Studies of Culture at a Distance." In *The Study of Culture at a Distance*, edited by Margaret Mead and Rhoda Métraux, 441–44. New York: Berghahn Books.

Mills, C. Wright. 1959. *The Sociological Imagination*. New York: Oxford University Press.

Modi, Narendra. 2013. "Narendra Modi on Islamic Terrorism on Big Fight after 9/11 Attacks." YouTube. 22 September. https://www.youtube.com/watch?v=fas-jaaZWWM.

Mudde, Cas, and Cristobal Rovira Kaltwasser. 2017. *Populism: A Very Short Introduction*. Oxford: Oxford University Press.

Mukherjee, Ramkrishna. 2009. *Why Unitary Social Science?* Cambridge, UK: Cambridge Scholars Publishing.

Müller, Jan-Werner. 2016. *What Is Populism*. Philadelphia: University of Pennsylvania Press.

Nader, Laura. 1974. "Up the Anthropologists—Perspectives Gained from Studying Up." In *Reinventing Anthropology*, edited by Dell Hymes, 284–311. New York: Vintage.

———. 2011. "Ethnographic Theory." *HAU: Journal of Ethnographic Theory* 1, no. 1: 211–19.

Navari, Cornelia. 2016. "Hans Morgenthau and the National Interest." *Ethics & International Affairs* 30, no. 1: 47–54.

Noordegraaf-Eelens, Liesbeth, and Willem Schinkel. 2011. "The Space of Global Capitalism and Its Imaginary Imperialism: An Interview with Peter Sloterdijk." In *In Medias Res: Peter Sloterdijk's Spherological Poetics of Being*, edited by Liesbeth Noordegraaf-Eelens and Willem Schinkel, 185–96. Amsterdam: Amsterdam University Press.

Nussbaum, Martha. 2012. *The New Religious Intolerance: Overcoming the Politics of Fear in an Anxious Age*. Cambridge, MA: The Belknap Press of Harvard University Press.

Parkin, David. 2007. "Introduction: Emergence and Convergence." In *Holistic Anthropology: Emergence and Convergence*, edited by David Parkin and Stanley Ulijaszek, 1–20. New York: Berghahn Books.

Powdermaker, Hortense. 1966. *Stanger and Friend: The Way of an Anthropologist*. New York: W. W. Norton.

Price, David. 2011. *Weaponizing Anthropology: Social Science in Service of the Militarized State*. Petrolia, CA: CounterPunch.

Radcliffe-Brown, A. R. 1940. "Preface." In *African Political Systems*, edited by M. Fortes and E. E. Evans-Pritchard, xi–xxiii. London: Oxford University Press.

———. 1952. *Structure and Function in Primitive Society*. Glencoe, IL: Free Press.

Raghunath, Leena. 2014. "The Believer: Swami Aseemanand's Radical Service to the Sangh." *The Caravan*. 1 February. https://caravanmagazine.in/reportage/believer.

———. 2017. "How Pragya Singh Thakur, Sunil Joshi and Swami Aseemanand Plotted the Samjhauta Express Blasts." *The Caravan*. 26 April. https://caravanmagazine.in/vantage/pragya-singh-thakur-aseemanand-samjhauta-express.

Ross, Carne. 2007. *Independent Diplomat: Dispatches from an Unaccountable Elite*. Ithaca: Cornell University Press.

Sahlins, Marshall. 1999. "What Is Anthropological Enlightenment? Some Lessons of the Twentieth Century." *Annual Review of Anthropology* 28: i–xxiii.

Schmitt, Carl. 1996. *The Concept of the Political*. Translated by George Schwab. Chicago: University of Chicago Press.

Shimko, Keith. 2010. *International Relations: Perspectives and Controversies*. Boston: Wadsworth.

Silverman, Sydel. 2005. "The United States." In *One Discipline, Four Ways: British, German, French and American Anthropology*, edited by Fredrik Barth, Andre Gingrich, Robert Parkin, and Sydel Silverman, 257–347. Chicago: University of Chicago Press.

Somadar, Tanya. 2010. "Fox Host Brian Kilmeade Says 'All Terrorists Are Muslim' In Defense Of O'Reilly's 'Muslims Killed Us' Remark." Thinkprogress.org. 15 October.

Spencer, Jonathan. 2001. "Political Anthropology." In *International Encyclopaedia of the Social and Behavioral Sciences*, edited by Neil Smelser, 1,628–31. Oxford: Elsevier.

Srivastava, Medha. 2012. "The Voting Rights of Prisoners: Examining the Indian Stand in Light of the Recent ECHR Decision in Scoppola v. Italy." https://humanrightsoncampus.wordpress.com/2012/06/11/voting-rights-prisoners-india-echr/.

Staff. 2018. "Quantico Hindu Terror Episode: Here Is Why Priyanka Chopra Is Under Fire." *Indian Express*. 10 June. https://indianexpress.com/article/india/quantico-hindu-terror-episode-here-is-why-priyanka-chopra-is-under-fire-5210489/.

———. 2019. "Eleven Muslims Acquitted 25 Years After Being Charged Under Anti-Terrorism Law." *The Wire*. 1 March.

Suskind, Ron. 2004. "Without a Doubt." *New York Times*. 17 October.

Trumpbour, J. 2003. "The Clash of Civilizations: Samuel Huntington, Bernard Lewis, and the Remaking of the Post–cold War World Order." In *The New Crusades: Constructing the Muslim Enemy*, edited by E. Qureshi and M. Sells, 89–130. New York: Columbia University Press.

The United Nations. 2015. "The United Nations Global Counter-Terrorism Strategy." A/70/674. Seventieth session. Agenda items 16 and 117.

van de Veer, Peter. 2016. *The Value of Comparison*. Durham: Duke University Press.

Verkaaik, Oskar. 2013. "Notes on the Sublime: Aspects of Political Violence in Urban Pakistan." *South Asian Popular Culture* 11, no. 2: 109–19.

Vincent, Joan. 1990. *Anthropology and Politics: Visions, Traditions and Trends*. Tucson: University of Arizona Press.

Waltz, K. 2000. "Intimations of Multipolarity." In *The New World Order: Contrasting Theories*, edited by B. Hansen and B. Hansen, 1–17. London: Macmillan.

Weber, Cynthia. 2010. *International Relations Theory: A Critical Introduction*. 3rd ed. London: Routledge.

White, Jonathan, and Lea Ypi. 2017. "The Politics of Peoplehood." *Political Theory* 45, no. 4: 449–65.

Wilson, Woodrow. 1918. "Woodrow Wilson's 'Fourteen Points.'" https://web.ics.purdue.edu/~wggray/Teaching/His300/Handouts/Fourteen_Points.pdf.

Wolf, Eric. 2001. *Pathways of Power: Building an Anthropology of the Modern World*. Berkeley: University of California Press.

Zulaika, Joseba. 2009. *Terrorism: The Self-Fulfilling Prophecy*. Chicago: University of Chicago Press.

AFTERWORD

Tim Ingold

I would like to thank all the contributors to this collection. It is a rare honor to have one's work subjected to such detailed critical scrutiny, and with such close—even forensic—attention. I should admit at the outset that the matters at stake in the troubled union of anthropology and ethnography are by no means as settled in my mind as they are on the page, and while I have endeavored to set them out as clearly as I can, the long-running argument I have been having with myself continues, and shows no sign of abating. Although there may not be—and perhaps *should* not be—any final resolution, I have thought it important to put these matters on the table so that they can be brought out into the open and properly debated. For too long, it seems to me, they have remained like a festering sore at the heart of our discipline, giving rise to a host of malignant side effects, not the least of which is our chronic inability to explain to the rest of the world, with clarity and conviction, what we anthropologists do and why we do it. I am therefore very pleased to see that my efforts to expose the tensions in the relation between anthropology and ethnography have borne fruit, in this collection as elsewhere, even if my critics have arrived at conclusions at variance with mine.

Ultimately, it comes down to a confusion of objectives. Since I have repeatedly been accused of being hostile to ethnography—an accusation leveled in this collection by Jeremy Walton—let me insist once again that this has never been my intention. Far from prosecuting what Walton calls a "scorched-earth campaign" against ethnography, my aim has been to liberate ethnography, to free it from the prison-house of method in which it has become enslaved to its anthropological masters; but by the same token, I aim to free anthropology to speak for itself, rather as the translator or interpreter of other people's voices. The ends of ethnography, I contend, are no better or worse than those of anthropology. They are simply different. One can join with others in a conversation about the conditions and possibilities of human life, or one can consider what they have to say as evidence from which to form an interpretation of their own ways of thinking and doing. But to attempt both at once would be to their mutual detriment. If an overdose of ethnography can do more harm than good to the anthropological patient, the converse applies as well: overdosing on anthropology is the death of ethnography. One causes anthropology to turn inward on itself into a degenerative study of its own ways of working; the other reduces the richness and subtlety of ethnographic writing to a catalogue of case studies standardized into ideal types for purposes of comparison.

Many otherwise sympathetic colleagues, however, tell me that I am making a fuss about nothing. They have long been engaged with their interlocutors in the kind of generous, collaborative, and speculative inquiry that I want to call anthropology. And yet they call it ethnography. Why? Because, they say, their inquiries are conducted by way of participant observation in the field. Call it what you will, anthropological or ethnographic, the resulting knowledge is produced in the company of others, at their own behest to be sure, but on sufferance of their hosts. Surely, these colleagues argue, we can have an in-house understanding of what we mean by ethnography that allows us to use the term with a degree of elasticity while still knowing, in our bones, what we are talking about. The trouble with this argument, however, is that such understanding does not extend beyond those already inducted into an anthropological sensibility. Outside our own circles, we have some explaining to do. And the fact is, we have not been very good at it. Not only is the anthropological voice conspicuous by its absence from the great debates of the day; there is also widespread public ignorance about what anthropology studies and what contribution it stands to make to human knowledge. Branding our contribution, and our voice, as "ethnographic" doesn't help in this regard. Why on earth use the term for a genre of study that is neither bound to any discernible ethnos nor graphic in intent?

In short, if we really want to get across what we anthropologists do, in a language that others will understand, then "ethnography" is about the worst possible word to choose. We are almost asking to be misunderstood. So why persist with it? The answers are to be found in Patrick Eisenlohr's trenchant contribution to this collection. They have to do with the establishment and confirmation of professional identity. I fully agree, with Eisenlohr, that anthropology is a calling, and that our commitment to it is professional in this vocational sense. There is, however, another sense of professionalism, relentlessly on the rise in the modern academy, which is founded on the meritocratic ideal of ascending expertise. The aspiring professional academic is drawn to study not for the love of it but for the purposes of qualification. It offers the means to stage a career. The tug of war between these two senses of professional commitment—between, as Walton puts it, "protean anthropological . . . participation/observation" and "the . . . professional imperatives that saturate and structure our discipline"—is all too familiar to every anthropologist who has spent time in the field in the prosecution of doctoral research. The fieldworker, all at sea in her host community, is unquestionably an amateur, driven by curiosity and care, but with next to no qualification in the ways of life into which she is drawn. Yet immediately on returning to the academy, this erstwhile amateur is required to assume the persona of the professional in a position to speak with authority on the matter of her research.

"Ethnography," in the armory of the career anthropologist, provides the means to pull this off. It allows for the novitiate experience of life in the field to be reshaped as a corpus of knowledge with which to claim a distinctive expertise. The anthropologist can now self-present as a professional, flaunting ethnography as the marker of his or her newfound intellectual authority. He has been there! And this, in turn, retrospectively colors the narrative of field research, which is recounted as an endeavor framed by a higher academic ambition that transcends the banality of quotidian life. This ambition, according to Eisenlohr, is no less than to pose "fundamental questions about the nature of social life." It is an ambition, he thinks, that separates the ethnographer-cum-anthropologist from a host of other characters—journalists, spies, activists, tourists, missionaries—who might also indulge in participant observation but to different and less exalted ends. In short, Eisenlohr mobilizes the concept of ethnography to police the boundaries of academia. No wonder he disagrees with me! For my purpose is just the opposite: to demolish the walls that divide the land of academia from the rest of the world, and to expose the conceit of its inhabitants—a conceit that lingers as an uncomfortable legacy from the colonial past—that they alone are equipped to tackle questions of so deep a nature as to elude ordinary folk. Are humans not all students of social life by the very fact of living it?

Surely, we need anthropology precisely because people around the world are as invested as we are in life's fundamental questions and, by that very token, have wisdom to share in the common task of fashioning a way to live, not just for the present but sustainably into the future. What, after all, would be the point of going to study with other people if we are already convinced that we have nothing to learn from them? This doesn't mean accepting everything they say or do, and I would certainly not subscribe to the relativist tenet that obliges us to recognize the intrinsic value of every way of life, a priori, on its own terms. Without this tenet, according to Eisenlohr, the pursuit of anthropology wouldn't make sense; yet from what he says about neo-Nazis in his native Germany, I doubt whether even he would assent to it, and no more do I. Indeed, I would be inclined to argue to the contrary that anthropology only makes sense if it is prepared to take a critical stance toward the lives it studies. This is a matter not of accepting diversity for its own sake, as a fait accompli, but of finding ways to *live together in difference*. While there are many people out there whose attitudes and conduct we might find abhorrent, to engage with them in critical correspondence might still be worth the effort, if only to firm up the grounds of our abhorrence and lend it a persuasive power it might otherwise lack.

Of course, circumstances might make this practically impossible. Correspondence—at least in today's world—may be more the exception than the rule in fieldwork, which, as Eisenlohr suggests, is more typically characterized by disjuncture and incommensurability in the relations between ethnographers and their hosts. Am I wrong, then, to take correspondence as the condition for participant observation? Eisenlohr thinks so. It is not clear to me, however, how the fieldworker can "exit out of correspondence," as he puts it, without also exiting out of participant observation. The mistake, surely, is not to describe all participant observation as a practice of correspondence, but to describe all fieldwork as a practice of participant observation. To participate is, by definition, to join with people in their activities; to observe is to follow what is going on. Nothing in either correspondence or participant observation implies that it is conflict-free or devoid of antagonism. It has nothing to do with a yearning for some kind of mystical oneness, as Eisenlohr—along with several other contributors to this collection—seems to think. Nevertheless, there are undoubtedly occasions on which the fieldworker, by force of circumstance, is either denied the opportunity to participate and observe or where the level of personal exposure it would entail—as Patrice Ladwig reports in his contribution—would be too much to bear. All may not be lost, however. Perhaps the research can be continued by other means, but then participant observation would not be among them.

It is worth recalling that I introduced the term "correspondence" as an alternative to the more usual notion of "interaction" in order to shift the emphasis from intentionality to responsivity, and to highlight how agency emerges from within the current of habitual action, in real time, rather than preceding it as cause to effect.[1] I did not introduce it with a view to imagining a world where all are immersed in blissful accord. Correspondence, in my understanding, crosscuts the Empedoclean division between love and strife. Several contributors to this collection, however, seem to place it all on the side of love, as opposed to strife. They consequently wonder, as Ladwig does, how it can accommodate the manifold cracks and contradictions of real life. The source of the misunderstanding seems to lie in my use of two keywords, in particular, to describe the dynamic of correspondence. These are "harmony" and "resonance"; and a word of explanation is needed about each. First, my understanding of harmony is based on the *armonia* of classical Greece, which referred to any means of joining (related to *armos*, "joint"). The bones of the body, the timbers of ships, the stones of temples, all were joined in harmony (Ilievski 1993). Our word "arm," of course, comes from the same root, and its ambiguity is telling. For the arms that hold another in their embrace are also instruments of combat, in which the thrust of each party meets the parry of the other. In harmony, indeed, love and strife, accord and friction, are mutually implicated (Ingold 2016: 12).

To invoke harmony, then, is not—as Eisenlohr, for one, seems to think—to dream of a pastoral arcadia, where all is sweetness and light. Ladwig takes this misapprehension one step further in speaking of "theologically inspired and harmony oriented undercurrents of theorizing, which leave no space for ambivalence." Whatever the theological inspiration may be for such theorizing—and I know of none—I hope to have made it clear that ambivalence is not so much absent from the idea of harmony as constitutive of it. With this idea, I merely ask that we pay attention to the joins in social life—to the sutures in which people are simultaneously stitched together and torn apart (Ingold 2015: 22–26). I am grateful to Arpita Roy for pointing this out, in her wonderfully insightful contribution. "Correspondence," as she correctly observes, "does not imply disregarding disagreements or conflicts." There can be no fusion without fission: singly they would lead to sclerosis, but together they bring about growth and transformation. And this brings me to our second term of contention, namely "resonance." I understand the term in a very precise sense, drawn from the ecological approach to perception, which refers to how the perceptual systems of skilled practitioners—their modes of seeing, listening, touching, and so on—are practically tuned to picking out environmental invariants from modulations in the flow of sensory stimulation.[2] My contention is that this resonant attunement—rather than any capacity to form interior mental representations—underlies our capacities of attention and response (Ingold 2001).

It is unfortunate that this precise sense of resonance has tended to evaporate into the aura of metaphysical overtones that have burgeoned around the term. Thus, Eisenlohr fears that with "resonant correspondence," anthropology itself would melt into the ether of numinous oneness. And for Ladwig, it implies nothing less than total immersion. A body so immersed, of course, would not actually resonate with its surroundings but dissolve into them. Drawing on the work of architectural design theorist Lars Spuybroek (2016), to which Ladwig also refers, I have adopted the word "sympathy" rather than "immersion" to describe the resonant coupling of persons and things in an environment (Ingold 2015: 23–25). By this, I do not mean to attribute such sentiments as warmth or compassion. Spuybroek is adamant that in his terms, sympathy implies no outpouring of affection, or even any judgment of taste (Spuybroek 2016: 120–21). It simply denotes an accord—a joining *with*—that comes from correspondence, from each person's taking into him- or herself something of the quality of the others to which they respond. In this sense, one could even speak—in Henri Bergson's famous example—of the sympathy of the wasp for the caterpillar that it stings, with surgical precision, at nine points along its body so as to paralyze without killing it (Bergson 1922: 183). And it is from the philosophy of Bergson, too, that I have taken the idea of holism, to convey an indivisible order of relations in which there are no parts as such, but only partial views of the whole (1922: 32). This order, like that of life itself, is processual, continually overtaking itself, and never complete.

Holism, thus understood, is absolutely opposed to totalization (Ingold 2011: 226; 2018b: 159).[3] For if, in the whole, every element gathers into itself its relations with all the others, the totality is the final sum of parts, each of which is exterior to every other. Thus when Ladwig writes that "immersion is often understood in a too totalizing way," he misreads not only correspondence as immersion but also holism as totalization. In Irfan Ahmad's contribution, this misreading takes a more sinister turn. For Ahmad, holism involves a totalization that is nothing less than global in scale. As such, it is divisible into parts at levels of segmentation ranging from the locality, through the region, to the nation–state. And it leads him to identify "people," quite incorrectly in my view, with these essentially political subdivisions of the global order. As such, "people" belongs within the same cluster of terms as "tribe," "nation," and "ethnicity." It denotes a sociopolitical entity. But this is absolutely not what I had in mind when, a quarter of a century ago, I defined anthropology as "philosophy with the people in" (Ingold 1994: xvii). Perhaps I was naive not to anticipate the way in which the idea of "the people" would be mobilized in the rhetoric of contemporary populism, as the signs were already there. In retrospect, it would have been better to leave out the offending article, rendering anthropology thus as "philosophy with people in." For I was thinking of people, simply, as a multiplicity of persons, not of "the people" as a singular entity.

Although I had yet to articulate the concept of correspondence as a going along together in difference, it was already there, implicitly, in the idea that persons are constituted in and through the history of their mutual relations. Nothing more is presupposed. Persons may be kings or commoners, old or young, male or female, even human or nonhuman. In Ahmad's worldview, however, we cannot refer to persons as people without wheeling in the connotations of sovereignty, nationhood, and status that attach to "the people" as a term of political rhetoric. By what word, then, should persons be known? It seems strange indeed to reject a definition of anthropology that includes reference to living people in favor of a concept of ethnography constructed on the root of a determinate *ethnos*. No term, indeed, does more than ethnography to craft the idea of "the people" as an entity, ripe for description. That's why, in carving out a domain of study for social anthropology, A. R. Radcliffe-Brown was so keen to distinguish the new field from ethnography. The reality we study as social anthropologists, Radcliffe-Brown insisted, "is not any sort of entity but a process, the process of social life" (Radcliffe-Brown 1952: 4). My lecture of 2007 (Ingold 2008), in which I first set out my ideas on anthropology and ethnography, was one of a series nominally dedicated to Radcliffe-Brown, and it seemed like a good opportunity to reclaim the processualism of his approach to social life, against the distortions visited upon it by his contemporary critics, notoriously E. E. Evans-Pritchard and Edmund Leach.

This does not, however, make me a follower of Radcliffe-Brown. He is not my "hero," as Ahmad seems to think. While I agree that ethnography should be clearly distinguished from anthropology, the grounds on which I draw the distinction are entirely different from his. Based on the neo-Kantian dichotomy between "idiographic" description and "nomothetic" generalization, Radcliffe-Brown (1951: 15) aligned ethnography with the former and anthropology with the latter. According to his explicitly positivistic agenda, ethnography would provide the objective facts from which theoretical generalizations could be drawn through systematic comparison. This procedure is consistent with the logic of totalization, and it is perhaps for this reason—because he confuses this logic with the logic of holism—that Ahmad jumps to the entirely mistaken conclusion that, for me, regaining anthropology's distinctive voice means restoring its nomothetic objective. Nothing could be further from the truth! What I show, rather, is that with a holism that is processual rather than totalizing, the opposition between description and theory, or between the idiographic and the nomothetic, can no longer be sustained. Thus, if anthropology and ethnography are to be distinguished at all, it must be along different lines (Ingold 2011: 237–38). My argument is that to practice anthropology is not to make studies *of* people but to study *with* them—a study that rather than educating us *about* the world, educates our *perception of* the world. And this bears directly on the question—which Ahmad also broaches in his contribution—of the relation between fact and truth.

Truth is not fact. On that, at least, we agree. Ahmad, following anthropologist Didier Fassin, situates truth *beneath* that which manifestly exists or occurs "on the surface of fact" (Fassin 2014: 41). Buried by deception or convention, it has to be unearthed. I hold, to the contrary, that truth lies *beyond* fact, in the opening of our perception that happens when those with whom we study begin to tell us how to perceive. It lies in the resonance of perceptual attunement (Ingold 2018a: 71–72). As Roy puts it so beautifully, "the finesse of participant observation entails the tuning fork of truth." So long as we are bound by the protocols of positive science, with its unassailable dichotomies between fact and value, subject and object, and theory and description, the road to truth will remain barred. Facts rear up and block the way, forbidding access to a beyond. Roy's report of the "unfailing inertia" with which the physicists she worked with separated human existence from physical nature mirrors my own experience with evolutionary biologists. Any challenge to the separation is met with blank incomprehension, often accompanied by a demand that it be supported by objective data. How science, in Roy's words, "finds harmony with nature on the pivot of sharp separations" remains profoundly puzzling, and is to my mind a source of considerable frustration. It points to a limitation of my approach, but I have yet to get my head around it. Meanwhile, I can only endorse Roy's acknowledgment of truth as "an awakening, a going forward, which comes to us, not extraneously, but in the ambit of self-discovery." We can know it only from the inside.

I would like to conclude with just two further observations. The first responds to Walton's call for new genres of writing that would take us beyond the sterile alternatives of ethnography and theory, and allow more room to breathe. It is a call I wholeheartedly endorse. Current academic writing—mired in verbal conceit, exclusively self-referential, and consumed by ever-lengthening bibliographies—is in deep trouble. Academic words, stripped of their power to move, touch, or evoke, are sequestered from affective commerce with the world of which they speak. This impoverishment is by no means the fault of ethnography, as Walton rightly notes. Behind it lie more powerful forces driving the global knowledge economy and manifested in the regimes of research assessment, peer review, and publication policy that increasingly hobble the practices of scholarship. If we are to oppose these forces and not succumb to them, we need to find ways of writing *with* the world rather than *about* it: ways more conversational than didactic, more dialogical than declarative—indeed more Socratic, in the sense adduced by Roy, according to which knowledge is not forcibly extracted through interrogation but brought forth in a process of gentle questioning and response or, in a word, through correspondence. Here, it is the *process* of writing, its performative aspect, that matters more than final outcomes. Perhaps it is not ethnography we need so much as "anthropography"[4]—an inelegant word, to be sure, but one that conveys an openness to alternative graphic modalities, including drawing and handwriting, as well as the "constellational writing" that Walton proposes.

My second observation concerns teaching. I'm profoundly grateful to Hatsuki Aishima who, alone among the contributors, brings out the challenges of teaching anthropology in the classroom. For teaching, and not ethnographic writing, is the other side of the ontological commitment that underwrites participant observation, and without which it would remain only half-formed (Ingold 2013: 13). It is no wonder that ontological commitment sounds to Eisenlohr like a vacuous surrender to oneness, or that Roy finds "bland and prescriptive" the idea of giving what we owe to the world for our development and formation. Both leave teaching out of the equation. Yet it is teaching that completes the cycle of commitment by giving back; without it we have nothing to offer. But what to give? This is not unproblematic, as Aishima shows by way of her experience of teaching courses in Modern Islam at the University of Manchester to a student audience that included many from local Muslim communities. Here, she found herself caught in the sharp divide between the "everyday Islam" familiar to her students and "lecture hall Islam"—the authoritative, academically sanitized version. Could there be a middle path between the two? I believe the source of the dilemma here is not internal to anthropology. It lies rather in the mismatch between two philosophies of education. How can we practice an anthropological education that would lead students *out* into the world, along paths of correspondence, in an institutional setting—that of the modern university—which still insists that education is about instilling *in* to students' minds knowledge that bears the seal of academic authority? For ultimately, that's what it all comes down to: not ethnography but education.

Tim Ingold is Professor Emeritus of Social Anthropology at the University of Aberdeen. He has carried out fieldwork among Saami and Finnish people in Lapland, and has written on environment, technology, and social organization in the circumpolar North, on animals in human society, and on human ecology and evolutionary theory. His more recent work explores environmental perception and skilled practice. Ingold's current interests lie on the interface between anthropology, archaeology, art, and architecture. His recent books include *The Perception of the Environment* (2000), *Lines* (2007), *Being Alive* (2011), *Making* (2013), *The Life of Lines* (2015), *Anthropology and/as Education* (2018), and *Anthropology: Why It Matters* (2018). He is also the editor, inter alia, of *Companion Encyclopedia of Anthropology* (1994).

Notes

1. I initially set out the contrast between interaction and correspondence in my book *Making* (Ingold 2013: 105–8), and returned to it in my Huxley Memorial Lecture of 2014 (Ingold 2016: 18).
2. The *locus classicus* for this approach to perception is in the work of psychologist James Gibson (1986). "The perceptual system," Gibson writes, "simply extracts the invariants from the flowing array; it *resonates* to the invariant structure or is *attuned* to it" (1986: 249—emphasis in original).
3. For very different assessments of holism in anthropology, compare the volumes edited by David Parkin and Stanley Ulijaszek (2007) and by Ton Otto and Nils Bubandt (2010).
4. Thinking that I had just coined an ugly neologism, I consulted the *Oxford English Dictionary*, only to discover, to my surprise, that the word "anthropography" already exists, having been invented in 1825 by the poet Samuel Taylor Coleridge, to mean "a Description of the different Races, and Varieties of Men, the effects of Climate, and Civilization." See https://www.oed.com/view/Entry/8426?redirectedFrom=anthropography#eid, accessed 11 June 2019.

References

Bergson, Henri. 1922. *Creative Evolution*. Translated by A. Mitchell. London: Macmillan.
Fassin, Didier. 2014. "True Life, Real Lives: Revisiting the Boundaries between Ethnography and Fiction." *American Ethnologist* 41, no. 1: 40–55.
Gibson, James J. 1986. *The Ecological Approach to Visual Perception*. Hillsdale, NJ: Lawrence Erlbaum.
Ilievski, Petar Hr. 1993. "The Origin and Semantic Development of the Term Harmony." *Illinois Classical Studies* 18: 19–29.
Ingold, Tim. 1994. "General Introduction." In *Companion Encyclopedia of Anthropology: Humanity, Culture and Social Life*, edited by Tim Ingold, xiii–xxxiv. London: Routledge.
———. 2001. "From the Transmission of Representations to the Education of Attention." In *The Debated Mind: Evolutionary Psychology versus Ethnography*, edited by H. Whitehouse, 113–53. Oxford: Berg Publishers.
———. 2008. "Anthropology Is *Not* Ethnography." *Proceedings of the British Academy* 154: 69–92.
———. 2011. *Being Alive: Essays on Movement, Knowledge and Description*. Abingdon: Routledge.
———. 2013. *Making: Anthropology, Archaeology, Art and Architecture*. Abingdon: Routledge.
———. 2015. *The Life of Lines*. Abingdon: Routledge.
———. 2016. "On Human Correspondence." *Journal of the Royal Anthropological Institute* 23: 9–27.
———. 2018a. *Anthropology and/as Education*. Abingdon: Routledge.
———. 2018b. "One World Anthropology." *HAU: Journal of Ethnographic Theory* 8, no. 1/2: 158–71.
Otto, Ton, and Nils Bubandt, eds. 2010. *Experiments in Holism: Theory and Practice in Contemporary Anthropology*. Oxford: Wiley-Blackwell.
Parkin, David, and Stanley Ulijaszek, eds. 2007. *Holistic Anthropology: Emergence and Convergence*. Oxford: Berghahn Books.
Radcliffe-Brown, Alfred Reginald. 1951 "The Comparative Method in Social Anthropology." *Journal of the Royal Anthropological Institute* 81: 15–22.
———. 1952. *Structure and Function in Primitive Society*. London: Cohen & West.
Spuybroek, Lars. 2016. *The Sympathy of Things: Ruskin and the Ecology of Design*. 2nd ed. London: Bloomsbury Academic.

INDEX

'Abd al-Halim Mahmud, 30–31
Advani, L. K., 132n12
aesthetics, 75
Africa, British imperialism in, 115–16
agencing, 100
Ahmad, Irfan, 3, 8, 12–13, 56, 103, 146–48
Aishima, Hatsuki, 3–4, 10, 149
alienation, 11, 72–74, 78, 82, 84–87, 88n2
Almond, Gabriel, 118
anthropological comparison, 9, 15n4, 104–7
anthropological knowing and knowledge, 27, 37, 39, 41, 46, 85, 117–18
anthropological writing, 21–23, 26–27, 46, 54–55, 106
anthropologists, interlocutors and, 11–12, 21–23, 30–31, 64–65, 93–100, 102
anthropology, 49. *See also specific topics*
  in classroom, practicing, 27–30
  connections in, 72–73
  crisis of representation in, 10, 21, 23–24, 32, 37, 40
  dark, 2, 11, 73–76, 80
  from description to correspondence in, 22–23
  discipline and method, 26
  as education, 7, 27, 32, 40–41, 74, 149–50
  future of, 4, 6–9, 128
  generalizations in, 47
  intrinsic values of, 97
  of Islam, 10, 24–28, 30, 32–33
  as nomothetic discipline, 7–8, 40, 104–5, 147–48
  philosophy and, 8, 12, 113, 146–47
  professionalism and, 142–43
  representation in, 10, 20, 24, 26–27, 32, 37
  research, rejected projects and, 98–103
  of science, 39
  social, 22–24, 115, 147
  teaching, 21–22, 27–30, 37, 149
  of terrorism, 112–13, 115, 129
  time and attention in, 96–98
anthropology and ethnography, 4–9, 141–44, 147. *See also* Ingold, Tim, on anthropology and ethnography
  from description to correspondence, 22–23
  disciplinary boundaries and demarcation, 12–13, 20, 31–32, 54
  education, teaching and, 27
  ethnographic methods and, 4, 20–21, 40, 82
  fieldwork in, 20, 93–98, 105–8, 113
  Islamic dream interpretation and, 26
  knowledge production in, 39–40
  participant observation and, 105, 107, 113
  representation, anthropological writing and, 26–27
  Sahlins on, 99
  tribes in, 119
antihistoricist theory of time, 58–59
Appadurai, Arjun, 23
The Arcades Project (Benjamin), 57–59
Ariès, Philippe, 88n7
A. R. Radcliffe-Brown lecture, by Ingold, 1, 7–8
Asad, Talal, 8, 10, 15n3, 24–25

Ashura rituals, 29–30
attention, time and, 96–98
attentionality, 73–75, 78–79, 98
awkward scale, 114, 122–27

Badiou, Alain, 132n10
Bangstad, Sindre, 102
Beattie, John, 116
Benedict, Burton, 101
Benjamin, Walter, 3, 11, 55–60, 64–65, 67n6, 68n7
Bergson, Henri, 146
Bharatiya Janata Party (BJP), 125–26
binary classifications and oppositions, 43
BJP. *See* Bharatiya Janata Party
Borneman, John, 118
Bourdieu, Pierre, 47, 85, 89n14
Bourgeois, Philippe, 81–82
Bowen, John R., 25
Breivik, Anders Behring, 122, 130
British imperialism, in Africa, 115–16
Buck-Morss, Susan, 59
Buddhist crematoria, death pollution and, 76–82
Buddhist death rituals and funerals, 3, 11, 73, 76

Canovan, Margaret, 119–20
care, knowledge and, 37–38, 46
caste, in Mauritius, 101
CERN (Conseil Européen pour la Recherche Nucléaire), 3–4, 10, 39, 42–45
Chakrabarty, Dipesh, 66n2
Chazan-Gillig, Suzanne, 101
Clifford, James, 22, 32, 85
Cold War, 15, 118, 124, 133n16
colonialism, 22, 24, 26, 72, 115–16, 119, 132n10
Comaroff, Jean, 114
Comaroff, John, 114
Companion Encyclopedia of Anthropology (Ingold), 131n5
comparative anthropology, 6, 9
comparison, 9, 15n4, 104–8
connection, alienation and, 72–73
Conseil Européen pour la Recherche Nucléaire (CERN), 3–4, 10, 39, 42–45

constellational writing, 3, 11, 59–65, 68n7, 149
constitutive resonance, 103–4
correspondence. *See also* Ingold, Tim, on correspondence
  of agencing, 100
  alienation and, 82, 86–87
  anthropology as, 20–21, 53–54, 66, 113
  attentionality and, 73–75, 78–79
  constellations and, 64–65
  from description to, 22–23
  ethnography and, 3, 7, 10, 54
  fieldwork and, 73, 99–100, 107, 144
  harmony, resonance and, 12, 145
  holism of, 86
  interaction versus, 144–45
  with interlocutors, 95, 99
  meshwork and, 95, 99–100, 107
  noncorrespondence and, 11
  nonobjectification and, 81
  ontological commitment and, 12, 95, 102–4
  ontology and, 50
  participant observation and, 72, 74, 100, 107–8, 144
  relations in, 72, 147
  resonant, 101–4, 146
  Roy on, 145
  tangentialism and, 83
correspondence thinking, 72, 81–82, 84, 86
crematoria, death pollution and, 76–82
crisis of representation, in anthropology, 10, 21, 23–24, 32, 37, 40
cultural anthropology, 1, 24

dark anthropology, 2, 11, 73–76, 80
dark ethnography, 74–75, 80–83, 86
death pollution, crematoria and, 76–82
description, 8, 15n4, 22–23, 37, 40, 47, 50
Dewey, John, 38, 48
dialectical thinking, 57–60
dialogue, of physicist and anthropologist, 43–44
dialogue form, Plato and, 36

dönme, 60–63
Douglas, Mary, 77
dream interpretation, in Islam, 26
dreams, antihistoricism of Benjamin
 and, 58
dualisms, in science, 42–46
Durkheim, Émile, 42–43, 130

Eckert, Julia, 121
education, anthropology and, 7, 27,
 32, 40–41, 74, 149–50
Egypt, 10, 20–21, 24–26, 29–32
Eisenlohr, Patrick, 3, 9–13, 65, 80,
 142–46, 149
empirical data collection, 105
empiricism, 38, 122
epistemology, 47–48
ethnic cleansing, 97, 120
ethnographers, interlocutors and,
 100
ethnographic encounters, 93–95,
 107
ethnographic methods, 4–5, 20–21,
 40, 53, 82, 105
ethnography. *See also* anthropology
 and ethnography; Ingold, Tim, on
 ethnography
 comparison and, 15n4
 conventional, 11–12
 correspondence and, 3, 7, 10, 54
 dark, 74–75, 80–83, 86
 description in, 37, 40
 dönme and, 61
 everyday life and, 96–97, 107
 fieldwork, 6–7, 10, 20–21,
  93–98, 105, 113
 immersion in, 4
 logical relations and, 4
 of Mauritian Hindu nationalists,
  102
 objectives of, 113
 politics, IR and, 123
 social anthropology and, 22
 sociology and, 130
 temporal distortion and, 54–55,
  57
 on terrorism and Islam, 123
 traditional ideas about,
  correspondence and, 3
 on tribes and "natives," 119
 writing and, 11, 22, 64, 142, 149
ethnonationalist movements, 102–3

Evans-Pritchard, E. E., 116, 147
everyday life, 20, 23, 25–26, 28–31,
 96–97, 107, 149

Fabian, Johannes, 96
fact, truth and, 148
Fadil, Nadia, 29
Fassin, Didier, 114, 128–29, 148
Faubion, James, 73, 85
Fernando, Mayanthi, 29
fieldnotes, writing, in anthropology,
 22
fieldwork, 11
 alienation and, 74, 84–86
 in anthropology, 8, 20–23,
  36–38, 41, 71–72, 80–81,
  87, 93–97
 in anthropology and ethnography,
  20, 93–98, 105–8, 113
 correspondence and, 73, 99–100,
  107, 144
 dialogic dimension of, 45
 ethnographic encounters and,
  93–95
 ethnographic methods and,
  20–21
 ethnography and, 6–7, 10,
  93–98, 105, 113
 everyday life and, 20, 23
 intentionality and, 97–98
 objectification and, 84, 86
 participant observation and, 71,
  74, 100, 144
 power and, 47, 49, 73
 on right-wing populists and
  ethnonationalists, 102–3
Fromm, Erich, 82

Geertz, Clifford, 1, 4, 8, 15n4,
 24–25, 118
Gellner, Ernest, 24, 47
generalizations, 47, 105–6
Geyer, Felix, 88n3
Goethe, Johann Wolfgang von, 48

Habermas, Jürgen, 80
hadīth, 24–25, 30. *See also* Islam;
 Muslims
harmony, 12, 41, 50, 79–81, 85,
 145
Heidegger, Martin, 103
hermeneutics, 106, 108

Herzfeld, Michael, 128
Hindus and Hinduism, 3, 12, 76,
    101–2, 121–22, 126–27
Hirschkind, Charles, 26
historical anthropology, 6, 9
historicism, 55–56, 66n2
historiography, 55–57, 64
holism, 3, 9, 12, 22, 38, 79, 84
    in anthropology and society, 127
    on awkward scale, 122–27
    Bergson on, 146
    of correspondence, 86
    locality and, 116–17
    Malinowski on, 119, 129
    participant observation and, 127
    politics, IR and, 113–15, 127, 129
    Radcliffe-Brown on, 129
    totalization and, 13, 146–48
    as translocal, 114
    tribes, anthropology and, 119
holistic truth, 95, 97, 101–2
holocultural comparison, 9, 15n4
human and nature dualism, in science, 42–45

ideal types, 105–7, 109n5, 142
idiographic and nomothetic sciences, 40, 105–6
immersion, 4, 74, 81, 146
improvisation, objectification and, 82–86
India, 12, 120–22, 125–27, 129, 132n14
Indian Penal Code (IPC), 121
Indonesia, 25, 31
Ingold, Tim, 67n4
    The Arcades Project by, 57–59
    Benjamin and, 56–58, 64–65, 67n6
    Companion Encyclopedia of Anthropology, 131n5
    on description, in ethnography, 37, 50
    on holism, 114
    on inquiry, 48–49
    on Radcliffe-Brown, 115
    Radcliffe-Brown lecture by, 1, 7–8
    on real life, 114, 128
    "That's Enough about Ethnography" by, 1–2, 112
    on truth, 46–49

Ingold, Tim, on anthropology
    aesthetics and, 75
    agencing, 100
    anthropologists and interlocutors, 95
    attentionality in, 75, 78–79, 98
    as comparative, 104–5
    discipline and method, 26
    as education, 27
    generalizations in, 47
    impersonal relations and, 42
    knowledge and care in, 37–38
    method, 49
    ontology and, 37–38
    participant observation and, 27, 48, 54–55, 71–72, 80
    "the people" in, 119, 129
    politics, IR and, 112–13, 129
Ingold, Tim, on anthropology and ethnography, 1–8, 10–14, 22, 31–33, 50
    anthropological writing and, 21–23, 26–27, 46
    correspondence and, 20–21, 53–54
    ethnographic methods and, 53
    fieldwork and, 20, 93–96
    knowledge production, 39–40
    observation, description and, 40
    observation, objectification and, 23
    theoretical generalizations, 105
Ingold, Tim, on correspondence, 41, 64–66, 71–73, 80–82, 84–85, 96
    anthropology as, 20–21, 53–54, 113
    attentionality and, 75, 78–79
    fieldwork and, 100, 107
    longing and, 109n2
    as meshwork, 95, 99–100, 107–8
    ontological commitment and, 95, 102–4
    participant observation and, 72, 100, 107–8
Ingold, Tim, on ethnography, 53, 93, 105, 113, 119, 128
inquiry, 4, 36, 38, 48–50, 128–29
intentionality, 97–98, 144–45
international politics, 118, 124–25, 132n8
international relations (IR), 3, 12, 124. *See also* politics, IR and

intersubjectivity, 7, 10–11, 41, 59
IPC (Indian Penal Code), 121
IR. *See* international relations
Islam, 3, 14
  anthropology of, 10, 24–28, 30, 32–33
  colonialism, Western scholarship and, 24
  demonization of after Soviet Union collapse, 124
  discourse in, 25
  dream interpretation in, 26
  in Egypt, 10, 20–21, 29–32
  ethnographic methods and fieldwork in researching, 20–21
  "everyday," 28–30, 149
  knowledge of, seeking, 30–33
  terrorism and, 120–27
  in university classrooms, teaching and learning, 21–22, 27–29, 149–50

Jackson, Michael, 84
Jenkins, Timothy, 72
Jetztzeit, 56–57, 64
Jog, B. N., 125

Kapferer, Bruce, 6
Keane, John, 124
Kennan, George, 124
Kingsolver, Ann, 131n5
Knodt, Reinhard, 72
knowledge
  anthropological, 27, 37, 39, 41, 46, 85, 117–18
  belief and, 44–45
  care and, 37–38, 46
  ethnographic data from field and, 23
  of Islam, seeking, 30–33
  logical relations and, 50
  Platonic dialogues and, 45
  power and, 24–25
  production, 26, 39–40
  textured historicity as form of, 59
Kopytoff, Igor, 84
Kovats-Bernat, Christopher, 82–83, 86
Kroeber, Alfred, 40

Laclau, Ernesto, 120

Ladwig, Patrice, 3, 11, 65, 99, 145–46
language, 38, 50, 105
Laos, 73, 76–77
Latour, Bruno, 130
Leach, Edmund, 1, 131n4, 147
Leibniz, Gottfried Wilhelm, 80
Lévi-Strauss, Claude, 1
logical relations, 4, 39, 42, 50

MacDougall, Susan, 1
Malinowski, Bronislaw, 36–37, 114, 116–17, 119, 127, 129, 131n4
Marcus, George, 32, 37, 85
Marx, Karl, 42, 82, 84–85
Mauritius, 12, 101–2, 109n5
Mauss, Marcel, 119
Mazower, Mark, 60
Mazzarella, William, 103–4
McLean, Stuart, 5
Mead, Margaret, 117–18
media, terrorism and, 12, 120–23, 125, 132n14
meshwork, 95, 99–100, 103, 107–8
Métraux, Rhoda, 117–18
Michelet, Jules, 58
Middle Eastern Studies program, Manchester, 27–28
Miller, Daniel, 109n3
Mills, C. Wright, 40
mimetic resonance, 104
Mintz, Sidney, 6–7, 9, 15n2
Mitchell, Timothy, 24
Mittermaier, Amira, 26
Modi, Narendra, 125–27
Morgenthau, Hans, 118, 130
morticians, 77, 79
Muhammad (prophet), 20, 25, 30
Mukherjee, Ramkrishna, 119
multidisciplinarity, 114–15
Muslims
  anthropology of Islam and, 24–28, 30, 32–33
  in Cairo, 20, 26, 30
  Egyptian, 25–26, 30–31
  everyday life of, 25–26, 28–31, 149
  in India, violence against, 121–22
  in Indonesia, 25, 31
  ritual prayers, 25
  students, 28–31

Sunni and Shi'a, 29–30
terrorism and, 120–25

national culture and national character, 118
national interest, of states, 118–19
National Investigation Agency (NIA), 127
nation-states, anthropology and, 114–21, 124
neoliberalism, 75–76
neo-Nazis, 103, 144
Neumeier, Emily, 68n7
New Mosque, in Thessaloniki, 11, 55, 57, 60–65
New World Order (NWO), 112, 124
NIA (National Investigation Agency), 127
9/11, 120, 122, 124–27
Nisaruddin Ahmad, 125
nomothetic discipline, anthropology as, 7–8, 40, 104–6, 147–48
nonanthropologists, ethnographic methods and, 4–5
noncorrespondence, 11
nonobjectification, 72–73, 75, 81
Nordstrom, Carolyn, 88n11
Norway, 122
NWO (New World Order), 112, 124

objectification, 3, 11, 20, 23, 72–73, 75, 81–86
objectivity, 83–84, 86–87
observation, 22–23, 38–40, 83–85. *See also* participant observation
ontological commitment, 40–41, 50
correspondence and, 12, 95, 102–4
participant observation and, 7, 12, 38, 149
ontology, 37–39, 50
Orientalism, 24–26, 32
Ortner, Sherry, 11, 75, 80
Ottoman Empire, 60–61, 63–65

Parkin, David, 127
Parry, Jonathan, 76
participant observation, 6
alienation and, 73–74
anthropology, ethnography and, 105, 107, 113

in anthropology, 22–23, 26–27, 31, 36–37, 41, 48, 71–72, 93–94, 99–100, 113–14
anthropology of terrorism and, 113
correspondence and, 72, 74, 100, 107–8, 144
fieldwork and, 71, 74, 100, 144
holism and, 127
Ingold on, 27, 48, 54–55, 71–72, 80
Malinowski on, 36–37
objectification and, 23, 72, 83, 85
ontological commitment and, 7, 12, 38, 149
truth and, 48, 148
particle and theoretical physicists, 43–46
Pels, Peter, 89n12
people, 13–14, 112–13, 119, 129
"the people," as category, 3, 12–13, 112–13, 119–22, 129, 146–47
phenomenology, 96, 98
philosophy, anthropology and, 8, 12, 113, 146–47
Plato, 36, 42, 45
political anthropology, 115–16
politics, 131n5
anthropological knowledge and, 117–18
enemies and, 124
international, 118, 124–25, 132n8
nation-states and, 115–19, 124
politics, IR and
anthropology and, 112–19, 123–24
ethnography, 123
holism, 113–15, 127, 129
Ingold and, 112–13, 129
"the people," 119–20, 129
Pollard, Amy, 88n6, 89n15
populism, 102–3, 120
postcolonialism, 22, 26
postmodernism, 10, 37, 47, 49, 72, 84–85
Powdermaker, Hortense, 114, 127
Powell, Colin, 124
power, 22, 24–25, 47, 49, 73
Priyam, Manisha, 4

Qur'an, 24–25, 30

Rabinow, Paul, 47
Radcliffe-Brown, Alfred Reginald, 7–8, 40, 105, 115–16, 127, 129, 131n4, 147
Radcliffe-Brown lecture, by Ingold, 1, 7–8
Ramhota, Pavitranand, 101
the real and the true, 113–14, 128–29
Realism, in IR, 124
reality, truth and, 46–49, 113–14, 128–30
real life, 101, 114, 128, 130, 145
"real time," 96–97
reciprocity, 49, 71, 75, 78, 81–82
Rees, Tobias, 5
relations, 4, 39, 42–43, 48, 50, 72, 146–47
religion, Western understandings of, 24, 29
representation, in anthropology, 10, 20–21, 23–24, 26–27, 32, 37, 40
resonance, 12, 103–4, 107, 145–46
resonant correspondence, 101–4, 146
right-wing populists, 102–3
Robben, Ton, 83
Roy, Arpita, 3–4, 10–11, 13, 99, 145, 148–49
Ryle, Gilbert, 8

Sahlins, Marshall, 6, 98–99, 101
Said, Edward, 10, 24, 26, 32
Salafism, 29
Santayana, George, 38
Sardesai, Rajdeep, 125
Schatz, Edward, 4
Schielke, Samuli, 29
Schmitt, Carl, 124
science, dualisms in, 42–46
Seeman, Melvin, 78
Shyrock, Andrew, 80, 88n10
Simmel, Georg, 83–84, 89n13
Sloterdijk, Peter, 103–4
Sluka, Jeffrey, 81
social anthropology, 22–24, 115, 147

social reality, 128
social sciences, 4–5, 20–21, 43, 101, 108, 128
social structure, 116–17
sociology, 44, 119, 130
Socrates, 36
Socratic dialogue, 36, 38–39, 45
Socratic inquiry, 4, 36, 38, 49
Soviet bloc, 124
Spuybroek, Lars, 74, 80
Starrett, Gregory, 25–26
Stewart, Charles, 67n5
subjectivity, 29, 47, 100
Sufism, 30–31
supersymmetry, 43–44
Swedenborg, Emmanuel, 79

tangentialism, 83
teaching anthropology, 21–22, 27–30, 37, 149
temporal alienation, 11, 73–74
temporal distortion, 54–55, 57
terrorism, 12, 112–13, 115, 120–29, 132n14
textured historicity, 3, 55, 57, 59–60, 64, 67n3, 67n5
Thailand, 73, 76–79, 85
"That's Enough about Ethnography" (Ingold), 1–2, 112
Thessaloniki, New Mosque in, 11, 55, 57, 60–65
thick description, 8, 15n4, 22, 47
Thompson, D'Arcy Wentworth, 48
time, attention and, 96–98
totalization, holism and, 13, 146–48
tribes, in anthropology and ethnography, 119
Trouillot, Michel-Rolph, 67n5
truth, 46–49, 95, 97, 101–2, 113–14, 128–30, 148
Turkey, 60–61, 63

Uberoi, J. P. S., 11
universals, 104–6, 108

value judgments, 105–6
van der Veer, Peter, 9, 118
veranda anthropology, 113–14
volition, 98, 100
voting rights, 120–21

Walton, Jeremy, 3, 11, 96, 141, 143, 148–49
Web, Alexander, 122
Weber, Max, 2, 49, 105–6, 108
Wedeen, Lisa, 4
Wertheim, W. F., 11
Wilson, Woodrow, 120–21
Witten, Edward, 44
writing
  academic, 149
  anthropological, 21–23, 26–27, 46, 54–55, 106
  constellational, 3, 11, 59–65, 68n7, 149
  ethnographic and, 11, 22, 64, 142, 149
  fieldnotes, 22
  across the gap, 53–55
  new genres, 148–49

Zulaika, Joseba, 124

www.ingramcontent.com/pod-product-compliance
Lightning Source LLC
Chambersburg PA
CBHW071710020426
42333CB00017B/2200